Flat Out Delicious

FLAT OUT
DELICIOUS

YOUR DEFINITIVE
GUIDE TO

SASKATCHEWAN'S
FOOD ARTISANS

JENN SHARP

PHOTOGRAPHY BY RICHARD MARJAN

TOUCHWOOD

Edited by Kate Kennedy
Original cover template by Colin Parks with design updates by Lara Minja
Interior design by Lara Minja
Maps by Eric Leinberger
All photos by Richard Marjan unless otherwise stated on page 337.

Library and Archives Canada Cataloguing in Publication

Title: Flat out delicious : your definitive guide to Saskatchewan's food artisans / Jenn Sharp ; photography by Richard Marjan.
Names: Sharp, Jenn, 1982- author. | Marjan, Richard, 1957- photographer.
Description: Includes bibliographical references and index.
Identifiers: Canadiana (print) 20190193166 | Canadiana (ebook) 20190193212 | ISBN 9781771513043 (softcover) | ISBN 9781771513050 (HTML)
Subjects: LCSH: Local foods—Saskatchewan. | LCSH: Food industry and trade—Saskatchewan. | LCSH: Food—Saskatchewan.
Classification: LCC TX641 .S53 2020 | DDC 641.01/3097124—dc23

TouchWood Editions gratefully acknowledges that the land on which we live and work is within the traditional territories of the Lkwungen (Esquimalt and Songhees), Malahat, Pacheedaht, Scia'new, T'Sou-ke and W̱SÁNEĆ (Pauquachin, Tsartlip, Tsawout, Tseycum) peoples.

We acknowledge the financial support of the Government of Canada and the province of British Columbia through the Book Publishing Tax Credit.

For my **Grandma Reg**
and **Grandpa Bert**.
You are always with me.

<hr>

For all those in Saskatchewan
passionately helping to build a
thriving local food system.

N   100 km

SASKATCHEWAN

La Ronge

2

Meadow
Lake

55

4

3

Prince
Albert

Nipawin

3

Lloydminster

Battleford   16

SASKATOON   11   2   6   Tisdale   Hudson
Bay

Humboldt   9

Biggar   5

Rosetown   7   Lanigan   16

Outlook   Yorkton

20   Fort
Qu'Appelle   10

11

21   Swift
Current   Moose Jaw   REGINA   9

Maple
Creek   1   1

4   2   Weyburn   13

13   Shaunavon   6   39

Estevan

CONTENTS

INTRODUCTION

———

Saskatchewan is called the Land of Living Skies because sunrise and sunset on these vast prairie landscapes are like nothing you've seen before. Some may call us flat and boring, but if you take the time to truly feel and experience Saskatchewan, this land will become part of your soul.

Growing food in the province is closely tied to that light. Animals have adapted and plants have evolved to thrive during hot summers where the sun sets after 8 PM and during the cold, short winter days. So too have the people. Everyone who visits us agrees: Saskatchewanians are the friendliest people in Canada. We have to be nice to each other in part to make it through -40°C! I also think our welcoming spirit comes from living in a place where the land feels limitless and your nearest neighbour might be miles away. While today the cities are home to the majority of the province's population of just over a million, many have rural roots that trace back generations—to a time when you always helped your neighbour especially during a frozen winter or a summer drought. (My great-grandma's family was fortunate to have a deep well of clean spring water during the Great Depression and didn't hesitate in sharing that liquid gold with people in need.)

Saskatchewan has a rich Indigenous history. Archaeologists have dated the first human settlements to 9,500 BCE. In the late 1700s, when the first European contact happened, there were four groups of inhabitants: the Cree, the Assiniboine, the Salteaux, and the Dene. Their descendants live on today, many of them working tirelessly to maintain their traditional ways of life for their families and communities.

◐ **The Regina Farmers' Market**

Unfortunately, there aren't (yet) many places to explore authentic Indigenous cuisine. The best spot in Saskatchewan is at Wanuskewin Heritage Park, where the executive chef works with elders to create modern dishes that respect and incorporate traditional ingredients—some of which are foraged from the surrounding Opimihaw Valley.

Over the years, Saskatchewan has welcomed newcomers from many regions of the world, from Eastern Europe and Asia to Central America and Africa. You'll see evidence of those diverse cultures throughout the province, especially in our ethnic eateries. Here, you can find Indian curry, Vietnamese spring rolls, Ukrainian borscht, and Mexican tamales. Nearly every Saskatchewan small town has a Chinese restaurant where you can order ginger beef alongside dry ribs and fries. The first Chinese immigrants began arriving in the 1880s, travelling east from BC after the Canadian Pacific Railway was completed. These immigrants helped establish towns along the new railway, many opening restaurants and laundries.

For a truly authentic Chinese dining experience, visit Jin Jin Cuisine Dumpling in Saskatoon, where the owner will encourage you to try the homemade dumplings and spicy chicken with chili peppers.

When I first talked to TouchWood Editions about this project, I hoped I would be able to find a hundred food artisans to profile. I had written about food in Saskatchewan for several years, focusing mainly on chefs and farmers in and around Regina and Saskatoon. I didn't know a lot about what was happening outside of those centres. So I started researching, asking chefs about their suppliers, talking to other food writers, and talking to farmers who then told me stories about their neighbours.

I began mapping out a big road trip, close to 20,000 kilometres all told, that would take photographer Richard Marjan and me as far north as Dore Lake and as far south as Minton on a heart-opening journey across this flat-out gorgeous province.

I launched a social media project, Flat Out Food, as a place to share the stories I learned along the way, to help promote small-scale producers and as a resource for consumers. I also began telling those stories through my column of the same name in the Saskatoon *StarPhoenix* and the Regina *Leader-Post*, along with regular features for CBC Saskatchewan and Eat North.

Local media was incredibly supportive of Flat Out Food. During the summer of 2018, I did several radio and TV interviews about the road trip and subsequent book. Thanks to that exposure, I had calls and emails from across the province from people recommending I stop in Wadena for a Boston cream doughnut or at the Osler Restaurant, a prime example of Saskatchewan's eclectic multiculturalism and likely the only place you can order butter chicken, cheese fondue, and a plate of kielke.

It boggled my mind. And my fears about not being able to find a hundred artisans quickly turned to an overwhelming feeling that I'd gotten myself in over my head. As it stands now, *Flat Out Delicious*, has 167 food artisan profiles. There could have been over 200 but I couldn't include everyone. I visited each person in this book, ate each chef's food, got to know each farmer's animals, and felt the dirt in each vegetable garden. It's for those reasons that I can personally recommend you support the artisans included in these pages.

Saskatchewan has an unbelievable number of people quietly doing their thing and contributing to a vibrant local food system. People here are known for their humbleness; bragging and boasting won't take you far in Saskatchewan. But that's part of the reason we're sometimes overlooked on the national scene when it comes to our culinary accomplishments. Beyond being the "bread basket of the world" or "so flat you can see your dog running away for three miles," what does the rest of the country know about us? And perhaps more importantly, what do we know? These are some of the questions I sought to answer.

Flat Out Delicious is about reconnecting us with our food, where it comes from and who is growing it. We weren't always separated from our food; farm-to-table was the norm for most of our grandparents. But these days many communities are overflowing with chain restaurants serving cheap, prepackaged food made off-site and chock full of preservatives and dyes. And many of us aren't sure where to even start in finding foods grown by local farmers. It's time to return home.

If there's one thing I've learned while writing this book, it's that your diet—whether you're vegan or carnivore—is not the determining factor when it comes to health, environmental, and economic impacts. What matters more is the way your food was grown and raised, and how far it had to travel to get to your plate. The bonus to buying food grown close to home is that it's often more nutritionally dense, which equals more bang for your buck. Meat producers usually offer affordable bulk buying options, too.

It's difficult for small-scale producers in Saskatchewan to compete with grocery stores' prices and buying power. It's expensive to grow food here and it's expensive to pay a living wage to agricultural workers. That's why food shipped here from Central America is so cheap—farmers there are paid next to nothing. It's the definition of modern-day slavery. There is always a cost behind cheap food.

Melanie and Kevin Boldt own Pine View Farms (page 85). Melanie says their prices are higher than in large grocery stores and explains why: "We price our meat based on what it costs us to raise that animal, process it, put it in the bag, pay all our expenses, and pay ourselves a living wage. You're getting the true cost of your food. Because something always pays for cheap food—whether it's the environment, the farmer, worker standards, or government subsidies that make food cheaper—and the taxpayer pays for that in the end."

I encourage you, dear reader, to get curious. Ask questions. Think of the food you're eating as being as important as your choice of doctor or your children's school. The best part about it is that you have the power to support a food system that will benefit Saskatchewan. The more money you spend at the farmgate store, the local farmers' market, on a community supported agriculture (CSA) subscription, on value-added prairie food products, at local grocers stocking Saskatchewan ingredients, and at independent restaurants doing their best to support Saskatchewan farmers, the more you will help build a robust local food system to be proud of.

To those readers who live in Saskatchewan, I hope these stories will make you proud. I think it's time to trade a little of our quiet humbleness for some well-earned bragging! To readers from farther away, I hope this book will change some of your assumptions about Saskatchewan. We are anything but flat and boring.

HOW THIS BOOK IS ORGANIZED

During the summer and fall of 2018, photographer Richard Marjan and I travelled all over Saskatchewan, visiting the artisans you'll read about here. And we barely scratched the surface of what our province has to offer. If you're coming to Saskatchewan to visit, be prepared to come back again and again once this expansive, soulful place and its welcoming people have pulled you in. From the clean northern lakes to some of the world's last remaining native grasslands in the south, we've got it all. Each region has a rich history and cultural gems to discover, along with unique food and restaurants.

Flat Out Delicious is divided into five regions: Northern, West Central, East Central, Southwest, and Southeast, along with a dedicated section for both Saskatoon and Regina. Each section's artisan profiles are organized alphabetically with maps telling you where to find the ones that welcome visitors. You can also page through the book in search of specific foods or experiences: artisan products; baked goods; tea and coffee; farmers' markets; foragers; fruits and vegetables; grains, seeds, and pulses; meat and poultry; cooking schools; and specialty foods.

You'll find eateries featured in association with chefs and restaurateurs. And each region has a watering holes section that lists fruit wineries, meaderies, distilleries, and breweries.

SASKATCHEWAN TERROIR

Terroir is a French term that means earth or soil. It also means "a taste of place" and can be traced to French winemakers attempting to understand the differences in wines through physical characteristics like the soil, climate, location, sunshine, and altitude.

The term is also used to describe food. It can come across as uppity but it doesn't have to. Saskatchewan's terroir is unique, and we are just beginning to understand and appreciate that. Our harsh climate has meant only the strong survive. The plants and animals that have evolved to thrive here embody a distinct taste-of-place.

Bison are a perfect example. Their story dates back to the ice age, when bison herds dominated North America. They successfully adapted to a warming climate and over thousands of years provided food, shelter, tools, and fuel for the Indigenous people, who revered them. These herds also played an integral role in the regenerative cycle that maintained grasslands and soil health.

In 1800, it's estimated over 60 million animals roamed from as far south as Mexico to as far north as Alaska. After European settlers arrived, a combination of overhunting and disease spelled disaster for the bison. By the turn of the century, less than a thousand animals remained.

Today, thanks to vigorous conservation efforts, there are about 225,000 bison in Canada and 250,000 in the United States. The wild herds, which number roughly 8,000 animals, live in parks and public lands. A leader in bison conservation, Les Kroeger, is profiled in this book (Rosedale Bison, page 87).

Saskatchewan is likely the coldest climate in the world where berry and fruit breeding thrives (via the University of Saskatchewan Fruit Program). Saskatchewan's wild mushrooms, like chanterelles and morels, are beloved for their small size, robust colour, and flavour. Fruits and vegetables taste sweeter here. Ancient grains grown here, like Red Fife wheat, spelt, and kamut, have a depth of flavour not found outside the province. Our mustard is strong, our alfalfa honey is floral, and our lentils earthy.

Our taste-of-place is also thanks to the legions of immigrants who have settled here during the last century, bringing their foods and cooking styles and integrating those with Saskatchewan ingredients. Saskatchewan truly is a multicultural melting pot, a place where you can taste your way around the world.

Each artisan in this book will help you further explore exactly what Saskatchewan terroir is all about.

WHO IS IN THIS BOOK AND WHY?
AND WHAT EXACTLY IS A FOOD ARTISAN?

The word artisan is a somewhat trendy term, in relation to food, and one that I was at first skeptical of. But when I thought about what it means, crafting food by hand, with attention to detail and time-honoured traditions, I realized Saskatchewan was built upon food artisans—from the Indigenous people who first inhabited these lands to the pioneer settlers. Whether they're fishing, brewing, distilling, foraging, or making chocolate, they all have one thing in common: the discovery that doing things a bit slower, the right way the first time, is what builds long-lasting success.

It wasn't possible to include everyone here, and I gave special consideration to those growing our food. They receive the least amount of the spotlight and deserve it the most. The farmers I included are using regenerative and organic techniques to rebuild soil health. They're raising animals holistically to ensure both the animals' health and that of the people who will consume the meat. These farmers—our stewards of the land—can save this planet. I believe regenerative and holistic agriculture is the way of the future and can make great strides in combatting our carbon footprint and climate change. If you're interested in learning more, I included educational resources at the end of the book.

While some of those producers are certified organic, many follow organic practices but aren't certified. It can be pricey and time-consuming, especially for vegetable growers who need to document each varietal to meet certification requirements. As I mentioned earlier, it's expensive to grow food here and the added cost of organic certification is simply not realistic for many growers. That's why it's always a good idea to talk to the people growing your food when you're able. Ask them how they raise their animals and how they grow their produce. Trust and a handshake go a long way. Or take the kids out for a visit to the farm. (All the places listed on each section's map accept visitors; just call ahead.)

The artisan makers and chefs in this book do their best to support the province's food producers. Since Saskatchewan's culinary scene varies widely outside Regina and Saskatoon, so too did my qualities for defining an artisan. This book features many professional chefs, most of whom honed their talents in larger centres before making their contributions to the province's culinary scene.

But I would be remiss if I left out the self-taught who are running bakeries, cafés, and restaurants in small towns. The ones who learned in their grandmas' kitchens are just as much artisans as those who studied abroad. They're all making food from scratch, with quality ingredients and devotion to method at the forefront, along with supporting the local food system and economy.

For me, this book has been an inspiring journey home. My family's agricultural roots run deep; both sides farmed in Europe and the

United Kingdom before immigrating to Canada in the early 20th century and continuing the tradition of growing food. Today, my brother and his family run a grain operation with my dad in southeastern Saskatchewan. They use both organic and regenerative agricultural techniques, and I could not be prouder of their commitment to growing healthy, nutrient-dense food for people.

In 2015, I left my career as a journalist in Saskatoon and moved to Spain, working at horse training facilities for two years. Ultimately, it wasn't the right career for me. I thrive in creating connections with people, writing, and storytelling. Plus, I missed my home too much. Yes, Spain's great but it's got nothing on this province! Creating *Flat Out Delicious* has made me fall newly in love with Saskatchewan. I am so excited to share it all with you. ∎

Disclaimer: It's likely that by the time this book is published, things will have changed for some of the artisans I've profiled. That's the nature of the business, especially for the chefs, who tend to move around a lot. If you feel that a person or product deserves to be in a future edition, please get in touch!

Facebook.com/flatoutfoodsk
Instagram.com/flatoutfoodsk
Twitter.com/JennKSharp

⊙ **Over the Hill Orchards in southeastern Saskatchewan**

Northern Saskatchewan

- Air Ronge
- Big River
- Christopher Lake
- Dore Lake
- La Ronge
- Loon Lake
- Meadow Lake
- Nipawin
- Prince Albert
- Shell Lake
- Spruce Home
- St. Walburg
- Waskesiu

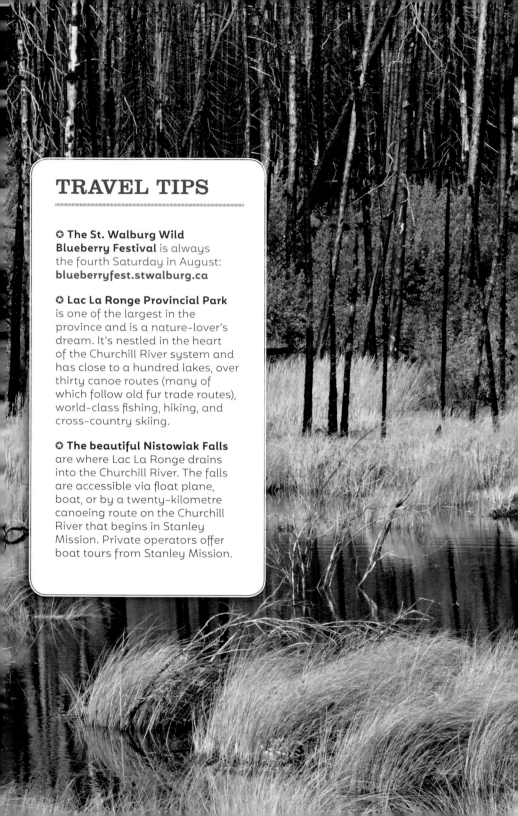

TRAVEL TIPS

✪ **The St. Walburg Wild Blueberry Festival** is always the fourth Saturday in August: **blueberryfest.stwalburg.ca**

✪ **Lac La Ronge Provincial Park** is one of the largest in the province and is a nature-lover's dream. It's nestled in the heart of the Churchill River system and has close to a hundred lakes, over thirty canoe routes (many of which follow old fur trade routes), world-class fishing, hiking, and cross-country skiing.

✪ **The beautiful Nistowiak Falls** are where Lac La Ronge drains into the Churchill River. The falls are accessible via float plane, boat, or by a twenty-kilometre canoeing route on the Churchill River that begins in Stanley Mission. Private operators offer boat tours from Stanley Mission.

P

ut simply, Northern Saskatchewan is pure magic. It's a wild, largely untamed, and untouched region of the province. If you think Saskatchewan is flat, you haven't been to the north!

For the purposes of this book, the region covers everything north of Prince Albert. It's home to lakes and breathtaking boreal forest, lying partly on the northern part of the Great Plains and partly on the Canadian Shield. Head to Lac La Ronge Provincial Park to take in the beauty and see the exposed Precambrian rocks. Campsites are situated on the shore and overlook the lake's islands.

Beautiful as the landscape is, it's difficult to grow food in the Northern region. Instead, Northerners are adept at fishing, foraging, hunting, and trapping. Traditional diets focus more on wild game and less on cultivated vegetable and cereal crops. Native berries have always been an important part of northern diets, and you can get your fill at the St. Walburg Wild Blueberry Festival.

Wild rice harvesting is prevalent here and Saskatchewan's organic wild rice is exported to markets throughout the world. The lakes and rivers are full of fish and quotas are closely followed to ensure the species' future health.

Chefs like Kevin Tetz, who ran the Boreal Bistro and Underground Supper Club in Prince Albert for years, strive to feature northern ingredients, from spruce bark crackers to wild morel mushrooms. Kevin now runs Executive Chef Services.

In recent years, several Indigenous communities have started market and community gardening initiatives, both to provide employment and to ensure food sovereignty in regions where it's expensive to bring in produce. Gardening consultant and northerner Murray Gray has helped many communities set up successful ventures, teaching them how to establish gardens in grow tunnels. ■

◕ Facing page: Lac La Ronge Provincial Park
Previous spread: A view from the road to Dore Lake

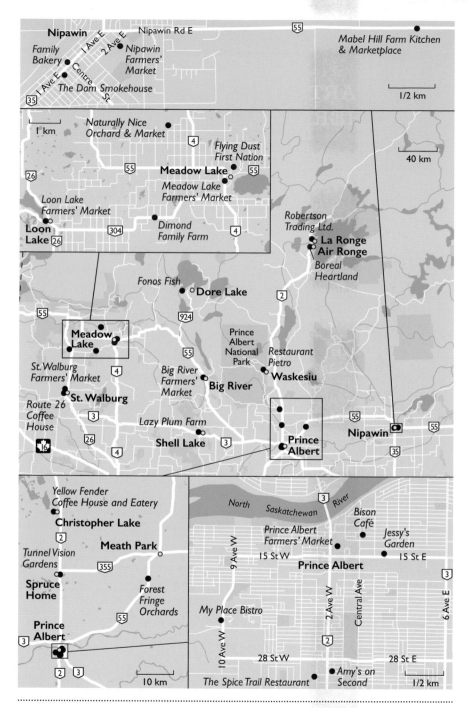

Note: Only artisans and producers who welcome visitors on site are shown on this map.

14

FOOD ARTISANS OF NORTHERN SASKATCHEWAN

Bison Café

1210 Central Ave, Prince Albert | 306-763-9095

Danielle Revale owns the Bison Café with her husband Edward.

■ **The Bison Café** holds dear memories for owners Danielle and Edward Revale. Both immigrated to Alberta from the Philippines and were hired as foreign workers in the food industry, which is how they met. The couple later moved to Prince Albert and Danielle began working at the Bison Café. They eventually bought the business and set down roots in the northern city. They were even married at the café.

The café is a welcoming place in downtown Prince Albert, offering a menu full of made-from-scratch eats and treats, along with a daily lunch special that often includes bison (try the hearty goulash).

Danielle didn't have a background in baking but started exploring how to make sweet treats when she and Edward bought the café. Her morning glory muffins are now a bestseller, but the cranberry flax, blueberry, and white chocolate muffins are definitely worth a taste, too.

When they first took over the business, the baking was outsourced but Danielle says, "We like it fresh—we know what's in it."

A chalkboard menu advertises the specialty coffee and espresso selection, made from Level Ground Trading's beans, a fair-trade importer based in Victoria, BC. "When we place our order, tomorrow they'll roast it and then send it."

The café's back room, which can be reserved for special events, houses the Red Door Gallery where local artists' work is on display and available for purchase.

Family Bakery

103 1 Ave W, Nipawin | 306-862-3600

■ **A good, old-fashioned bakery** is hard to find, but not in Nipawin. Family Bakery was started in 1975 by brothers Peter and Barry Stoicescu. Albert Walker's first job after high school was as their night baker, a role he's kept for over forty years. When the brothers decided to retire, Albert and his wife, Cris, bought the business.

It's truly a family operation for the Walkers. A few years ago, their son Justice began training under Albert when he finished high school. He's now one of the bakers. His shift begins at 11 PM doing prep with two other employees until Albert arrives at 2:30 AM to begin the baking, which finishes at 7 AM.

"He's talking about buying us out at some point down the road. And that's good because there's not a lot of from-scratch bakeries left anymore," says Cris. And speaking of from-scratch, their doughnuts are made daily. Get there early to try the bestselling coconut long johns. Or perhaps an apple pastry, cinnamon bun, cream puff, or éclair is more your style.

All the handmade pastries aside, the bakery is best known for bread. They bake between 1,000 and 1,200 loaves daily. "When it sold, people kept saying, 'Oh, I hope they don't change the recipe for bread.' I told everyone not to worry," Cris says, smiling. She even has a customer who drives four hours from La Ronge to buy a case of bread each month.

Family Bakery supplies stores in Cumberland House, Red Earth Cree Nation, and Carrot River, along with grocery stores and restaurants in Nipawin.

From left, Albert, Justice, and Cris Walker own the Family Bakery in Nipawin.

My Place Bistro

2345 10th Ave W, Prince Albert | 306-922-2299 | myplacebistro.ca

■ **Randy Whitter** knows the draw of a good cinnamon bun in Saskatchewan. At his sunny little Prince Albert café, the sticky sweet cinnamon buns are served hot from the oven every morning. "My baker comes in here at 5 AM and rolls, kneads, cuts, forms, and pans. We make the real gooey ones ... lots of syrup on them," he says with a smile. Cinnamon buns are made every morning except Friday when the oven is reserved for homemade bannock, which has become another hit at My Place.

Randy wants to feed people fresh wholesome food. "I think that in a society of fast food, if you're a real foodie, you realize that we have lost the art of cooking in a lot of cases." That's why everything on the menu is made from scratch. If cinnamon buns aren't your jam, try a Morning Magic Muffin. The house specialty is full of apples, carrots, pineapple, and roasted pecans.

Hannigan's Honey near Shellbrook supplies all the sweetness in My Place's baking and tubs are for sale at the café.

Light lunches include wraps and sandwiches served with salad, the regular cabbage soup, or a daily soup feature. There's cakes, pies, and tarts, along with gluten-free options for after your lunch. "Lunch is designed so that you've got enough room for a cookie or that little piece of confetti square." Sign me up, Randy!

✪ Make sure to stop by Dr. Java's Coffee House in Prince Albert for more homemade baking, lunch items, and coffee roasted on site.

Randy Whitter at My Place in Prince Albert.

Route 26 Coffee House

299 1st Ave, St. Walburg I 306-392-0710

■ **Saskatchewan is full of hidden food gems.** Take Route 26 Coffee House, a café tucked away in St. Walburg, for example. Peggy and Bert Cowan converted their historic house into a café in 2017. Route 26 serves espresso-based coffees, homemade baking (try the legendary cinnamon buns), and light lunches. Everything from the fig compote on the turkey croissant, to the coleslaw on the pulled pork focaccia is made from scratch.

Warm wooden tones, paintings, and antiques artfully link café culture to Saskatchewan history. An upstairs deck and three outdoor patios—one of which has a pond and waterfall—make the place eclectic and inviting. But all the welcoming décor in the world would be for naught if it weren't for the Cowans' hospitality. Route 26 has cemented its place in St. Walburg as a community gathering place.

Bert and Peggy Cowan of Route 26 Coffee House.

Peggy says she wants parents to feel comfortable. "It's so hard for women to get together when they have little kids." High chairs, toys, and a book-borrowing area all help that vision. An outdoor, fenced-in kid zone with a patio means parents can sip a latte and chat while their kids play.

Bert's carpentry is on display at the outdoor bar, built with reclaimed hundred-year-old barn wood. The bar top incorporates smoothly sanded holes where horses were once tied. An Artisan's Garage in the yard displays Bert's barn wood furniture collection, handsome reminders of Saskatchewan's agricultural roots.

✪ St. Walburg is known for the annual Wild Blueberry Festival in August, but Route 26 makes the village worthy of a visit year-round.

Amy's on Second

2990 – 2nd Avenue W, Prince Albert | 306-763-1515 | amysonsecond.com

Amy Hadley opened
Amy's on Second in 1986.

■ **What does it take** to run a successful restaurant for over three decades? Not many know the answer, but Amy Hadley has an idea. She opened Amy's on Second in 1986. "I am really proud of the fact that I've stuck to what I believe in," she says.

Those beliefs include a commitment to quality food made almost entirely from scratch, investing in wonderful staff, and providing customers a personalized experience.

Amy's is known as a place to taste wholly Saskatchewan foods, like wild rice from La Ronge or pickerel caught by Air Ronge's mayor Gordon Stomp and his family. The commitment to local food extends to the community. The restaurant's coffee comes from Prince Albert roaster Dr. Java's Coffee House, and artwork by people in the area hangs on the walls.

A chalkboard menu, designed nightly by Amy's head chef Kyle Novicki, entices customers at the door. On my visit, Novicki featured a pearl barley risotto with pumpkin seeds, goat cheese, and butternut squash, along with a hearty Italian-style bison ragù.

"I like food to be as local and as fresh as possible. I don't like frozen—that drives me insane. It's a little hard in Saskatchewan winters though," says Novicki.

He makes the focaccia daily—you'll get a healthy slice before dinner comes out. And leave room for pastry chef Lindsey Wilkinson's delectable creations, like chocolate layer cake.

"I'm really blessed with the staff I've had over thirty-two years," says Amy. And Prince Albert is blessed to have this long-standing gem of a restaurant.

Diana Bird

Prince Albert | 306-930-1597

■ **Diana Bird believes** wild, foraged, seasonal, and homegrown foods are the way for Indigenous people to regain their health. Diana uses her background in psychology and social work, combined with a passion for cooking, to help teach Indigenous people in Prince Albert how to eat better. She does it through a multi-faceted approach: canning workshops and healthy, traditional meals via her catering company. She teaches at First Nations health centres and cooks for elders when they are sick.

Diana is a member of I-Collective, an autonomous group of North American Indigenous chefs and activists. A cookbook she co-wrote with her family in 2015 got the group's attention and they asked her to give a keynote presentation during an Indigenous food symposium (a family emergency prevented her from attending).

"We're all Indigenous chefs who are experimenting with Indigenous foods in North America and South America. A lot of what we're trying to do is raise awareness of the foods that you can forage in your local backyard."

Food security and sovereignty are causes close to her heart. "My love of food started when I realized that so many Indigenous people do not know how to cook. They don't know how to eat healthy and, because of that, there's so much diabetes, cardiovascular disease, heart disease, obesity—and there's a way around that."

Diana Bird serves up a traditional Indigenous lunch.

Diana is from the Montreal Lake Cree Nation, a hundred kilometres north of Prince Albert. "We hunt, we fish, we gather, we berry pick, and I grew up with those foods my whole life."

The Dam Smokehouse

206 1 Ave W, Nipawin | 306-862-3617

■ **Southern BBQ** is alive and well in northeastern Saskatchewan. Faron Saufert always wanted to get into the industry. He previously worked in agriculture retail, and on a work trip, he was eating at a St. Louis BBQ joint and it got him thinking. "One day, I woke up and said, 'I'm done in ag.' And we took the plunge into this industry."

Faron Saufert owns the Dam Smokehouse in Nipawin.

Faron, his wife Andrea, and sister-in-law Stephanie Ylioja do all the cooking. Faron's daily chalkboard menu featuring items like The Village Idiot (a smoked gouda stuffed Angus burger) or Porky Pig's Revolt (pork belly with cheddar, jalapeño, spicy mayo, and BBQ sauce) have become famous in town.

Faron's always loved cooking. He learned from his mom. "I don't think you have to be a trained chef in order to love cooking. If you have a passion for it, you can make it work."

Their business motto is to support as many Saskatchewan companies as possible. "Coming from the ag side of life, I know how hard farming is. To me, you try to support that as much as you can," he says. The bar only stocks Saskatchewan craft beers and spirits, and that motto applies to the food, too. Bison comes from a ranch near Codette and vegetables from a grower in the area.

The menu combines different BBQ styles, from Texas brisket to St. Louis ribs and Carolina pork butt, with homemade sauce. The pork gets a rub made by Prairie Smoke & Spice BBQ, whose Regina owner, Rob Reinhardt, Faron consulted for advice before opening his restaurant.

Mabel Hill Farm Kitchen & Marketplace

Nipawin | 306-862-2040

Michael Brownlee opened Mabel Hill Farm Kitchen & Marketplace in early 2019.

■ **People in the Nipawin area** got a wonderful New Year's gift when chef Michael Brownlee opened Mabel Hill Farm Kitchen & Marketplace in early 2019.

Michael's formative years were spent helping grow food. His grandparents run Rudy's Fruit and Vegetable Farm near Carrot River. Michael's chef career first took him to Holland College's culinary arts program in Prince Edward Island. He later appeared on the TV series the *Prairie Diner* and worked at Saskatoon's Ayden Kitchen and Bar.

The farm beckoned him home—Michael thought he'd give growing food full-time a chance. He soon realized he missed cooking too much, though, which led to purchasing the Mabel Hill site and developing a business that combines his two passions. Although he's quick to say it's not fully farm-to-table, it's pretty darn close. "We do our best with what we can get from around the area. We make a conscious effort to get as quality products as we can."

The upscale farmhouse is situated at the top of Mabel Hill. The restaurant's floor-to-ceiling windows give a view out to a four-acre garden and

→ **Mabel Hill Farm Kitchen & Marketplace**

orchard. A fireplace blazes in the winter, and seating on the wrap-around verandah is ideal in the warmer months.

"I wanted to see what's possible—what you can grow every day and every year and how it can be changed into something absolutely beautiful." Guests are invited to walk through the gardens, sampling the produce before sitting down for a meal. "The idea is to offer a sense of place."

The contemporary food is all made fresh, from hand-rolled pasta, homemade buns, and house-cured bacon and charcuterie. Much of it can also be purchased at the marketplace store, which includes homemade perogies, cabbage rolls, pies, and preserves—a "dying art for the younger generation" that Michael wants to reinvigorate.

For Michael, cooking has never been about winning competitions or making it onto best restaurant lists. "This restaurant is about building a community: giving the community something to be proud of and offering something that's completely unique to the area."

Heidi O'Brodovich

Yellow Fender Coffee House and Eatery
215 Main St W, Christopher Lake I 306-982-4240

■ **Heidi O'Brodovich** learned everything she needed to know about cooking from her mom, Connie Freedy.

Connie grew up on a farm in rural Saskatchewan and also raised her children on a farm, teaching Heidi baking and pickling, and taking her to pick wild berries.

In 1979, the family moved to southern France for a year when Heidi was ten. Connie and her partner were both avid painters; the family studied art history and, of course, fell in love with French culture and food. "In France, so much is about the taste and presentation of the food and the ceremony of eating," recalls Connie.

Later in life, Connie earned her Red Seal certification in pastry arts, which was "always a dream."

As a young woman, Heidi worked for Parks Canada, but the lure of creating food for people was strong. The year her daughter Emily (a budding pastry chef in her own right) was born, she

Chef Heidi O'Brodovich and her mom Connie at their Yellow Fender Coffee House and Eatery.

quit her job and began a small catering business. She and Connie opened the Yellow Fender Coffee House and Eatery in Christopher Lake in 2004.

The duo's devotion to feeding people from-scratch food made with love paid off. They operated for over a decade year-round, then scaled back to seasonal for several years before Connie retired in 2019.

Along with ingredients sourced from area gardeners, farmers, and fisheries, the café also sells a variety of homemade baking, French bread, custom pastries, and cakes.

The café is for sale, but Heidi's not going anywhere: "Food is always going to be a part of what I do. It's my passion."

Restaurant Pietro

955 Waskesiu Drive, Waskesiu | 306-663-9534
restaurantpietrowask.wixsite.com/restaurantpietro

Owner Garry Gagne serves up a tableside Caesar salad at Restaurant Pietro.

■ **Dining out at the lake** doesn't have to mean burgers and fries. If you're in Waskesiu, there's an elegant and refined dining option. Longtime friends Evan Niekamp and Garry Gagne, who once owned a locally famous pizza joint in Waskesiu, opened Restaurant Pietro in 2014.

Garry takes care of the front of house with outstanding hospitality skills cultivated over a long career in the service industry. He worked at Saskatoon's upscale steak house John's Prime Rib (it's now closed), before opening his first restaurant in Waskesiu.

Evan is the executive chef and focuses on rustic Italian food. His five-mushroom ravioli combines shiitake, oyster, butter, chanterelle, and enoki mushrooms with gorgonzola, encased in pillowy soft homemade pasta. Make sure to order a tableside Caesar salad for two, prepared by Gary, in the restaurant's elegant and welcoming dining room.

Steaks are another highlight and the menu features several cuts, including a bone-in filet mignon. Evan learned his skills from a Swiss master butcher and does all the butchering for the restaurant. Each tender steak is cut by hand and everything on the menu is made from scratch. "I want it completely understandable. Big flavour and great quality ingredients," Evan says.

Restaurant Pietro is open seasonally from May to September. Call for reservations and make sure to visit Gary's other business, Evergreen Coffee + Food, if you're in the area. Get there early. Morning lineups can stretch right out the door for a coffee made with beans roasted by Venn in Saskatoon.

The Spice Trail Restaurant

2902 2 Ave W (Unit #1, South Hill Mall), Prince Albert | 306-970-9442

thespicetrail.ca

■ **Harinder and Sheena Rai** faced a few obstacles when they first opened their Indian restaurant, chiefly educating people about authentic Indian food. "People think Indian food is curry," Harinder says with a smile, adding that generic curry powder does not make a dish authentic.

It's the spices that form the heart of Indian cooking. Harinder buys his wholesale, then grinds and makes custom mixes in-house. The whole process is a bit like chemistry. "The spices that we use need to be activated. They need to be brought to the right heat, at the right time, in the right sequence."

Everything on the menu is made from scratch, right down to the kabab, which Harinder grinds himself. "I don't buy ground beef that you get in the store. It has to be the right consistency, the right amount of fat and meat to get the right product."

Harinder attended culinary school in India, but more importantly learned from his grandmother: "I prefer homemade, grandma food." The Spice Trail's menu focuses on northern cuisine, from the Kashmir region where Harinder was born, with things that he grew up with, like saffron tea served in a traditional pot. Northern Indian handiwork pieces are also for sale in the restaurant, decorated to make one feel transported to South Asia.

The couple opened the restaurant in 2015. Four years later, they opened Kashmere Restaurant on Broadway Avenue in Saskatoon.

Sheena and Harinder Rai own the Spice Trail Restaurant in Prince Albert, along with Kashmere in Saskatoon.

Boreal Heartland

319 Husky Ave, Air Ronge | borealheartland.ca

■ **Northern Saskatchewan's** boreal forests are full of medicinal and nutritious treasures that Indigenous people have been using for centuries.

Randy Johns launched Boreal Heartland in Air Ronge in 2018 as a division of the non-profit Keewatin Community Development Association. The goal is to create jobs for local workers and to promote the various uses for boreal herbs and plants to the world market. Boreal Heartland has been working with a skin care company, which places large orders for dried fireweed. Randy is working on growing wholesale orders with other companies.

Boreal Heartland employs local foragers.

"We have high unemployment rates in our region," he says. "This gives local harvesters and foragers the ability to make some income. We want to build the non-timbered forest products sector in northern Saskatchewan."

For Randy, the business is as much about respecting Indigenous knowledge as it is about helping people make a living. First Nation and Métis harvesters are paid 5 percent extra (everyone is paid by the pound). Many harvest plants from their traditional traplines.

An advisory committee of Indigenous elders helps ensure a balance is maintained between marketing and respecting plants' uses. "We need to be careful of the ethics of using plants traditional to Cree and Dene people. We don't claim medicinal benefits with our products," explains Randy.

Boreal Heartland's products include a line of herbal teas and dried wild mushrooms. Purchase them online at SaskMade Marketplace in Saskatoon, or at the organization's store in Air Ronge, which sells other local goods, like haskap berry jam, wild rice flour, and tree fungus artwork.

Randy welcomes school groups and guided tours to the Air Ronge headquarters.

Curtis Reid
Big River | 306-469-7501

Curtis Reid is a forager in Northern Saskatchewan.

■ **Curtis Reid** has been tree-planting for years, but it was only about a decade ago that he really started paying attention to all the life in the forest. "What grows on the ground is different than what grows through the canopy of the tree," he says. "They're two different worlds and they support all different kinds of animals and flora. It's really incredible."

It was a fellow tree planter who taught him how to forage for chaga. The mushroom, which in Saskatchewan grows on paper birch trees in the boreal forest, has been gaining popularity for a range of health benefits. Chaga is purported to help support the immune system; lower cholesterol, blood pressure, and blood sugar; and slow aging.

Chaga's not all Curtis finds in the forest, though. He's harvested and sold Labrador tea, fireweed leaves, yarrow, wild sarsaparilla root, valerian roots, balm of Gilead buds, and wild mushrooms. "Foraging is a very fluid thing. You have to be open to change as not everything is available all the time."

Robert Rogers's *The Fungal Pharmacy* is Reid's foraging bible. "So much of what he talks about is right out the back door here in Big River. Once you start to pay attention to how everything works together in this natural environment, it's quite astounding."

Find Curtis's foraged chaga, complete with tea-steeping instructions, at the Heart of Riversdale Community Market & Café in Saskatoon and the Wandering Market in Moose Jaw—and inquire at those stores about bringing in his other foraged goods or give him a call to place a larger order.

Flying Dust First Nation

Meadow Lake | 306-236-4437 | flyingdust.net

Band member Gladys Cardinal works in Flying Dust's garden.

■ **The Riverside Market Garden** supplies fresh organic produce year-round for Flying Dust's 1,200 band members, ensuring food security for the Meadow Lake First Nation.

The garden is Flying Dust's economic development manager Albert Derocher's baby. He put together the proposals and has been with it since day one. What started as a two-acre plot to feed the community has grown to a 65-acre farm that includes washing equipment, a climate-controlled storage room (they have fresh potatoes until April), a farmgate store, and a commercial kitchen.

Free-run organic chickens supply thirty dozen eggs daily for people in the community. The band also has cattle and a herd of bison. They keep a few freezers filled with fish, wild game, and beef for band members. Youth go on mandatory hunting trips and everyone shares the meat.

"They all have to learn how to make a fire and survive in the bush," says Albert. "We want to get our young people to understand who they are, where they come from, and to make sure they've got some strong roots."

The First Nation has its own abattoir and people pitch in with butchering the game meat. "We use every piece of the animal. Nothing goes to waste."

They collaborate with Thomas Fresh to grow certified organic potatoes, onions, and carrots, and sell to Sobey's. They also sell produce to Saskatoon businesses, like Thrive Juice Co., and donate thousands of kilograms of potatoes to food banks across the province.

Michael Rooney is the equipment and irrigation manager at Flying Dust's potato processing plant.

The Riverside Market Garden hires about fifteen employees from the First Nation each year, five of whom are certified horticulturists.

The decision to grow organic was an easy one. "We want healthy food, food that we know hasn't had something put into it that's not good for you," says Albert. Saskatchewan isn't typically known for its potato crops, but the soil at Flying Dust is an exception. Tests showed their soil is full of nutrients that make for ideal potato-growing conditions. A ten-year land management plan ensures crops are rotated effectively and soil health is maintained. "Feed the land to feed the people."

Albert's goal in starting the garden was to ensure food sovereignty for Flying Dust's members. "When our people are having a rough time, instead of giving them a cheque to go buy groceries, we have food for them."

It's a beautiful sight to see during the fall harvest, the gardens full of people, others stopping by to pick up veggies for the week. Later in the season, canning nights are held with all that produce to help feed people over winter.

A new heated greenhouse with grow towers is just outside the elementary school. Children from Kindergarten to Grade 4 spend half a day in the greenhouse each week, lending a hand with planting, weeding, and harvesting, while ensuring a future generation of farmers for the community.

All are welcome to stop by the garden and farmgate store.

Jessy's Garden
Hwy 302 E, Prince Albert I 306-922-3103

Bonny Sanderson runs Jessy's Garden in memory of her daughter Jessy.

■ **Ten years ago,** Bonny and Melvin Sanderson's daughter died at age twenty-one from a drug overdose. The couple wanted to create a place that would memorialize Jessy and the work she did with those less fortunate. The best way to do that was by feeding people. "While she was alive, she gave to the homeless. She took care of whoever she could," says Bonny.

After Jessy's death, the couple built a memorial creek and waterfall on their yard east of Prince Albert. Three large vegetable gardens followed. Jessy's Garden initially offered a handout program, providing free vegetables to people in the Prince Albert area. The Sandersons fed over five hundred people in the first three years. It became cost prohibitive, and they've since changed the model to a "hand-up": In exchange for volunteering in the garden, people can take home as much fresh produce as they need. Vegetables are available for purchase at a reasonable price.

The garden is a multi-purpose site. Bonny takes school groups on tours in the fall and gives workshops on container gardening for city dwellers. The Sandersons organize vegetable orders for seniors who can't get to the property to pick. They donate vegetables to Diana Bird, who makes batches of soups and stews for Indigenous elders. "We don't want anyone to go without. This is where this food is meant to go."

In the fall, they host a big harvest event. Once volunteers have taken what they need for the winter, the remaining thousands of kilograms of produce is donated to social service agencies.

Naturally Nice Orchard & Market

Meadow Lake I 306-240-7266 I naturallynice.ca

■ **It's easy to find** Vicki and Roger Cockrum's stall at the Meadow Lake Farmers' Market. It's the one with an almost constant line of people hungry for homemade baking, honey, fruit, and vegetables.

A few years ago, the Cockrums were ready for a change from their 9 to 5 gigs. They dreamed of customers coming to pick produce at their farm and Naturally Nice Orchard & Market took on life. They began by planting six thousand haskaps in 2014, followed by a market garden and beekeeping. The bees pollinate the garden and provide honey for Vicki's bread, preserves, and baking—her haskap and rhubarb crumble is a top seller.

The couple had kept a large garden for thirty years with their three children; changing it to an intense planting operation wasn't too difficult. She and Roger rotate their crops in raised beds, employ minimal tillage techniques, and use landscape fabric and flame weeding to keep the weeds down. The plants that need extra nutrients receive a top dressing of alfalfa pellets and manure.

After the haskaps were established, the Cockrums added raspberries, strawberries, sour cherries, apples, blackcurrants, plums, and rhubarb to the orchard.

Vicki and Roger Cockrum at the Meadow Lake Farmers' Market.

Vicki makes preserves using a combination of these fruits, which also feature prominently in her baking and even in some of the honey.

"We love the haskap berries," she says. "We love how nutritious they are for you—that's our main crop."

Naturally Nice is at the Meadow Lake Farmers' Market every Friday and at Loon Lake's market on Saturdays from June until October. Farm visits are welcome.

Tunnel Vision Gardens

Spruce Home | 306-961-3650

■ **A short drive north** of Prince Albert takes you into Saskatchewan's dazzling Lakeland region. Tunnel Vision Gardens is just south of the region and has supplied customers in the area with bountiful produce for about fifteen years.

Wes and Sarah Detillieux run Tunnel Vision, but it was a venture Sarah started with Wes's mother. The business transitioned when the couple bought high tunnels, one of which is devoted solely to the biggest, brightest strawberries (over 2,400 plants) you're likely to see. Another houses melons and a variety of other vegetables, like bell peppers. The grow tunnels were an excellent addition, explains Sarah. "They help to extend the season, bring things on a little earlier, and keep them going later."

The Christopher Lake Farmers' Market lacked fruit growers and Sarah saw an opportunity, not only for filling a niche but also as a way to teach her four children lifelong skills: "The importance of healthy eating and the importance of working hard for a living, with the hope that one day they will take over or at least use what we've taught them."

Crops like root vegetables, massive cabbage, and Swiss chard thrive in the outdoor gardens. The couple also operates a grain farm and when Wes isn't in the field, he's helping Sarah in the garden. So too are the kids and the grandparents, who live on the neighbouring property. "There is no way I could do this on my own," Sarah says.

Along with the Christopher Lake Farmers' Market, Sarah anticipates selling at the Prince Albert market in the future. To see those strawberries in the tunnels for yourself, just give Sarah a call for directions to the farm.

Sarah Detillieux of
Tunnel Vision Gardens.

Robertson Trading Ltd.

308 La Ronge Ave, La Ronge | 306-425-2080 or 1-888-414-4422

Robertson Trading Ltd. has been open since 1967 in La Ronge.

■ **Robertson Trading Ltd.** has been a northern Saskatchewan institution since 1967. In an area of the province where the people are spread thin, and community gathering spots thinner still, the store on La Ronge's main drag has stood the test of time.

The building is home to a historical Indigenous cultural collection that includes buckskin jackets, beaver felt top hats, and a birch bark canoe. It all hangs from the ceiling's rafters, making for one heck of a unique shopping trip. The second floor also housed CBC's one-person northern bureau office for decades.

It's a genuine trading post, where raw furs are bought and sold, along with local food products (like wild rice and mushrooms) and everything from moccasins and beadwork to birchbark bitings and leathercraft by northern Indigenous artists.

Scott Robertson and his siblings own the business. Scott's sister-in-law Diane manages the store. Scott's dad Alex started the business, after working in the fur industry for the Hudson's Bay Company. Alex amassed the historical collection over the years by trading with and buying from local people. "People needed money, or they wanted to sell things to him because there was a trade happening," explains Diane.

Artwork lines the back wall, from lesser-known artists to the likes of Roger Jerome, who in his sixties painted a mural for the Legislative Building in Regina and met Queen Elizabeth II and Prince Philip. Myles Charles, a painter whose work depicts life on the Plains for Aboriginal people, happened to be there the day I visited. He attended art school in 1968. When asked if he still paints, he replied with a smile, "That's all I do."

→ Robertson Trading Ltd.

Artist Myles Charles with store manager Diane Robertson.

The trading post buys artwork (from as far away as Stanley Mission and Fond du Lac) outright and doesn't take a commission, in order to help provide artists with a small source of income. "We're just trying to help them out. A lot of them don't have that extra money."

The second floor houses the most treasured artwork. It's a collection that spans Saskatchewan's Indigenous history and each piece, like a birchbark berry basket, has its own story of origin. World-renowned birchbark bitings by La Ronge's Sally Milne are up there, too.

Guthrie Winn, the trading post's butcher for over thirty-five years, is legendary in these parts. Many even make the drive from Prince Albert for his bacon, roasts, and smoked brisket. The wall separating Winn's butcher shop from the rest of the store is lined with ribbons and awards, about a dozen from the once illustrious processed meats competition held during Agribition Week in Regina (new food safety regulations caused the competition's end).

Winn makes everything in-house, including fifteen fresh sausage varieties. "Ours is all beef trimmings. It's a better-quality product going in so hopefully better quality coming out," he said.

That wall beside his butcher shop also holds a number of fascinating historical photographs, like one showing huge bins of furs at the trading post back in the day when people still made a living from the trap lines. Diane points to one old picture of Alex with ten thousand muskrat skins and said, "I don't even think we bought one or two hundred this year."

While some pelts (mostly bought as souvenirs) are for sale in the store, they ship most to the North American fur auctions where global buyers snatch them up. "The only thing that's going extinct is the trapper. There's lots of fur out there," says Diane.

The Dimond Family Farm

Meadow Lake I 306-234-2221 I thedimondfamilyfarm.com

▪ **Minda Dimond** says grass-fed beef has three benefits: "To the animal, to the environment, and to the people who ingest it." She and her husband, Colin, and their three children, Bo, Owen, and Charlie, switched their conventional cow-calf operation to a direct-to-market farm in 2015. They added chickens, goats, and sheep, and moved to rotational grazing and grass-finishing their small cattle herd. "I want [our customers] to understand where their food comes from and the difference between our local food compared to commercial food," she says.

The Dimond kids do nearly all of the chicken work (they need a little help moving the pens). One of Minda and Colin's goals in running the farm, where they rely on solar power and grow or raise almost all their own food, was to educate their kids. "They will grow up with actual real-life skills. It sets them up with a work ethic and a way to think critically when things go wrong," Minda says.

Minda makes cheese from their goats' raw milk. She purchases pasteurized milk to make goat cheese for market. She'd love to have a pasteurization facility but says, "for the average person, it's a little cost-prohibitive. And our market is small."

They'd like to expand to bigger urban centres (grass-fed meat has been slow to catch on in the area) but that would detract from her other goal: "We try to do everything as local as possible—support the local economy and feed our community."

The family's booth is at the Meadow Lake Farmers' Market. They take online orders and welcome visitors interested in sustainability and regenerative agriculture to the farm.

Left to right: Bo, Minda, Charlie, and Owen Dimond.

Lazy Plum Farm

Shell Lake | 306-841-7779 | lazyplum.org

■ **Lazy Plum Farm** is a place unlike anywhere else in Saskatchewan. Situated at the end of a dirt road that winds through the boreal forest, the farm is home to a rare group of heritage breed animals.

Tyler Rendek and Dianne Manegre raise Icelandic sheep, Tamworth pigs, and Tibetan yaks. Turns out, yaks thrive in Saskatchewan winters. The same goes for Icelandic sheep and Tamworth pigs, which are direct descendants of European wild pigs and were first brought to Canada in the 19th century. "They're just so winter hardy and suited to this climate," says Tyler.

Tyler Rendek and Dianne Manegre of Lazy Plum Farm.

The couple started raising yaks six years ago. The yaks' dense, woolly coat means they don't lose body heat as easily as cattle in the winter and they're feed efficient. The Icelandic sheep, with their furry round bodies, inquisitive faces, and elaborate curved horns, make vigorous additions to the farm. When the couple began raising Tamworths in 2005, they couldn't find anyone breeding the pigs in Saskatchewan. (They've since helped build up the province's breeding stock.) Tamworths take longer than commercial pigs to reach market weight and don't do well in large-scale confinement operations. However, their meat is nutty and sweet, with an uncommon depth of flavour.

"The breeds that we're raising now in the barns are all driven by economics and not necessarily by considerations on the quality of the meat or the appropriateness of the animal to its environment," explains Dianne.

Lazy Plum Farm's products, from grass-fed yak, beef, lamb, pork, and heritage chicken, can be ordered online with delivery or farmgate pickup options. Farm tours can also be arranged.

Fonos Fish

Dore Lake | 306-832-4450 | reelwomansretreat.com

■ **Jonathon Fonos** has always been a fisherman and he likely always will be. He started Fonos Fish over fifteen years ago from his home at Dore Lake. The lake is full of Saskatchewan's best pickerel, along with ample pike and whitefish.

Jon Fonos at Dore Lake.

Jon has built a loyal customer base for his "from lake to plate" business over the years for two simple reasons: quality and consistency. His process hasn't changed much in fifteen years; he fillets and debones every fish he catches. (His kids, both teenagers, help out on weekends.) It's all frozen within hours of coming off the lake. You can't get fish much fresher than that! "I just haven't ever found anybody that I would let fillet a fish for me to sell. Nobody's came close," he says.

Several Saskatoon chefs have been customers for years. "[They're] pretty loyal and pretty fussy, like me, which is what they should be. There's no such thing as being too fussy with somebody else's food."

Jon grew up in the same lakefront yard where he lives today. Northerner to the bone, he learned how to fish, harvest wild rice, raise animals, hunt, and trap from an early age. (He trapped his first lynx at just six.)

For a time, Jon sold to a fish marketing corporation but the low and non-negotiable prices drove him to find another option. Fonos Fish has a permanent stand at the Saskatoon Farmers' Market.

✪ Bev's Fish & Seafood is another great spot to pick up wild-caught Saskatchewan fish in Prince Albert.

NORTHERN SASKATCHEWAN FARMERS' MARKETS

Check the website for current hours prior to your visit.

Big River Farmers' Market
Hwy 55, next to Tourist Information
Wednesdays and Saturdays
10:00 AM–2:00 PM
May to September

Loon Lake Farmers' Market
North of Legion Hall, school area
Saturdays 9:00 AM–3:00 PM
late June to Labour Day Weekend

Meadow Lake Farmers' Market
Old Museum Building
Hwy 4 South
Fridays 10:00 AM–2:30 PM
May to October
facebook.com/
meadowlakefarmersmarket/
306-240-7266

Nipawin Farmers' Market
Centennial Arena parking lot
Thursdays 7:45 AM–Noon
May to October

Prince Albert Farmers' Market
Gateway Mall
Hours vary
facebook.com/buylocalpa/
or www.pafm.ca

St. Walburg Farmers' Market
Town Campground
Fridays 3:00 PM–6:00 PM
May to September,
December Christmas Market
facebook.com/pages/category/
Community/St-Walburgs-Farmers-
Market-666522170087679/
306-248-7574

NORTHERN SASKATCHEWAN WATERING HOLES

Check the website for current hours prior to your visit.

Forest Fringe Orchards

Prince Albert
(see website for directions to farm)
306-930-6229
forestfringeorchards.ca

Tours: By request.
Winery, U-pick, and farm store.

SASKATCHEWAN'S WILD RICE

The journey from northern lakes to dinner plates

After a day of howling winds and overcast skies, the sudden stillness at sunset was almost startling. The sun began to descend toward the horizon over Meeyomoot Lake. Rays of light poked through the clouds and coloured the sky burnt orange, pink, and yellow.

The Muirhead family had been at the ready all afternoon, waiting for the wind to die down, so they could get back out on the water and continue harvesting wild rice. It's an unconventional harvesting scene—lightweight aluminum airboats gliding over the water's surface and a buzz boat waiting to collect the harvest—but one that's vital for the province's northern economy.

Apart from wild rice's delicious nutty flavour and nutritional value, what has helped make it popular all over the world is its sustainability. Wild rice is an organic food source grown in harmony with nature. Harvesters in Saskatchewan go to great lengths to ensure the province's pristine northern waters stay that way. The Muirheads are some of the industry's newest arrivals and are working to create a more robust local market for the high-fibre grain.

◐ **Harvesting wild rice on Meeyomoot Lake.**

⊙ **Chase and Larissa Muirhead and their daughter Violet.**

A few years ago Larissa and Chase Muirhead and their family took over a long-standing wild rice operation on Meeyomoot Lake. The pair both have careers in non-agricultural sectors but when the wild rice opportunity came, they jumped at the chance.

Family friend Lynn Riese first obtained a lease to harvest wild rice from Meeyomoot and several smaller lakes in the area just east of Prince Albert National Park, over thirty years ago. (Riese also exports wild rice via his company, Riese's Canadian Lake Wild Rice.) Provincial regulations stipulate that only northern residents can hold leases on lakes where wild rice grows. Riese and his family built a camp on an island at Meeyomoot—the area can only be accessed by float plane—and acquired all the necessary harvesting equipment.

When Riese wanted to pass along the business to another family, he approached Garth, Chase's father. Although the Muirheads didn't have an agricultural background, they wanted to try. In 2015, the family began a two-year crop sharing agreement with Riese to learn the ropes and Against the Grain Organic Wild Rice was born.

The Muirheads got lucky. Those were high-yielding rice years. But then—typical in agriculture—that high was followed by an extreme low. "Our first year on our own was the worst year on record," says Larissa. That first year was tough for other reasons, too.

Industrious beavers dropped six trees on the camp, destroying two harvesters and several cabins. A plow wind tore apart a buzz boat. And the docks washed away in a storm. "It was pretty interesting to go through all of the really bad things in one year," she says, laughing.

Family members, including Chase's sister Katy, take turns working during the harvest season from late August to October. Sometimes, the whole clan is living at camp together. "For us, this is a family affair," says Larissa. The camp is full of laughter and comradery. Larissa and Chase's young daughter Violet loves camp life, playing with her cousins and immersing herself in nature. "It's a great place to raise a kid and have them out here. It means a lot," says Larissa.

A Cessna 180 float plane came with the camp and the family hires a pilot each season during harvest. Chase also has his pilot's licence and in their off-time, the couple explores islands in the area, foraging wild foods. Larissa is an apothecarist, skilled at using northern plants for health remedies.

The area's bounty is almost hard to believe. Chanterelle mushrooms colour the hill on one island peach and deep orange. Other islands overflow with blueberries and cranberries.

The camp island, like all the rest, is full of fir trees and bushes. The Cessna floats in the water, tethered to a small dock on the shoreline. The plane does double duty as a ride for people and provisions, and wild rice transport. The camp is a rugged, rustic affair of simple log cabins, all heated by wood-burning stoves. One cabin doubles as

⊙ Cosette, Garth, and their daughter-in-law Larissa Muirhead.

the cookhouse, a propane-fuelled stove and small countertop the only space to prepare meals for up to ten. A big coffee kettle sits at the ready for those cold nights when the crew comes in wet and chilled to the bone from harvesting. There's a small shower room (that, thanks to a generator, has hot water), an outhouse, and a shed full of tools.

It's hard work. To be a wild rice harvester, one must also be adept at mechanics. There's no way for the harvesting equipment to leave the lake when repairs are needed. There's stress about what yields will be like that year, breakdowns, and the weather. And, of course, there's all the planning that goes into living in a remote area.

Larissa never envisioned her husband as a farmer but has witnessed a huge change in him. "When Chase comes in on the harvester after a big day, the smile on his face is just priceless."

Wild rice is North America's only native cereal crop. It's a grass plant that originated in the Great Lakes region. Saskatchewan's climate and soil limit agricultural opportunities in the north. However, shallow lakes and slow-moving rivers that formed on the ancient rocks of the Precambrian Shield are an ideal habitat for wild rice.

According to a University of Saskatchewan publication, northern entrepreneurs who invested time and resources were responsible for the now flourishing international trade in the province's wild rice. Wild rice was introduced to Saskatchewan in the 1930s to provide food for muskrats and waterfowl to enhance hunting and trapping opportunities. The commercial industry took off in the late 1970s.

Before the propeller-driven airboats were introduced, people used canoes for harvesting. One person sat in front and paddled, while the second bent stalks over the boat's side with a short, tapered stick and used another stick to tap off the rice.

Modern harvesters (most of which are handmade) have wide flat-bottomed aluminum hulls fitted with collecting trays. As the harvester moves through the rice stands, rice grains hit an angled screen on the header and fall into the tray. After several passes, the harvester dumps the tray into a buzz boat. The rice is shovelled by hand into bags, which are later taken to the dock for air transport to the mainland (up to ten flights a day at the height of harvesting). A bus later takes the bagged rice to a processing plant in La Ronge.

⬆ **Nicole Lemire and Gordon Charles shovel rice into bags.**

Jeanne Gress manages the La Ronge Wild Rice Corporation. At the modest facility on the edge of town, wild rice is finished, cured, dried, and bagged before it goes to export companies. Much of the work is done outside.

"It's a wonderful product (and) it has a lot of nutritional value," Jeanne says. But although wild rice is sought-after elsewhere in the world, the high-fibre grain isn't a staple at many Saskatchewan dinner tables. "As people get more familiar with it, it'll catch on," says Larissa, who posts recipes on Against the Grain's Facebook page. "But people just either don't know about it or aren't really aware of how healthy it is."

The Muirheads' wild rice, like much of that grown in northern Saskatchewan, is certified organic and requires minimal inputs. Wild rice is an annual plant. Reseeding is only necessary when it's been wiped out by fluctuating water levels. The family keeps a portion of their harvest each year and markets it throughout Saskatchewan under their own label; the rest is exported internationally.

Meeyomoot Lake is a magical place. Aside from the camp, it's a part of Saskatchewan seemingly untouched by humanity. Towering fir trees on nearby shorelines are set off by green stands of wild rice in the sparkling blue water.

Wildlife is abundant here—geese, ducks, moose, muskrats, beavers, deer, fish, and the odd black bear. Larissa's handiwork in the outhouse is required bathroom reading for newcomers to camp: steps outlining what to do if you encounter a bear.

"You know there's something about this place as soon as you get here, it just grabs you," she says. And she's right. Even though it's a short plane ride to the closest grid road, it feels like thousands of miles away from civilization.

The sun disappeared on the horizon that day, as Chase moved the harvester through the rice stands, golden rays highlighting his face. He and his family have found their happy place and it's one that also provides a nutritious, sustainable food source to thousands all over the world. ■

◈ **Chase Muirhead runs the wild rice harvester on Meeyomoot Lake.**
◈ **Following spread: A heritage Icelandic lamb at Lazy Plum Farm.**

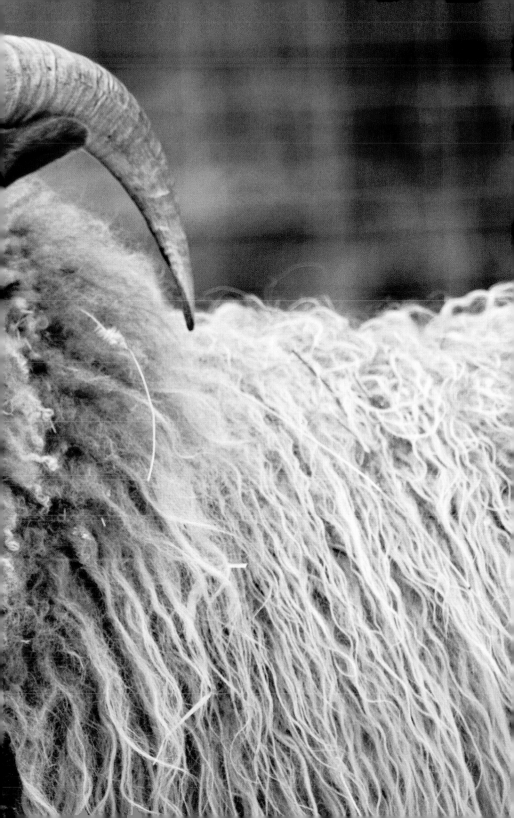

West Central Saskatchewan

- Battleford
- Biggar
- Blaine Lake
- Crossmount
- Denzil
- Dundurn
- Grandora
- Hanley
- Hepburn
- Lloydminster
- Martensville
- North Battleford
- Osler
- Outlook
- Parkside
- Paynton
- Perdue
- Radisson
- Richard
- Rosetown
- Rosthern
- Saskatoon
- St. Louis
- Vanscoy
- Waldheim
- Warman

TRAVEL TIPS

✪ **Learn more about the region's Doukhobor pioneers** on a guided tour and sample bread baked in a clay oven at the Doukhobor Dugout House, near Blaine Lake: **doukhobordugouthouse.com**

✪ **The Seager Wheeler Farm** educates visitors on the farm's famous founder who immigrated to Canada in 1885. Wheeler developed new grain and horti-culture varieties (including three types of wheat), and helped publicize the Prairies' agricultural potential. Tours are held in the summer and a September harvest dinner features homemade food with fruit and produce from the farm's orchards and gardens: **seagerwheelerfarm.org**

West Central Saskatchewan is full of places to explore and learn. Intriguing national historic sites give a sense of place, helping to tell the story of West Central Saskatchewan's past.

North of Rosthern, the Batoche National Historic Site educates visitors on the Northwest Resistance of 1885. A traditional way of life was forever changed during this historic battle between the Métis and First Nations, and General Middleton's Canadian Forces.

Poundmaker Cree Nation is west of North Battleford and includes a museum and historic site atop Chief Poundmaker Hill. Saskatchewan's Northern Plains Cree culture and traditions are detailed in the museum's collections. Elders and storytellers from the community share stories from the Battle of Poundmaker, which took place on the site during the Northwest Resistance. Much of this oral history has not been recorded anywhere and is often left out of Canadian history.

A large concentration of Saskatchewan's Mennonite population settled in the West Central region. Today, that means this is where you come to find the best Mennonite sausage in the province, along with traditional food you'll be hard-pressed to find elsewhere in Saskatchewan. While there are over a dozen Mennonite butcher shops in the Warman/Osler/Rosthern region, Riverside Meats has consistently won top honours at the annual Lord of the (Sausage) Rings competition, held in Osler.

Small-town grocery stores stock homemade items like kielke noodles and roll kuchen, a fried pastry usually served with watermelon. PS Liquor & Market is a wonderful specialty grocery in Osler that stocks everything from homemade summa borscht soup and baking to local produce, honey, and other Saskatchewan-made food products.

↻ Previous spread: **Two of Hal Jadeske's goats at Red Barn Dairy.**
↻ **A flowering flax field in West Central Saskatchewan.**

Saskatoon is home to likely the world's only drive-thru perogi restaurant, Baba's Homestyle Perogies, Kindersley's annual Zest of the West festival features dozens of Saskatchewan restaurants, along with distilleries and breweries, and Lloydminster's Exhibition Association holds a Harvest Feastival in October with gourmet menus featuring locally produced ingredients. In July, the Farmyard Market near Martensville hosts Perogyfest, an outdoor party with local bands, Mennonite sausage, and, of course, homemade perogies. In August, Petrofka Orchard's AppleFest celebrates the harvest season with wagon rides, homemade food, music, and children's activities. ∎

⊙ **Steven Guenther checking his crops at Living Soil Farms north of Osler.**

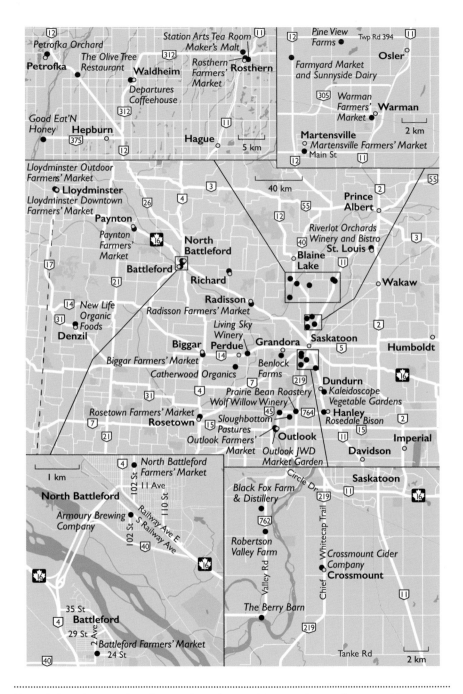

Note: Only artisans and producers who welcome visitors on site are shown on this map.

WEST CENTRAL SASKATCHEWAN ARTISANS

Departures Coffeehouse
3019 Central Ave, Waldheim | 306-716-6548

Sophia Kim and Gun-Sang Yoon own Departures Coffeehouse.

■ **A café housed** in a charming little red-roofed building in the heart of Waldheim is helping change people's minds about just how good small-town food can be. In fact, Saskatonians even make the journey to Departures Coffeehouse as there's nothing quite like it anywhere else.

Sophia Kim and Gun-Sang Yoon, a couple from South Korea, opened Departures in 2014 along with their daughter Liv. Waldheim's charm and proximity to Saskatoon appealed to them.

Sophia specializes in authentic Korean dishes, like dumplings and bulgogi. Staple ingredients, like red pepper powder, soybean paste, and sesame seed oil come from her family's South Korean farm. In the summer, gardener friends supply the vegetables. The menu also features Canadian dishes, like salads, sandwiches, and pizza, all made from scratch. Liv handles much of the baking and her desserts have become legendary in these parts. The café offers a gourmet espresso drink menu, organic loose-leaf teas, specialty teas from Korea, and homemade milkshakes.

"We pride ourselves on being an interaction-based (rather than transaction-based) business. Sophia is gregarious and loves getting to know our customers," says Liv. They happily take requests from customers for future menu items. Liv's gluten-free coconut flour chocolate chip cookies are a big hit and came from a customer request. When the Buddha bowl trend hit, the café put out a prairie version, using local vegetables and Sophia's soy sauce, made using her homemade veggie stock to amp up both nutrition and flavour depth.

The travel-themed café hosts different artisans' work throughout the year and live music nights.

Prairie Bean Roastery
Outlook | prairiebean.coffee

■ **Prairie Bean Roastery** was born out of a Seattle transplant's desire for freshly roasted coffee. "I moved to Canada and everyone drinks canned coffee. That's not a thing!" laughs Valerie Ylioja. She, her husband, Nick, and their seven children live on an acreage near Outlook, where roasting endeavours began in earnest several years ago with a Value Village popcorn popper.

The couple toured Diedrich Roasters' plant in Idaho before purchasing one of the company's coffee roasters. It's an automated beauty that delivers a consistent, elevated coffee experience.

They launched Prairie Bean Roastery in 2017, offering carefully crafted coffee blends with names that evoke life on the Prairies. (The Gale Force espresso is my favourite.) Coffee labels match the whimsical prairie aesthetic—the result of a vision to connect the coffee to Saskatchewan.

Their beans come from a variety of origins and are sourced through Café Imports, an American company focused on empowering farmers with price, traceability, and long-term partnerships.

The roastery has a partnership with Simply Grounded Coffee Gallery. Their two Saskatoon cafés serve a custom house blend drip coffee, made by Prairie Bean, and serve the roastery's espressos as well.

"That's been cool to see the bigger relationships that we've built," says Valerie. "We wanted to roast coffee for the average person and make it affordable. Everybody can afford to drink fresh coffee."

Prairie Bean Roastery is also sold and served at several other locations. Check the website for details, online ordering, custom design, and roasting inquiries.

Nick Ylioja roasting coffee beans.

Station Arts Tea Room

701 Railway Ave, Rosthern | 306-232-5332 | stationarts.com

■ **You won't find hip philosophies** at the Station Arts Tea Room, just home-cooked food all made from scratch in a kitchen that began life as an adjunct to the Arts Centre and became a destination in its own right. "From our earliest days, we just call it home cooking," says owner Dennis Helmuth of the restaurant he and his sister Joan Yoder began running over two decades ago.

"We work with material on hand, out of the garden, procure as local as we can," he says, adding they're not fanatical about being wholly local. "I challenge any decent kitchen to cook without lemons or olive oil."

The Tea Room's meals are reminiscent of Grandma's kitchen: simple, hearty, and honest. The small menu features sandwiches, salads, homemade dessert (the cream pies are the stuff of legends), and a daily soup, served with a thick slice of whole wheat bread made from organic flour stone-milled on site.

Wild blueberries, cranberries, and lingonberries show up on the menu, as does smoked farmer's sausage from Carmen Corner Meats, Grandora Gardens' tomatoes, and cherries from the Seager Wheeler Farm.

The Tea Room is open daily for lunch and occasionally offers a set dinner menu to coincide with performances at the Arts Centre, which is all housed inside a renovated CN Railway station.

Station Arts, a cooperative for performing and visual arts, opened in 1990. It includes an art gallery and summer theatre lineup. "It's a multi-sensual experience at the Arts Centre," says Dennis. "We feel very fortunate that our town has something like this."

Dennis Helmuth at the Station Arts Tea Room.

Good Eat'N Honey

Hepburn | 306-946-4217

Ian Eaton and the high school students he employs unloading beehives.

■ **North of Saskatoon,** Ian and Verna Eaton run a booming family-size honey operation. They keep between 650 and 700 hives. About 350 of those are producing colonies, while the rest are nucleus hives (starter colonies that are building in population for the next year).

The couple sells the majority of their product to Bee Maid Honey. They keep a portion of the sweet clover and wildflower honey to sell under their Good Eat'N Honey label: "The best of the best," says Ian. "It's just got that little bit better flavour to it with a nice and soft buttery texture."

In his decades as a beekeeper, Ian has become a keen bee observer. He refers to their dance, the bottom-wiggling jig bees use to alert the colony to nectar or pollen: "I can actually watch a bee dance and I know where it's telling its girlfriends to go ... I see them dance and say, 'Okay, they're all going south.' And then I look, and sure enough, there's a field of something blooming south."

→ Good Eat'N Honey

....

The Eatons' bees produce a lot of honey—anywhere between 114 and 160 kilograms per hive each year. Sometimes it comes in so fast it splashes out of the hives' frames. The bees work quickly to bring the moisture content down to around 18 percent and preserve the honey. "Sometimes we'll see thousands of bees out on the front of the hive fanning, trying to pull the air through to dehydrate that honey."

Each bee gives about an eyedropper's worth of honey, 70 percent of which is water. "So you can imagine the volume that each tiny bee [gives]." And yet, as a group, they bring in massive amounts. "We're starting to think of the hive as one organism that all works together."

Maybe we could all take a lesson from the bees.

Find Good Eat'N Honey in the Hepburn, Waldheim, Craik, and Blaine Lake Co-op grocery stores; Nutters stores in Moose Jaw, North Battleford, and Prince Albert; Herbs 'n' Health in Saskatoon; and Smokehaus Meats in Martensville. Verna and Ian enjoy sharing their bee knowledge; give them a call if you'd like to visit.

Farmyard Market and Sunnyside Dairy

Martensville | 306-242-8949 | farmyardmarket.ca

■ **A small dairy** north of Martensville made headlines in Saskatchewan in 2018 when it announced plans to open the province's first creamery in recent times. Bas and Martha Froese-Kooijenga own Farmyard Market and Sunnyside Dairy where they have thirty milking cows. "We produce the milk on the farm and if we can process it and sell it from our yard—for us, it is a nice option," says Bas.

The creamery opened in spring 2019. It includes a coin-operated Swiss milk dispenser—the second of its kind in Canada—so customers can buy milk on tap. The milk is non-homogenized, which means the fat molecules are not broken down and the cream rises to the top.

The couple operates the Farmyard Market on their property, a farmgate store where they sell their grass-fed beef and pork, homemade baking and perogies, along with products from other local farmers, market gardeners, beekeepers,

Martha and Bas Froese-Kooijenga own Farmyard Market and Sunnyside Dairy.

and craftspeople. Martha was raised on the farm with eleven siblings, and she remembers her mom always sold cream, cottage cheese, and eggs.

The Froese-Kooijengas' small dairy herd lives outside for much of the year. Bas names each cow and calf; when he's milking the cows, he takes the time to groom and pet each one. "We try to keep the cows happy. That's the goal."

It used to be a common practice to buy milk directly from small dairies in Saskatchewan. For Martha, being able to sell her cows' milk is a return to a simpler time. "It's old fashioned and I like that. And people are excited about it, too. There's a trend [toward] off the farm foods, the way it used to be."

The farmgate store is open year-round; directions are on the website. Watch for details about the farm's annual summer Perogyfest.

Red Barn Dairy

Richard | 306-380-8612

■ **After thirty years** of milking cows, Hal Jadeske retired and moved to the lake. He soon got bored and decided he needed to work with animals again. The growing demand for goat milk in Saskatoon's ethnic communities convinced him to buy a herd (he has about seventy goats now) and build a pasteurization facility at his farm.

He spent about a year getting his licensing in place with the Saskatchewan Health Authority. It was a long process, mainly because he was the first in his region to acquire the licence.

Hal Jadeske at Red Barn Dairy.

He opened a stall in 2017 selling certified organic goat milk at the Saskatoon Farmers' Market. "The farmers' market has been a good place for me to grow. I've been able to develop quite a loyal customer base."

By the following summer, Red Barn Dairy's goat cheese was also available.

Hal's parents both died from cancer several years ago. He said it made him rethink his retirement plans and his life. "I said, 'Well, heck! I'm not going into a ten-by-ten room to die. I might as well be out here having fun doing something.'"

Thus far, raising the goats has been "wonderful," although building a market for his products have taken longer than he expected. "Getting up in the morning and working every day is not an issue, it's second nature. But goats are way more fun than cows."

Red Barn Dairy's goat cheese is also available at Dad's Organic Market and the Heart of Riversdale Community Market & Café in Saskatoon.

The Olive Tree Restaurant

Hwy 12, Hepburn | 306-945-5551

Georgia Sinaki owns the Olive Tree Restaurant.

■ **As soon as Georgia Sinaki** set foot in Saskatchewan, she knew she was home. More specifically, it was the landscape near the North Saskatchewan River, south of Blaine Lake, that drew her in. She liked it enough to leave the island of Crete, where she trained and worked as a chef, and establish a new life for her two daughters.

She and her partner Michael Pantermarakis have created a warm, welcoming restaurant with excellent homemade Greek food, organic wine, and hospitality, which makes it all the more worth the drive. It may be a location in the middle of nowhere, but that mattered little to Georgia. Nor did it matter to her when friends said it would be difficult without a deep fryer. "That kind of thing, you can find in little towns everywhere," says Georgia. "I wanted to do something unique, use local products and extra virgin olive oil from Greece."

Over a decade later, she's stayed true to her word. Her Greek and Mediterranean food, from moussaka to tzatziki and spanakopita, are made from scratch and with love. Ingredients are from producers in the area, apart from the herbs and olive oil. The olive oil comes from Michael's family's olive farm in Crete and is also sold in the adjoining food market.

The Olive Tree is an eclectic place full of antiques that reveal its past lives (as a gas station and diner). In 2019, extensive renovations, including an olive tree mural on the ceiling, made the space just that much more welcoming.

The Berry Barn

830 Valley Road, Saskatoon | 306-978-9797 | berrybarn.ca

Natalie and Grant Erlandson with their dogs at their idyllic Berry Barn, located on the South Saskatchewan River.

■ **Warm summer days** attract a steady convoy of vehicles driving south of Saskatoon to the end of Valley Road where the famed Berry Barn awaits. It's here where locals often take out-of-town guests to pick the region's namesake berry or to enjoy a homestyle meal in a restaurant with the prettiest views for miles.

Grant and Natalie Erlandson bought the property and orchards over two decades ago. They built a restaurant, filled with antiques and country charm, along with a wide patio that offers sweeping views of the river.

Grant says their goal is to bring the farm life to city folks. "We were raised on the farm and thought everyone had a connection to the farm. But that's not the case. It's really getting lost now, even in Saskatchewan."

In the fall, a greenhouse becomes a kids' fun zone, then later morphs into a haunted house in October. Life-size farm equipment toys dot the grounds. There's even a pedal cart track and an ice cream shack. And, of course, you can take the kids out berry picking. Family fun and berry picking aside, the Berry Barn's gift shop stocks their house preserves, along with other Canadian-made collectibles, and a case of homemade baking beckons.

The Erlandsons have shared their passion for growing food with visitors from all over the world. "They come for the beauty. The serenity of it," says Grant, as he points to the view of the South Saskatchewan River, in all its glittering glory.

Floating Gardens

Osler | floatinggardens.ca

■ **Winter doesn't mean an end** to fresh vegetables, thanks to Floating Gardens. In 2011, siblings Chris and Rachel Buhler, with help from their family, started a hydroponic greenhouse operation. The siblings had read a stat that said Saskatchewan produces less than 5 percent of its own fruits and vegetables. "The food security of that is a really big problem. That was a big factor in us starting," says Chris.

Today, they grow twenty-six crops. Their vibrant tomatoes, eggplants, and cucumbers burst with flavour and are the biggest sellers.

The hydroponic system allows plants to grow on average six times (or even up to fifteen times) faster than if those plants were grown in soil outdoors. "Per square foot to grow in a greenhouse is so much more expensive than growing outside—it's ridiculous. We need things to grow faster in order to make money," says Chris.

It's expensive to heat the greenhouse in the winter. Chris says their prices are higher than your average grocery store vegetables for several reasons. "To ship stuff in from other places costs around 5 percent of the cost of your final product. Our heating and even our staff time is a lot more expensive here than it is in Mexico or in the United States. The system is not aimed at helping the environment. The system is aimed at big corporations making money."

Pre-order vegetables via their website or through Local and Fresh. Visit their stall at the farmers' markets in Saskatoon and Regina.

Chris, along with his sister Rachel Buhler, own Floating Gardens.

Grandora Gardens

Grandora | 306-668-4598 | grandoragardens.com

■ **Grandora Gardens** is a favourite stop for many at the Saskatoon Farmers' Market. The table overflows with tubs of bright tomatoes, crunchy bell peppers, and vibrant little chili peppers. And everyone who visits has received the cucumber talk at one point: Did you know fresh cukes don't need to be refrigerated?

Fred and Pat Gittings' vegetables are insecticide-free and grown with biological controls. They were one of the first operations in Saskatchewan to use specific bugs to control crop-eating pests.

After many years in the business, the couple is retiring but they won't soon be forgotten. They started with a relatively small greenhouse in 1991 as a second income for Pat. They later decided to go all out and make a living growing food. "We added another greenhouse and then we sold all those cucumbers, and so we added two more greenhouses. And we just kept adding to the operation," recalls Pat. "I enjoy the growing. If I had my choice, I would be out in the plants every day."

Today, the greenhouses take up an acre of land on their farm west of Saskatoon. They employ twelve people during the growing season and sell cucumbers to six Co-op grocery stores in Saskatchewan.

For Fred, when people tell him that Grandora's tomatoes are the best they've eaten, "It's been rewarding in that sense more than anything else. I think it's more a social philosophical bend. We're supplying a local need and meeting people at the market, talking to them and educating them."

Fred and Pat, you will both be missed. Saskatoon veggie lovers look forward to the greenhouses' future with a new owner.

Fred and Pat Gittings opened Grandora Gardens in 1991.

Kaleidoscope Vegetable Gardens
Dundurn | 306-262-0646

■ **Adithya Ramachandran** has loved gardening since he was a child. In 2011, he and his wife, Jennifer Menat, began an urban farm in Saskatoon. "I saw there was an opportunity for unique, niche vegetables," he says.

Adithya Ramachandran and Jennifer Menat own Kaleidoscope Vegetable Gardens.

The couple used row covers and low tunnels for growing in rented backyard gardens around the city but soon found the travel time inconvenient. In 2013, they bought a property near Dundurn, built high tunnels, and have expanded the operation several times since then.

"I wanted to manage a farm that was low carbon. That's why I don't use any heat in my tunnels," explains Adithya, adding that they collect rain water for irrigation. "I try to be environmentally friendly and work with the seasons rather than try to defeat them, but at the same time, I use row covers to extend the season."

The couple has set themselves apart by growing heirloom vegetables, like Asian and Italian eggplant, tomatillos, and Japanese turnips, along with Spanish Padron peppers. They strive to grow the most flavourful varieties. Their kabocha squash is just one example. "In my opinion, that's the best kind of squash you can find. It's so dense and starchy, the flavour gives you a lot of satisfaction when you eat it. It's a cross between sweet potato and egg yolk."

Crop selection is tailored to the season. During the winter, both the soil and the gardeners get a well-deserved rest.

Find Kaleidoscope's stall at the Saskatoon and Regina farmers' markets. Inquire about CSA subscriptions as they may begin offering farm shares in 2020.

Mumm's Sprouting Seeds

Parkside | 306-747-2935 | sprouting.com

Mumm's Sprouting Seeds sells a variety of microgreens.

■ **The company farmers** Maggie and Jim Mumm founded in 1982 is still going strong in Parkside, Saskatchewan. In the beginning, alfalfa was the main crop on their mixed organic farm. They looked into the natural foods market for alfalfa sprouts and started a small sideline business. Their first contract was with a company in Vancouver and it grew from there.

"In the early years, it was quite slow growth," recalls Maggie. "Now, we have somewhere between eighty and one hundred different varieties of seeds to grow sprouts and microgreens."

Everything is certified organic and always has been. "We were just totally committed right from the beginning."

In 2000 the Mumms moved the business from the farm to an old curling rink in town, acquiring more staff over the years. Today, their daughter Lisa is partway through a buy out plan to take over the operation.

They still grow some of the specialty sprouting seed crops on the farm, but most are sourced from organic farmers in Saskatchewan. The Mumms work with organic operations outside Canada for seed that doesn't grow well here.

Everything is packaged and shipped from the Parkside facility, to people growing sprouts on their kitchen counter right up to large orders for commercial spreaders that sell to restaurants and grocery stores. They have customers throughout Canada and the United States.

The website is an excellent resource for anyone getting into growing sprouts and microgreens, both for personal use or as a business. Free shipping is available within Canada on orders over $25.

Petrofka Orchard

Hwy 12, Blaine Lake | 306-497-2234 | petrofkaorchard.com

■ **Petrofka Orchard** is a wonderful place to while away a warm summer afternoon. The forty-six-acre orchard lies along the banks of the North Saskatchewan River and guests can take tours or self-guided hikes on the grounds. Bring a fishing rod or a picnic basket (or both!) and bask in the beauty, or enjoy a freshly baked apple cinnamon bun at a picnic table overlooking the orchard.

The orchard's name pays homage to the original owners' Doukhobor roots. The Doukhobors were a group that fled religious persecution in Russia and settled in the nearby Petrofka village in 1899.

Petrofka Orchard began as an apple orchard. The original owners worked with the University of Saskatchewan's fruit department on new Saskatchewan-hardy apple varieties. The current owner, fruit breeder Diana Fedosoff, develops new varieties and grows trees for the U of S.

She bought the orchard in 2014 and added haskap, sour cherry, and plum trees, along with a thousand more apple trees. The business side expanded with over fifty products and help from her two children and brother-in-law.

A farmgate store stocks those products, such as iced sour cherry green tea, apple mustard, and apple breakfast sausage, along with meat, baking, and produce from local farmers. The biggest sellers are homemade orchard fruit pies and traditional Doukhobor bread made in a clay oven using a centuries-old recipe.

School tours and tours for seniors are available. Watch the website for details about a late summer apple festival.

"I love people. I like visiting with people. I like bringing kids out here and teaching them where their food comes from," says Diana.

✪ Hafford is a scenic thirty-minute drive west of Petrofka. The town's A & M Bistro & Bakery makes it worth the trip.

Diana Fedosoff in her apple orchard.

Riverbend Plantation and HomeQuarter Coffeehouse & Bakery

110-405 Avenue B S, Saskatoon | saskatoonberry.com
or homequartercoffeehouse.com

■ **The Whittington family** has been growing Saskatoon's namesake berry for decades in their Valley Road orchard. Grace, Lee, and their children own Riverbend Plantation, a large value-added food company making everything from jams and syrups to pemmican and pie filling. Riverbend Plantation is perhaps most famous for its chocolate-covered saskatoon berries—a staple gift to pack in the luggage when a Saskatonian goes abroad.

Grace said they grow and promote saskatoons because the berry is part of Saskatchewan's culture. And when they started the orchard, it was difficult to grow anything except saskatoons. "There weren't a lot of cold-hardy plants then." Saskatchewan's climate is perfect for the nutritious fruit, which explains why the berries were revered for centuries by Indigenous people.

Lee explains the lifetime commitment they've made to planting saskatoons. (Their oldest bushes were established in 1981.) "Through renovation and regrowth, we manage a healthy, vigorous orchard. This means pests and disease are minimized and the bushes are able to handle weather or disease challenges."

For years the Whittingtons also ran a café at the Saskatoon Farmers' Market, selling homemade baked goods and their fruit products. In late 2018, they opened HomeQuarter Coffeehouse & Bakery. HomeQuarter serves seasonal main dishes and desserts that celebrate Western Canadian ingredients in a welcoming farmhouse kitchen atmosphere.

Riverbend products and berries are available on their website, at HomeQuarter, at Co-op grocery stores across Western Canada, and at the SaskMade Marketplace. Note: The farm at Riverbend is not open to the public.

Lee Whittington with her saskatoon berries at Riverbend Plantation.

Robertson Valley Farm

380 Valley Road, Saskatoon | 306-382-9544

facebook.com/robertsonvalleyfarm

■ **Joan Merrill's face** lights up when she talks about the years-old friendships made with customers at Robertson Valley Farm. "When somebody comes in the door and says, 'I'm so glad you're open,' it almost makes me weep. It's so kind."

One elderly man has been coming for decades. A former chef, he's particular about his veggies. Staff know to go out to the greenhouse and to find his favourite tomatoes—that's the kind of service that has built Joan's loyal customer base.

Joan Merrill with a customer at Robertson Valley Farm.

Robertson's origins lie with clientele Joan describes as "Saskatchewan winter survivalists—people from a generation that pickled, canned, and preserved, and put down frozen peas and beans, and made handmade perogies and cabbage rolls."

After the popular book *The 100 Mile Diet: A Year of Local Eating* was released in 2007, a younger generation began coming out to the farm. "It was the best thing that ever happened to local production," she says of the book, which explores a couple's journey eating a local, sustainably sourced diet, and exposes the environmental harms of eating exotic foods shipped from afar.

She and her husband Don Robertson took over the business in 1997. Before that, they helped his parents run it for ten years, their now-grown children spent many a day running through the garden rows.

The farmgate store is open seven days a week during the growing season and sells everything you'd expect to find in a typical Saskatchewan garden, plus local honey and BC fruit. There's even a Prairie Sun ice cream stand and a bookshelf full of works by Valley Road authors. Visit in the fall for U-pick pumpkins.

Black Fox Farm & Distillery

245 Valley Road, Saskatoon | 306-955-4645 | blackfoxfarmanddistillery.com

John Cote and Barb Stefanyshyn-Cote own Black Fox Farm & Distillery.

■ **Since launching in 2015,** Black Fox Farm & Distillery has been giving others in Canada's microdistillery scene a run for their money. Owners John Cote and Barb Stefanyshyn-Cote's hyper-local approach means most every ingredient used in the distillation process comes from their own farm just minutes south of Saskatoon.

Eat North claims Black Fox's small-batch spirits are some of the most sustainably made in all of Canada—no small feat! One way that's accomplished, besides growing their own ingredients on their eighty-acre farm, is by creating a complete ecosystem. Distillation by-products are composted back into the flower gardens.

Prior to 2015, the couple were grain farmers. Instead of expanding the farm to support their family (they have four children), they chose a career path that brings them closer to their customers. "We want to share our passion for agriculture," says John of their flower farm and the artisanal spirits they produce.

→ Black Fox Farm & Distillery

The couple studied agriculture and travelled extensively, learning at other flower farms and distilleries. "We realized that a lot of the things that were done in other countries could be done here and we just hadn't gone that route," says Barb.

That route is all about Saskatchewan's unique terroir. "These really long days, cool nights, and harsh winters make for phenomenal products—not only on the flavour side but for the depth of colour in the flowers."

Because sugar cane doesn't grow in Saskatchewan, you won't find rum at Black Fox. You will find a mustard-infused gin though. It all ties into the Saskatchewan identity that harkens back to the province's agricultural roots: a time when resources were limited and people made do with what they could grow or source locally. That pride of place is resonant at Black Fox. "That's why we grow 90 percent of what goes into our bottles. It's artisanal. It's craft. It's us. And you're not going to be able to replicate this anywhere else in the world," says Barb.

Depending on the gin, they'll use everything from pumpkin and calendula flowers to rhubarb and cucumbers grown on the farm. Along with vodka and liqueurs (it was a raspberry liqueur that got them started on the distillery path after their six-acre fruit orchard produced more than they could sell), they've also got whisky that's tucked away in aging barrels.

Black Fox is open year-round for distillery tours and in the warmer months, there are weekly date night offerings when people can sip a gin and tonic and pick flowers in the fields. Watch for the annual summer lily festival and fall pumpkin festival.

The booming agri-tourism side of Black Fox's operation is all about getting people out of the city and experiencing the farm on a sensory level. As Barb says, that's what will help reconnect people to the land and to agriculture.

Living Sky Winery

Perdue | 306-290-1693 | livingskywinery.com

Sue Echlin owns Living Sky Winery with her husband Vance Lester.

■ **In an orchard** that gives back to the nature that surrounds it, fruit destined for bottles of Saskatchewan's award-winning winery grows. Sue Echlin and Vance Lester's Living Sky Winery produces seasonal ciders, table and dessert wines—of which their Juliett cherry port-style has been their biggest award winner.

Mingle, a 100 percent local spritzer, is the latest venture for Living Sky in partnership with Black Fox Farm & Distillery. Living Sky's rhubarb and raspberry haskap wine, combined with Black Fox's gin and honey, has been a bestseller. "It was a natural partnership with Barb and John [of Black Fox]. We were both named Canada's Outstanding Young Farmers. Our value systems are the same around the environment and agriculture," says Sue.

That approach to agriculture was informed by Vance's background as a biologist. The pair designed their orchard to be as sustainable as possible, with an eye to protecting the wild bee population. The land surrounding the orchard is kept planted with alfalfa, and isn't made into hay until late July, providing habitat and pollen sources. They never use chemicals.

The couple planted their orchard in stages, beginning in 2006, so everything would ripen together. The winery launched in 2010. The Okanagan's Forbidden Fruit Winery inspired them to start Living Sky. They tracked down Forbidden Fruit's winemaker, who was living in Thailand at the time, and flew him to Saskatchewan. "He was really instrumental in the beginning to teach us. I can't imagine trying to do it without help like that."

While some years have been rough (hail wiped out nearly the entire fruit crop in 2018), Sue just smiles and gives that resilient farmer adage: "Harvest as much as you can when you can and then accept that next year you might not have anything."

Maker's Malt

4020 Saskatchewan St, Rosthern | 306-717-6099 | makersmalt.com

■ **It's a farm-to-glass story** of the finest order. Barley grown and malted in Saskatchewan winds up in the province's finest craft breweries' creations. A small farming collective (each member has experience growing high-quality malt barley) in Rosthern own Maker's Malt, Saskatchewan's first craft malting facility.

Owner Matt Enns had watched craft beer's popularity grow in the United States over the last decade, and along with it, craft malting facilities. As the craft beer movement took hold in Saskatchewan, Enns and the farming collective knew the time was right to provide local craft brewers with a malt supply tailored to their needs.

Matt took a hands-on course at the Canadian Malting Barley Technical Centre in Winnipeg and joined the Craft Maltsters Guild. State-of-the-art craft malting equipment came from a family-owned business in Wisconsin.

Maker's Malt produces both base and specialty malts for craft breweries. "We bridge the gap for malt they can't get in North America, like boutique-style malts and bespoke malts."

In 2019, the company partnered with SeCan on the Bow Project, which offered bow barley (developed at the University of Saskatchewan) to fourteen local craft breweries—each one made a specialty beer using the new single malt.

Ensuring a consistent end product starts in the farmers' fields. The collective uses a no-till farming approach to conserve soil moisture and limit erosion. Crop rotations also enable long-term soil health in the province's best barley-growing region.

Today, there are about fifteen small-scale breweries in Saskatchewan, and Maker's Malt, which opened in 2018, is taking orders from across the Prairies.

Maker's Malt is Saskatchewan's first craft malting facility and is owned by a small farming collective.

New Life Organic Foods

Denzil | 780-806-3605 | newlifeorganicfoods.ca

■ **The history** at David and Valerie Witzaney's organic farm dates back over a hundred years: They're third-generation farmers on the land homesteaded in 1911. The Witzaney family, which includes eleven children, decided to make the grain and livestock operation certified organic in 1999. Since then, David says he's learned a tremendous amount about soil health and how it determines food's nutrient value.

Using cattle in the crop rotations, along with intensive grazing (smaller pastures that are rotated daily), has been hugely beneficial. Since the animals can't wander a large pasture eating only their favourite vegetation, it makes better use of the land. The animals' manure and the vegetation they've trampled improves soil health by providing concentrated organic matter. "We're seeing the soil rebound," says David. "I've seen different plants grow that I didn't plant—so you know the biology is getting better."

When an organic processing mill came up for sale in 2007, the family "jumped at it." David says running the mill is worth the work and marketing effort, especially when he meets customers with health issues. "If we feed people good food, it's going to change our healthcare system." That adage applies to feeding the land, too: "What we keep putting in will affect the outcome."

Visit New Life's stand at the Saskatoon Farmers' Market or check the website for delivery details. If you'd like to visit the farm and pick up your order, just call ahead. And watch the website for details on their annual open farm day.

David Witzaney of New Life Organic Foods.

Benlock Farms

Hwy 672, Grandora | 306-668-2125 | benlockfarms.com

Tom Blacklock with one of his prized Speckle Park bulls.

■ **Tom and Shawnda Blacklock's** annual February bull sale has become the event of the year. It's held in the loft of their red hip-roofed barn, where everyone enjoys a day of home-cooked food, drinks, and socializing. In 2019, the couple marked Tom's sixtieth birthday with themed food and the biggest party to date.

The farmhouse dates back to 1917 but the barn goes back earlier than that: "They always built the barn before the house," says Tom with a smile. Tom's roots in the cattle business go back generations. His maternal great-grandpa and grandpa were members of the Canadian Angus Association. Today, about 75 percent of the Blacklock herd goes back to the original one started in 1910. The family has always been in the seed stock business; that is, breeding registered cattle with documented pedigrees.

The Blacklock brothers on Tom's dad's side were some of the only auctioneers around and everyone knew the Blacklock name—his uncle even auctioneered at the historic Calgary Bull Sale.

The annual bull sale is when people come from miles around for their chance to get some of the Blacklock genes (Angus and some Speckle Parks)

→ **Benlock Farms**

for their own herd. "The bull sale has turned into a great thing. We just really appreciate all the support that we get," says Tom.

He says Benlock Farms is typical of Saskatchewan cow-calf family operations and that fact fills him with pride. "The whole industry [makes] their first priority animal welfare. People that are just driven in terms of monetary gains don't stay in the cattle business. It's people that are passionate and really enjoy working with livestock.

"As a province and as Western Canada, we can take a great deal of pride in our cattle business."

Benlock Farms operates a year-round stall at the Saskatoon Farmers' Market, selling their homegrown beef and talking to customers about their forage-based feeding system that's supplemented with grain. "To suggest that a growing calf when it's -30°C in February shouldn't have a little energy in its ration isn't practical. Energy is a bad thing if it's not balanced. If you're eating potatoes for 90 percent of your ration, that's not good either," explains Tom.

All are welcome at the annual bull sale or contact the couple if you'd like to visit the farm. And be sure to stop in at Shawnda's new venture, Little Market Box, in Saskatoon.

Catherwood Organics

Hwy 655, Perdue | 306-237-9286 | catherwoodorganics.com

■ **In 1997,** Les and Betty Hamm switched over to organic farming, an anomaly in Saskatchewan at the time. "There was a lot of doubt," recalls Les. "Even myself, I had doubts. The neighbours looked at us very strange. We were the hippies of the area," he adds with a laugh.

They got into organic farming after a year with a devastating drought and a staggeringly high chemical and fertilizer bill. "We found that if we didn't have big bills, it was a little easier to sleep at night."

Over the years, the neighbours have changed their minds, amazed by the crops the Hamms grow without inputs. Half the farm is left in green fallow for the year to control weeds and save moisture, while the other half is seeded on a rotational basis.

Along with the grain farm, the couple raises heritage Berkshire pigs, cattle, goats, poultry, and Guernsey family milk cows. The Hamms, their three children, and twelve grandchildren all drink the cows' raw milk. Les finds it strange that it's illegal to sell raw milk to the public while high sugar and high caffeine drinks (marketed at youth) are legal. "You can get Red Bull. I don't understand it but that's just the way it is," he says with a smile.

Five generations of Betty's family have farmed the homestead. Raising pastured animals was a natural fit. "We realized that's the way we wanted to bring up our kids and why not raise the animals yourself?"

Visit the website to place an order and if you'd like to pop out to the farm, just call the Hamms and they'd be happy to host you.

Betty and Les Hamm
with their baby goats.

Original Family Farm

Vanscoy | 306-222-4413 | originalfamilyfarm.ca

Regan and Tracy Sloboshan run Original Family Farm.

■ **Regan and Tracy Sloboshan** run Original Family Farm, home to poultry, a grain operation, hay land, and a large bison herd. They began acquiring their bison herd years ago, when prices were relatively affordable. "We thought, 'Oh, what the heck. We'll start with a few bison,' … it grew into a pretty big herd," says Tracy of their four hundred animals.

Aside from injuries that come from the bulls pushing each other around and fighting for dominance, they're independent animals. "When they have a calf, you'll notice one's off in the bush by herself. You'd be silly to help them—they seem to know what's best. They are hardy."

The Sloboshans have been farming their entire lives. "Every farm girl grows up loving her animals so that's the best part of it."

The couple is always diversifying, giving themselves different income options to keep up with fluctuating commodity prices. "We want to be self-sustaining. We have our own feed mill to make our own feed." To that end, they've also built an abattoir at the farm and employ butcher Rob Thompson. Rob ensures top quality in everything from fresh bison and poultry cuts to sausages, lasagna, and pot pies. It's a provincially inspected facility and the butchering is done on site. "I always tell customers we're hoof to plate," he says.

Original Family Farm has stalls at the Regina and Saskatoon farmers' markets, along with the community markets held in the London Drugs and Peavey Mart parking lots in Saskatoon. Online ordering is also available.

Pine View Farms

Osler | 306-239-4763 | pineviewfarms.com

■ **Pine View Farms' products** are sold throughout Saskatchewan and are synonymous with quality. Their meat is labelled all-natural. It's a term that can be misused, but for Melanie and Kevin Boldt and their sons, all-natural is something they take seriously in their animal husbandry practices.

The Boldts raise their poultry and livestock on a GMO-free vegetarian diet without growth-promoting medications or hormones. Lower stocking rates mean animals have ample access to pasture and that pasture isn't over-grazed. "It's basically traditional old-fashioned farming, quality over quantity," explains Melanie. "We're not a high-volume kind of place but we need to do enough to make our farm sustainable economically. Because we're smaller, we can pay more attention to the smaller details."

Pine View Farms started in 1998, pretty much by accident. The Boldts were married, farming grain and cattle with Kevin's parents, and needing to expand the farm to support the two families. In a serendipitous turn of events, the Boldts purchased Kevin's great-grandfather's homestead. (His wife and their eighteen children homesteaded it beginning in 1901. It was later sold in the 1950s.)

Melanie and Kevin Boldt of Pine View Farms.

→ Pine View Farms

The small farm came with a poultry barn and abattoir, and kick-started the couple's agricultural diversification ideas. "We didn't really do the research. We kind of bought more on our heartstrings than anything," says Melanie. "We needed a place to launch our lives. We jumped in with both feet and then fear takes you the rest of the way because you learn as you go."

As the years went by, they realized where the opportunity was in Saskatchewan: a direct-to-consumer meat business. "In our opinion, there's always profitable little market niches left behind in the wake of the big guys. Agri-food is about large-scale commodity production, high volume, low margin, but there's little niches." That opportunity meant they could be "price setters not price takers," and not at the whim of global markets, trade agreements, and exchange rates.

Raising, processing, marketing, and selling their own animals gave them an incremental profit margin that has made the farm sustainable. "By having a branded product that's different from what you can get in the grocery store, we can compete and carve out a little place for ourselves."

Pine View Farms has a farmgate store and offers online ordering. Delivery is available throughout Saskatchewan (free in the Saskatoon area), as are discounts for picking up your order at the farm. The website lists stores carrying their products.

Rosedale Bison

Hanley | 306-544-2869

■ **At Rosedale Bison,** the herd's living conditions mimic how the animals thrived for thousands of years before humans intervened. Les Kroeger is the president of the Saskatchewan Bison Association and advocates for low-stress handling and animal welfare. His 150-strong herd of North American Plains Bison is kept on a strict diet of native prairie grasses. "This animal has adapted to convert grasses and forages of poorer quality into a very high-quality protein."

Les Kroeger of Rosedale Bison.

They don't require shelter in the winter and do best when handled as little as possible. "They're indigenous to this part of the world. They've been here for thousands of years and adapted quite well."

Les says bison are just "amazing to watch" and he's spent many a summer day admiring his herd. "They look clumsy. But they can be running full speed and turn on a dime with no effort. It's because of the mass in the front end, they can spin their backhand around so fast."

Les, his wife Kathy Grad, and his dad began the operation in 1989. Les also works with the University of Saskatchewan on reproduction techniques, like artificial insemination, to help bison conservation efforts. Since bison were almost completely wiped out from overhunting and disease in the 19th century, their gene pool is small and there are several diseased wild herds in North America.

Slaughtering is done on site, which means less stress for the animals and better meat quality. Les sells some of his products direct off the farm. Rosedale Bison is available at SaskMade Marketplace in Saskatoon.

Sloughbottom Pastures

Outlook | 306-856-3033 | sloughbottom.ca

■ **At Sloughbottom Pastures,** Justine and Kalevi Lustig focus on cattle genetics to breed animals that will do well with their holistic management practices, such as mob grazing and low-stress livestock handling. "We want a cow that's a smaller frame, that can maintain herself on a lower amount of feed but still be healthy," explains Justine. "We're focusing on a strong genetic base that's going to get us that small frame and hardy cow that we want."

To that end, they've developed their herd using Angus, Luing, and Longhorn bloodlines. The Luing is a breed developed on the island of Luing in Scotland. They're a cross between a Shorthorn and a Highlander. "The Highlander has long hair and moderate size. Shorthorns are bigger and beefier," says Kalevi. The combination results in a well-marbled end product from a hardy animal.

Pasture is carefully managed. The animals are frequently moved in the mob grazing set-up in which a large group of cattle graze a small area over a short time frame. It's an efficient method, which prevents overgrazing and encourages productive grasses to grow.

Another focus for the farm is a custom winter-feeding program where they bring in outside cattle from farms that follow similar holistic practices.

"We can't take on a cow that needs babysitting because our cows are fairly self-sufficient," says Justine.

The couple sells beef cuts and bulk beef direct to customers and offers delivery to Saskatoon and Outlook. They also welcome farm visitors and tours—just call ahead.

Justine and Kalevi Lustig with their children at Sloughbottom Pastures.

WEST CENTRAL SASKATCHEWAN FARMERS' MARKETS

Check the website for current hours prior to your visit.

Battleford Farmers' Market
Battleford Furniture's parking lot
Thursdays, 8:00 AM–Noon
May to September

Biggar Farmers' Market
Legion Hall, 118 Main Street
Tuesdays, 3:00 PM–5:00 PM
June to September

Lloydminster Downtown Farmers' Market
Olive Tree Thrift Store
5002 51st Avenue
Thursdays, 11:00 AM–5:00 PM
May to September
facebook.com/Lloydminster-downtownfarmersmarket/

Lloydminster Outdoor Farmers' Market
4515 44th Street
Thursdays 11:00 AM–5:00 PM
Saturdays 10:00 AM–4:00 PM
DTFMLloydminster.com
facebook.com/Lloydminster-downtownfarmersmarket/

Martensville Farmers' Market
Curling rink, 555 Main Street
Thursdays, 3:00 PM–7:00 PM
June to August
facebook.com/Martensville-farmersmarket/

North Battleford Farmers' Market
Living Faith Chapel
Saturdays, 8:30 AM–Noon
May to September

Outlook Farmers' Market
Beside the post office
Fridays, 8:00 AM–Noon
May to September

Outlook JWD Market Garden
North of town on Mackenzie Street
Fridays, 9:00 AM–6:00 PM
May to August
306-867-9419

Paynton Farmers' Market
Baseball diamonds off Highway 16
Tuesdays, 4:00 PM–6:00 PM
June to September

Radisson Farmers' Market
Behind the Red Bull Restaurant, inside the hangar
Fridays, 11:00 AM–6:00 PM
May to October

↻ Previous page: **The Lustig children playing at Slough-bottom Pastures.**

Rosetown Farmers' Market
Rosetown Elks Hall
Thursdays, 3:00 PM–5:00 PM
June to September

Rosthern Farmers' Market
6th Street, beside the library
Fridays, 11:00 AM–2:00 PM
May to October
facebook.com/Rosthern-District-
Farmers-Market-249939582036826
306-232-5273

Warman Farmers' Market
City Hall parking lot
107 Central Street
Thursdays 2:00 PM–6:00 PM
May to October
facebook.com/Warman-
FarmersMarket/
306-931-2206

WEST CENTRAL SASKATCHEWAN WATERING HOLES

Check the website for current hours prior to your visit.

Armoury Brewing Company
702 102nd Street, North Battleford
306-445-2739
armourybrewing.com

Tours: By request.

Crossmount Cider Company
30 Glen Road, Crossmount
306-374-9884
crossmountcidercompany.ca

Tours: By request.
Tasting room & event space

Riverlot Orchards Winery and Bistro
St. Louis
306-422-5411
riverlotorchards.ca

Tours: By request.
Winery and bistro open seasonally

Wolf Willow Winery
Outlook
306-867-9463
wolfwillowwinery.ca

Winery and restaurant open
seasonally

ON THE HUNT

Carson Albert-Checkosis is still tired from an early wake-up call, but what he sees makes him spring to life. On a mid-November morning, the sun is just beginning to light up the shoreline of a large slough in a hunting area about sixty kilometres east of Lloydminster.

As Carlin Nordstrom drives Carson (age fifteen) and two class-mates into a clearing, a large black shape becomes visible across the frozen water. A cow moose is rooting through the bush and eating her breakfast. Carlin tells Carson to prepare his rifle. The excitement in the air is palpable as Carson loads and sights the gun with Nordstrom's help. The group, which includes Shawnee Smallchild and Ariah Baptiste-Cameron, walks around the far end of the water to get in as close as possible before taking a shot.

It's 8:30 AM on the first day of a four-day hunting trip. Carson has been out hunting once before but has never shot an animal. Before he is able to take a shot, the moose disappears in the bush.

"[She] gave us the slip!" says Carlin.

He drives the group around the far end of the slough, before taking the students on foot to track the moose.

The sun is coming up over the treeline, beams shooting through the clouds. There isn't a hint of wind, the only sound the occasional woodpecker's tapping. It's cool, but not cold—in other words, a perfect day for hunting.

They eventually find her. Carson quickly readies the rifle and takes the shot, his emotions, he later says, a mix of anxiety and

○ Bison at Les Kroeger's ranch.

 Carson Albert-Checkosis sights his rifle before the hunt.

eagerness. A loud boom punctuates the morning's quiet and stillness, echoing across the prairie.

It's a clean shot through the shoulder, which hits the lungs and puts the moose down immediately.

"Wow," Carson exclaims. "That was exciting."

A big smile is plastered on his face, his forehead glistening with sweat.

"I was kinda happy," he says of killing the moose. "But kind of sad—a little bit—for taking out a life that could probably have lived for so many more years. But it's meat now."

It's just 10 AM. By 12:30, the moose will be gutted, skinned, and quartered, the meat in the truck, the students loaded up to go back to the cabin and share the day's stories with waiting elders.

Carlin leads the Oskayak Minowin Project, which is funded by Health Canada. It's a land-based healing initiative he started with a group from Poundmaker Cree Nation, located two hours northwest of Saskatoon. In the fall of 2018, all Poundmaker's youth from Grades 7 to 10 went on multi-day hunting and fishing trips (followed by ice fishing trips in the winter), learning how to harvest healthy and sustainable food sources for their community.

"We really want these kids to come away with … confidence in being able to skin an animal, process the animal, butcher the animal and cooking skills," says Carlin, who works with Saskatchewan Indigenous youth in a variety of programs. They also attended empowerment, mental health, and wellness workshops.

The group travelled everywhere from English River and Lac LaPlonge in the north, to the Cypress Hills country in the south. The students were all given rods during the fishing trips. "The hope is that they take the fishing rod home, take family members, and teach that what they've [learned] and can carry this on to other family members to learn these important skills."

Each participant also receives a set of hunting knives. Carlin teaches everyone how to sharpen their knives before gutting the animal. Later in the day, they'll need the knives for butchering. What the group doesn't eat will be used at Chief Poundmaker School's lunch program.

Gutting a moose is no simple task. "Shooting it is the easy part," Carlin says with a smile. It takes considerable strength and skill to

○ Carlin Nordstrom shows Carson Albert-Checkosis, Shawnee Smallchild, and Ariah Baptiste-Cameron how to field dress the moose.

↑ **Carson Albert-Checkosis hauls out meat after his kill.**

first open the animal's body and second, remove the innards without contaminating the meat. Carlin demonstrates the technique he's honed over years of experience, deftly separating the innards from the carcass. Carson helps him remove the heavy mass. Next, everyone begins the lengthy skinning process.

Steam erupts into the air; the students' bare hands, which are covered in blood by now, stay warm thanks to the carcass's lingering heat. The first smell to hit the nostrils is the iron scent of the blood spilled here today. It's mixed in with excrement, released during the animal's last moments. The innards emit a raw odour. All combined, it makes for primal bouquet.

All three students tackle the work without complaints. "It makes me feel really happy that we can give meat to our community and feed all the kids," says Carson.

The project's healing aspects cannot be underestimated. Nordstrom points to the intergenerational effects of residential schools and other hardships Poundmaker youth have faced. "It's about getting them out into a new opportunity and experience that they would have never had—and giving them a chance to empower themselves, learn a new skill, and be in a positive environment."

Once the skinning is finished, Nordstrom shows them how to quarter the animal. Carson hoists a large leg quarter over his shoulder, smiling proudly as he realizes his own strength, and carries it to the waiting truck.

Lastly, Carlin removes the moose's nose—nothing is wasted. An elder from English River First Nation, Violet Janvier, will boil it for soup later that night at the cabin. Along with being an assistant cook for the Oskayak Minowin Project, Janvier also teaches the youth traditional hide tanning, cooking, and smoking methods.

Carson's appreciation for Nordstrom and the project is obvious. "I would really love to do this again. Even though this is our first day, I'd love to come out much more."

For Nordstrom, who has been hunting and fishing since he was a boy, the students' transformational experiences are proof of the value of the project, which has received funding to continue for the next several years. "Driving down today, thinking about how happy these kids are to be out here and how excited they were—for me to be able to do something that I love and teach these kids these skills and see all the positive results—I'm pretty happy." ■

Saskatoon

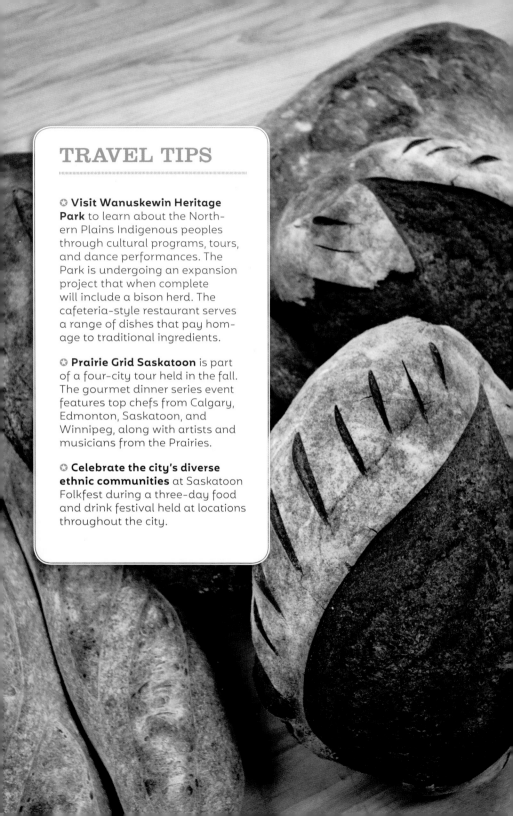

TRAVEL TIPS

✿ **Visit Wanuskewin Heritage Park** to learn about the Northern Plains Indigenous peoples through cultural programs, tours, and dance performances. The Park is undergoing an expansion project that when complete will include a bison herd. The cafeteria-style restaurant serves a range of dishes that pay homage to traditional ingredients.

✿ **Prairie Grid Saskatoon** is part of a four-city tour held in the fall. The gourmet dinner series event features top chefs from Calgary, Edmonton, Saskatoon, and Winnipeg, along with artists and musicians from the Prairies.

✿ **Celebrate the city's diverse ethnic communities** at Saskatoon Folkfest during a three-day food and drink festival held at locations throughout the city.

3

Saskatoon, my home, is called the Paris of the Prairies because, well, the city is gorgeous. It's made more beautiful by the welcoming, engaged citizens, many of whom are helping Saskatoon's local food system thrive.

One of those engaged citizens is Gordon Enns. He works toward securing a robust, affordable and accessible local food network. Gordon is the executive director of the Saskatoon Food Council, which aims to improve the city's food economy, enrich our food culture, and reduce hunger.

CHEP Good Food Inc. has established over fifty community urban gardens, including in core neighbourhoods and at schools, where a range of Indigenous and newcomer families grow food together. Station 20 West is a community enterprise centre in the heart of the westside core neighbourhoods. The Boxcar Café serves a menu of from-scratch, healthy food at affordable prices and offers culinary employment and skills training opportunities.

Saskatoon is a city on the rise, with thriving tech, bioscience, and entrepreneurial sectors, and is home to several global mining companies' head offices. The University of Saskatchewan is renowned for its agricultural research.

In 2017, the city welcomed the Remai Modern art gallery (and its outstanding Shift Restaurant), which helped make Saskatoon the only Canadian destination on the *New York Times*'s list of 52 Places to Visit in 2018. Saskatoon's culinary scene has been keeping pace with all the development and has really begun to stretch its legs. Like a fine wine, we just keep getting better.

Favourite spots, like St. Tropez Bistro and Taverna Italian Kitchen (both of which have rooftop gardens), remain excellent places to eat because of their chefs' commitment to quality ingredients, prepared

○ Previous spread: **Summon in beautiful Saskatoon.**
○ **Fresh loaves at the Night Oven Bakery (profile on page 114).**

with love. Aroma Resto Bar and Odd Couple continue to up their game and stay relevant in the city's ever-changing restaurant scene.

Despite the short season, Saskatoon has a booming food-truck industry (check out the Foodtruck Wars Street Festival in July). Saskatoon knows how to make the most of summer. Outdoor festivals are on offer nearly every weekend. Many make food a focal point, like Ukrainian Day in the Park and Vesna Festival.

YXEats is all about the Riversdale neighbourhood's diverse independent restaurant scene, while Taste of Saskatchewan is the time to sample a range of restaurants' signature dishes.

New microdistilleries and breweries pop up on the regular—celebrate World Gin Day at Black Fox Farm & Distillery and make sure to tour Lucky Bastard Distillers's beautiful boutique distillery. Crossmount Cider Company is just south of the city and offers summer yoga and cider-tasting events, in addition to cidery tours year-round.

There are several excellent from-scratch bakeries, such as Nutana Bakery and Nestor's Bakery (both make mouth-watering doughnuts) and Earth Bound Bakery and Kitchen, the perfect spot on Eighth Street for a hearty homemade lunch.

Third wave coffee culture is in full force (but there are still plenty of diners where you can get a hearty breakfast and a good ol' cup of brewed coffee, too).

The newest roaster, Venn Coffee Roasters and its awe-inspiring latte art, is tucked away in an alley in the city's artistic hub, Broadway. Cafés like Citizen, City Perks, Collective Coffee, d'Lish by Tish, Museo, and Prairie Ink are neighbourhood gathering spots, thanks to homemade food, from-scratch baking, quality light lunches, and good coffee. And the Broadway Roastery will always be a Saskatoon institution. Pro tip: Take a decadent Café Broadway (hazelnut espresso with steamed chocolate milk and chocolate whip) to the outdoor seating area and soak up the sun. ∎

⊙ **Guests at Wanuskewin's Han Wi Moon Dinner roast bannock on a hill overlooking the South Saskatchewan River.**

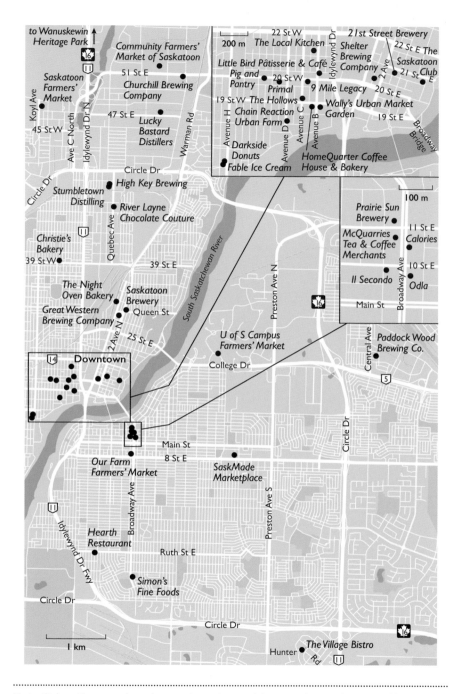

Note: Only artisans and producers who welcome visitors on site are shown on this map.

SASKATOON ARTISANS

Fable Ice Cream

633 Avenue H South | fableicecream.com

Jordan and Lauren Ethridge
with Quill at Fable Ice Cream.

■ **It took just two days** for Jordan and Lauren Ethridge to sell out of their rich and creamy artisanal treat when they first opened Fable Ice Cream in 2017.

Fable's ice cream is all made from scratch – even the waffle cones. "We value quality food," says Lauren. "The opportunity to contribute something to the local food scene excites us. Ice cream lends itself really well to so many ingredients and flavour combinations, so it's a lot of fun to experiment with."

They use organic milk (or cashew and coconut milk for their vegan varieties), organic cane sugar, and as many local flavouring ingredients as possible—there's no end to the creativity at Fable. Their rhubarb comes from a vendor at the Saskatoon Farmers' Market, the chocolate is from Those Girls at the Market, and fruit comes from nearby orchardists.

The company's name reminds us all of a simpler time, when many a hot summer day was spent trying to make a melting ice cream cone last forever. "We knew we wanted our name to evoke a certain feeling. We wanted it to feel whimsical and childlike. And Fable captured that well," says Lauren.

Fable features a standard six-flavour menu (including salted caramel) along with seasonal picks and a vegan option or two. They've also added espresso and specialty coffees to their pretty little Riversdale shop.

Fable Ice Cream is open year-round, except for a winter break in January. Everyone's on a diet then anyway, right?

✪ Homestead and Jerry's are Saskatoon's famous homemade ice cream shops. Try an ice cream sandwich at Homestead or an artisanal gelato at Jerry's. Lineups stretch around the park for Homestead's chocolate-covered cheesecake on a stick at the annual Taste of Saskatchewan festival.

Meat Chops

306-262-0068 | meatchopsleathershop.com

■ **Chelsey Parker** is shaking up Canada's beef jerky market with Meat Chops, a prairie-bred, grass-fed product. "Eat meat. Craft leather. Respect cow." Parker's meat mantra is one of conscious consumerism. "It's about looking at the whole picture and knowing you're using what you have."

Chelsey handmakes the jerky in Saskatoon from whole cuts of beef, using simple ingredients and zero fillers. Her grass-fed beef is from a federally inspected abattoir, which sources from Saskatchewan ranchers who raise their cattle using regenerative agriculture methods. Ranchers who do things like rotational grazing with their herd not only benefit the animals but also the natural environment. "These suppliers are land stewards—that's a lot of what I've learned about grass-fed," she explains.

Besides fuelling the Prairies with jerky, education is huge for Chelsey. She encourages her customers to think critically: Where does your meat come from and what type of food production system are you supporting with your hard-earned cash? "If you have a high-quality meat in less quantity, it's way better for you."

She knows her jerky is up against stiff competition. The big guys can bring the price of their larger-sized packages down to half of what she charges. But she's confident Meat Chops' taste will win out as she strives to move Canadians' snacking habits toward quality products. "I know this is bold, but I want to be Canada's best grass-fed beef jerky company. I want to change your snacking options out there."

Meat Chops is sold throughout Saskatchewan. (Visit the website for retail locations.)

Chelsey Parker owns Meat Chops, prairie-bred, grass-fed beef jerky.

River Layne Chocolate Couture
39-1736 Quebec Ave | riverlayne.com

■ **In 2018 Faye Moffatt left her job** as a senior market analyst at Cameco to open River Layne Chocolate Couture. Her artisanal chocolates are stunning: She hand-paints each one's design using coloured cocoa butter. "People want something unique. They appreciate the artistic part of it before they even bite into the chocolate."

A lavender and lemon chocolate is painted in a whimsical fashion, reminiscent of a field of flowers, while the chai vanilla bean has a striking copper lustre dust design. "Let it melt in your mouth. That's how you get the most flavour," she says.

Faye Moffatt and her chocolate shoe.

Making artisan chocolate is a labour-intensive process. It can take Faye three days to make a single batch. She first paints the designs on the mould. "I try and match some of the designs to the flavours. For others, I try to be artistic and play and have fun."

Next, the chocolate is poured. Faye uses the finest quality chocolate available, all imported from France and Belgium. Once it sets, she pours one of seventeen flavours, before the two-step finishing process, which includes a River Layne stamp on the bottom. The filling is all cream ganache-based, which means the texture will never feel grainy. "It's really delicious art."

Faye, who grew up on a farm near North Battleford, shared a sweet ritual with her dad. Every Christmas they made chocolates to give away as gifts. "It was always a really fun thing that I remember doing as a kid."

✪ If you're after small-batch, artisanal truffles, visit Coco + Muse: cocoandmuse.com.

Those Girls at the Market
812 16th Street W | 306-850-5671 | thosegirlsatthemarket.com

■ **Those Girls at the Market** began as a fun passion project for two then-university students excited about raw chocolate. But it very quickly evolved into a full-fledged business.

Sisters Julianna and Ying Tan both have backgrounds in fitness and nutritional counselling. "Whenever we hear chocolate, we associate it more with candy bars," says Julianna. "Whereas cacao is very dense in nutrients." Raw chocolate has several

Julianna Tan making chocolate.

health benefits: It's rich in magnesium and antioxidants, along with epicatechins—flavanols that help maintain or gain muscle mass.

They keep their organic chocolate simple and never add artificial flavours or colouring. There's just three ingredients: cacao paste, cacao butter, and a touch of maple syrup. To add flavour, they use organic whole ingredients or pure essential oils (like peppermint in the mint chocolate).

The sisters opened their Saskatoon Farmers' Market booth in 2014, thinking it would be a summer project. Their raw chocolate was a big hit. "We stayed up all night making chocolate so that we could come back to the market on Sunday," says Julianna. "We sold out in two hours, and thought, 'What have we got ourselves into?'"

Since then, the sisters' chocolate has grown in popularity—enough that Julianna has made it her full-time job. "Every day I look forward to getting up and making chocolate. It's just such a cool gig to have. I feel really grateful that I'm able to do this every day with my sister." Be sure and visit their new Riversdale shop, just around the corner from Darkside Donuts.

Christie's Bakery
420 33rd Street West | 306-244-0506

Il Secondo
802C Broadway Ave | 306-384-0506

■ **In an age** when dollars are king, time is money, and the bottom line is everything, there's pressure to mechanize, cut corners, and use mixes. However, good bread takes time and care, says Tracey Muzzolini. "It is a conscious choice to honour artisanal techniques and traditions. We are the key-keepers of the classic techniques and we feel a responsibility to use, perfect, and teach these techniques so that they will not be lost forever."

The Christie brothers operated out of a house on Avenue E before building the bakery on 33rd Street in 1932. Tracey's parents, Ennio and Janet Muzzolini, bought the bakery in 1966 and it's been in the Muzzolini family ever since. Ennio was a baker by trade and the couple thought it would be a good opportunity to provide for their growing family. "The banks would not lend them money, so they borrowed money from my uncle Paulie," explains Tracey. "He sold a parcel of his farmland to pay for the loan. They worked hard and paid the loan back in one year."

In 2010, the family opened Il Secondo to diversify their offerings. It's a cozy place to while away the afternoon, sipping a craft beer and eating a wood-fired pizza.

Today, three generations work at the two locations and will never stray from the artisanal techniques upon which the bakery's reputation was built. "Knowing and understanding the complexity of bread making and keeping a consistent product for the customer during extreme weather fluctuations makes us feel very proud of the bread we make."

Tracey Muzzolini owns Christie's Bakery and Il Secondo.

✪ Saskatoon has several bakeries worth a visit, including Nutana Bakery (fresh doughnuts and pastries) and Earth Bound Bakery and Kitchen (rustic bread). Visit Griffin Takeaway or Leyda's for gluten-free bread and baking.

Darkside Donuts

631 Avenue H South | darksidedonuts.com

■ **Saskatoon's first specialty doughnut shop** opened in late 2018 to much anticipation. Bryn Rawlyk wanted to offer the city a playful shop to celebrate and showcase the ridiculous, via wild doughnut flavours. Weeks of social media teases had got people fired up about sourdough doughnuts.

Bryn owns the Night Oven Bakery, where flour from locally sourced grains is milled on site and baking is done in a wood-fired oven. However, the Night Oven, a French boulangerie, "isn't really the appropriate place to be making weird and wacky and colourful doughnuts," says Bryn. Hence, the Darkside venture, where made-from-scratch dough-nuts are the star.

"It's very delicious and it's a good performer," says Bryn of the sourdough brioche doughnut base used at Darkside. The idea to open Darkside came from the doughnuts' "wild popularity" at the Night Oven and customers requesting them.

Darkside Donuts is Saskatoon's first artisanal doughnut shop.

Darkside takes a thoughtful approach in naming doughnut flavours. The Cranberry Flats Fritter is named for a popular hiking and beach spot well known to Saskatonians. A classic honey dip is called the Kitako, after a local honey producer. New flavours are announced on Darkside's social media feeds and weekend lineups can stretch out the door.

In addition to experimental flavours, a few consistent, classic styles are available daily, and Darkside always features a vegan option. Look for cake doughnuts and old-fashioned varieties in the rotation, too. Brewed coffee is available, as is online ordering.

✪ If you're in the mood for something heartier before that doughnut, slip around the south corner of the building to the hidden gem Gangster's Italian Sandwiches. Order a locally made Calabrese and Genoa salami sandwich or a meatball sub.

Little Bird Pâtisserie & Café

258 Avenue B South | 306-384-4663 | thelittlebird.ca

A customer admiring French pastries at Little Bird Pâtisserie & Café.

■ **At Little Bird,** Saskatoon's finest French-style pâtisserie, there are three elements that make good baking: ingredients, method, and love.

Kim Butcher and her business partner, Tasha Altman, built their café on fine teas, artisanal baking, and homemade food, but also on community. "We live in a province of makers and doers, where tradition is a critical component of maintaining connection to our families, neighbours, and the land under our feet," says Kim.

Little Bird's decadent pastries, like the cruffins (a croissant muffin with various fillings—try the fig), French macarons, and cakes are huge sellers. They offer high tea service in their beautiful space, with its high ceilings, antique furniture, and vibrant local artwork on the walls.

Little Bird's food is made from scratch, using real ingredients. "You wouldn't believe the amount of butter, flour, sugar, and farm eggs we go through each week! To understand the complexities of what we make from scratch, we must first understand the ingredients."

Pastries like the French macarons require finesse—Kim studied in Paris to learn how to make them. Ingredients are weighed to the exact gram and mixed by hand using a unique spatula stroke. Each shell is hand-piped. "We do it this way because it was the way we, and generations of pastry chefs and bakers, were taught. There is no machine out there that replicates the delicate touch of human hands."

Perhaps the most important piece of it all is love. "Any chef out there will tell you they do what they do because they're absolutely, head over heels, in love with ingredients and methods."

McQuarries Tea & Coffee Merchants

708 Broadway Avenue | 306-242-6016 | mcquarries.ca

■ **A stroll on Broadway** isn't complete without a stop at McQuarries Tea and Coffee Merchants, where hundreds of glass jars, brimming with loose-leaf tea, fill the wooden shelves and antique scales sit on the countertops.

The business opened its doors in 1929 in downtown Saskatoon. It was called Dickson's Tea Coffee & Cocoa. Russ McQuarrie managed it for the Dickson company, before buying and renaming the business in the '50s.

Today, Adam Anton owns the store, which relocated to Broadway in 1975 when Adam's dad bought the business. "It's been the central hub of our family," says Adam. "For us kids, the business has always been there. Some of my first memories were of this place." Adam and his brother Evan worked at McQuarries starting in high school. (Sadly, Evan has passed away.) Since he took over, Adam hasn't changed much about the shop. After all, it's a business model that's always worked: fresh products at great prices with good old-fashioned customer service.

McQuarries is best known for loose-leaf teas. Since the market demand for tea exploded in the mid-2000s, they've brought in hundreds of additional varieties.

They also carry sixty coffee blends from three Canadian suppliers. Adam stocks a variety of fair-trade, organic, and single origin coffees and encourages customers in that direction. The McQuarries' house blend is a mixture of South American and Indonesian beans. The recipe dates back to Russ's time—his old recipe book still exists.

McQuarries offers delivery service, and it's often Adam who will come to your door.

Adam Anton owns McQuarries Tea & Coffee Merchants.

The Night Oven Bakery

629B 1st Avenue North | 306-500-2350 | thenightoven.ca

■ **The smell of baked bread** mingles with a slight whiff of campfire inside the Night Oven. The bakery is the result of owner Bryn Rawlyk's tireless commitment to artisanal methods and connecting people to local whole grains. He's part of an exclusive group—there's just a handful of bakers in North America doing in-house milling and using wood-fired ovens.

Grains come from a range of Saskatchewan organic farmers. Marc and Anita Loiselle supply Red Fife, rye, and Rouge de Bordeaux wheat; Carberry wheat comes from a high school friend of Bryn's who runs Maida Vale Farm. Einkorn comes from Prime Grains Inc., a farmer-owned company that markets certified organic heritage products.

It's then milled at the bakery, in a stone mill Bryn built. Unlike industrial flour mills, which use stainless steel rollers that break the grain to specific sizes and can remove the bran and germ, a stone mill spins very slowly. "It's a cooler process and doesn't activate any of the nutrients in the grain. And because it's a whole grain process, the product at the end is a complete food."

That slow process is what the Night Oven is all about. "Ingredients make a good product and also procedure and process make a good product. You can't rush sourdough and you can't fake it. If you do it properly, it shows."

Bryn built the bakery's wood-fired oven after extensive research and experimenting with the design in a backyard project. Using the oven for the business aligns with having to care for the process during each step. "You can't use this oven and not be an active participant in using it."

The Night Oven makes a range of breads, rustic French-inspired pastries (and even to-die-for vegan croissants). The flour is available for purchase at the bakery. Stop in on a Friday evening for pizza night.

Bryn Rawlyk in front of his wood-fired oven at the Night Oven Bakery.

Three Foragers Bee Co.

306-514-3633 | threeforagers.ca

■ **Angela Seto and Andrew Guran,** along with his family, started Three Foragers Bee Co. to share their love for raw honey. The couple is also happy to talk about honey's environmental sustainability. Unlike other sweeteners, local honey only requires minimal energy costs to produce, refine, and transport. "Honey is literally a byproduct of flowers," says Angela.

Andrew grew up beekeeping with his grandparents. Three Foragers is now comprised of three generations. The beekeeping and honey processing is done on the Guran family farm outside Saskatoon.

Bees were new to Angela but she quickly "became obsessed. Bees are a really interesting creature. They're so smart. I like learning how they work, learning how to take care of them."

Providing food to people close to home is a priority for the couple. "Saskatchewan honey is so good and it's just being melted down, heated,

Angela Seto of Three Foragers Bee Co. at the Saskatoon Farmers' Market.

and added to products when really the community here should be able to taste the stuff that we produce in our own province," says Angela.

Three Foragers also has a line of honey caramels (sold in compostable bags), made with their honey and a minimal amount of other ingredients. Angela says it took a bit of work to make candies with honey as the star. "Honey is a little finicky. It's very moisture absorbing, so it's not as easy as using sugar."

Visit Three Foragers' stall at the Saskatoon Farmers' Markets or check the website for other Saskatchewan retail locations. Their honey is also sold in Co-op grocery stores (under the Co-op Gold label), in Save-On-Foods across Western Canada, and in Whole Foods stores in British Columbia.

Prairie Sun Brewery

650 Broadway Avenue I 306-343-7000 I prairiesun.ca

Cameron Ewen and Heather Williams at the new Prairie Sun Brewery on Broadway.

■ **Heather Williams and Cameron Ewen** founded Prairie Sun Brewery in 2013 with a vision of helping build Saskatchewan's craft beer industry. It's a vision that's been wildly successful, thanks to the duo's inventive beers (like Honey Hemp red ale with Kitako Lake thistle honey), community engagement, and, most recently, a vibrant new family-friendly brewery and restaurant.

In 2019, Prairie Sun moved into the spot, purpose-built for the microbrewery, on the site that once housed the historic Farnam Block on Broadway. The gastropub concept houses an off-sale and deli, where sandwiches are made with locally sourced pastured meats and bread that Joel Kroeker (of Baeker Kraeker) makes with Prairie Sun's beer.

The restaurant features traditional dishes elevated with Prairie Sun's unique beer spin. Beer and agriculture are incorporated into the food, whether it's via a beer-infused sauce or crunchy barley on salads. Spent grains from the brewing process are dried and ground into flour for pizza dough, or given to farmers.

"Saskatchewan is agriculture," says Heather. "Our big values are community and tourism—bringing people into the brewery and telling them all about Saskatchewan." Prairie Sun sources from several producers, touring their farms before buying. Holistic animal management is part of the story told to brewery customers. The story also includes brewery tours that educate about agriculture and beer's origins. The Farnam Block's history takes centre stage, and staff even study with the Saskatoon Heritage Society. "We feel the responsibility to pay respect to who came before us and tell that story."

The Pig and Pantry
523 20th Street W | 306-202-7827

■ **A small craft butcher** is changing the local palate for pork in Saskatoon. Chef Jordan Lohneis launched the Pig and Pantry in 2016 with a stall at the Saskatoon Farmers' Market and now does a brisk business at his new butcher shop. Jordan's nose-to-tail philosophy means that, along with standard cuts and artisanal sausages, there's also bone broth, curries, country paté, and deep, rich pork heart ragù available that use the not-so-familiar animal bits—and help us all play a part in supporting a sustainable agriculture system.

Whether it's bacon, pork rinds, andouille sausage, or a thick chop from a heritage Berkshire pig, Jordan's products are made from pastured animals sourced from small family farms that share his vision of sustainability and animal welfare. "The quality of meat is directly related to what the animal eats and its living environment," explains Jordan. "We prefer to work with smaller farmers who have the ability to closely monitor the animals' access to fresh pasture and to balance their diet with the right amount of grains and legumes."

Jordan worked in Canadian restaurants before moving on to gigs at Michelin-starred spots in London, England. Witnessing the way London chefs showcased their region's farmers and ingredients inspired him to return home and do the same. He landed the role of sous chef at Ayden Kitchen and Bar when it opened and helped develop the charcuterie program there before setting out on his own.

Contact Jordan for custom meat processing and wholesale inquiries or stop in for a daily sandwich special. Hint: Try his smoked sausages. (The smoked mushroom and cheddar is my favourite.)

Chef Jordan Lohneis owns the Pig and Pantry.

✪ For the best artisanal charcuterie in the city, be sure to visit the Cure, which is owned by two chefs, at the Saskatoon Farmers' Market or call 306-715-0967.

Saskatoon Spruce

306-290-9011 | instagram.com/saskatoonspruce

■ **Kevin Petty** makes small-batch artisanal cheese in a style modelled after an 18th-century European recipe. He launched Saskatoon Spruce in late 2018, inspired by a cheesemaker he met in the Swiss Alps and by a French monk in Manitoba.

Saskatoon Spruce's small-batch artisanal cheese is sold at the Saskatoon Farmers' Market.

Kevin trained with Brother Albéric, a monk at the Notre Dame des Prairies monastery near Holland, Manitoba, who made Fromage de la Trappe cheese with unpasteurized milk for sixty years. Brother Albéric is now retired and was the last person in Canada making cheese using traditional Trappist techniques. "He handmade everything and used raw milk. He aged his wheels on wooden shelves," says Kevin.

Saskatoon Spruce's Welsh Caerphilly is a dry hard cheese that crumbles easily. It delivers a flavour that becomes more robust when it's served at room temperature (all the better if you've got a nice chutney or marmalade to serve alongside). Kevin makes traditional raw milk cheese because it provides ample bacteria varieties. His milk, bought through SaskMilk, always comes from the same dairy and is triple tested before Kevin uses it for cheese.

To meet food safety regulations, Kevin ages it for at least sixty days. He uses spruce boards for aging, cut from trees near Big River. "Cheese ages so well on spruce. That was the whole drive—the relationship between the cheese and the wood and the humidity exchange." The spruce-aged cheese gives a taste of Saskatchewan terroir in every bite.

Saskatoon Spruce has a stall at the Saskatoon Farmers' Market and is sold at the Bulk Cheese Warehouse.

Calories
721 Broadway Ave | 306-665-7991 | caloriesrestaurant.ca

Taszia and Karan Thakur bought Calories in early 2019.

■ **Calories is a Saskatoon**—and really, a Saskatchewan—institution. It opened over thirty years ago on Broadway Avenue and the hardwood floors of the quaint little spot have felt continuous footsteps ever since. Whether you're coming in to gaze longingly at the breathtaking dessert cooler, sip a glass of organic wine, nibble away at Calories' famous quiche, or for a sumptuous dinner spread, it's truly a spot that celebrates Saskatchewan's vibrant local food system. And children are always welcome

In 1986, chef Remi Cousyn's vision to open a coffee shop that focused on real ingredients and flavour changed Saskatoon's culinary scene for the better. Calories has evolved over the years into the restaurant and community-gathering place it is today.

It's an ethos built on simple, local, and delicious food that Calories' new owners will continue to promote and support. Long-time staff members Taszia and Karan Thakur bought Calories in early 2019 when Remi retired. "I have the same vision Remi has had over the years—local, organic, and

119

3

→ Calories

keeping it in the community," says Taszia, Calories' executive chef. "That's what Calories has always been about and that's what I'm about, too."

Calories's commitment to sustainability, community, and health means the chefs maintain relationships with area producers and food suppliers, sourcing organic as much as possible, and making everything from scratch with raw ingredients. Additives or preservatives are never used, and the baking is chock full of real butter. It makes Calories an ideal place for anyone with dietary restrictions, since staff know exactly what's in each dish.

Taszia's seasonal feature sheets change every two months, based on what she can get from her suppliers. It keeps things fresh for guests, while preventing boredom and renewing culinary passion for the cooks in her kitchen.

The serving staff maintain a high level of professionalism, thanks to Karan's proficient management style. This is a place where you'll find an unpretentious yet educated staff who make the experience truly one to remember. "We stress the quality of service and knowledge every server has about our menus," says Karan.

The couple, who met when they worked at Elk Ridge Resort, say that for any independent business to work, it has to be a community effort. "We keep the money in the Saskatoon market and it's important to us that our money stays here," says Karan. "It's important to us to build that relationship with local people."

"In turn, we hope the locals of Saskatoon keep coming in," adds Taszia.

If you both keep doing what you're doing, there's no fear Saskatonians will ever stop supporting Calories.

Darren Craddock

The Village Bistro | 110-250 Hunter Rd

Chef Darren Craddock at the Village Bistro.

■ **Chef Darren Craddock,** a Toronto transplant who has called Saskatoon home for a decade, has built a career the envy of many a young cook. He trained as a chef in England for seven years, with an apprenticeship at a Michelin-rated country house hotel. A stint in Perth, Australia, followed before coming back to Canada to work everywhere from Toronto's King Edward Hotel under chef John Higgins to the Fairmont Jasper Park Lodge.

Back in his hometown, he was married with two young children and had a work day and commute totalling over fourteen hours. It wasn't feasible. He found a position as the Riverside Country Club's executive chef and moved to Saskatchewan. He's won a number of competitions over the years and has represented Saskatoon at the Canadian Culinary Championships.

Darren has taken a step back from demanding positions in recent years and from his role with the Canadian Culinary Federation Saskatoon Branch. "I got fed up with the stress, not sleeping at night, not spending time with my family."

Since 2018, he's been the Village Bistro's executive chef, serving fresh, quality comfort food in a casual and cozy atmosphere. The bistro also provides dining service for residents at the Village at Stonebridge, an independent-living retirement community. While being at the bistro is different from what he's used to, "it's still creative. I still love cooking. I don't know what else I would do. It's given me that clarity and that balance."

Scott Dicks
Odla | 801 Broadway Ave | 306-955-6352 | odla.ca

■ **True farm-to-table restaurants,** backed by a farmer, aren't common anywhere. Farming and owning a restaurant are both risky ventures, with little certainty and often slim profit margins. Saskatchewan is lucky enough to have several farm-backed restaurants (although none are able to source 100 percent from their farms).

The newest one on the block, Odla, opened to much fanfare in 2019. The city always embraces new restaurant openings, and this one was helped along by chef Scott Dicks and the reputation he'd built in the culinary community.

His career began in Calgary, training at the Southern Alberta Institute of Technology (SAIT) and cooking at Vintage Chophouse. He moved to Vancouver and worked at Feenie's and Boneta, and was Les Faux Bourgeois's head chef. In 2014, he came to Saskatoon and spent two years at the Hollows and Primal before launching Rural and helping establish the Local Kitchen. He collaborated with other culinary entrepreneurs and built his own brand with private dinners, classes, and pop-ups.

Chef Scott Dicks at Odla.

→ Scott Dicks

He learned a lot about the food people truly enjoy. "Every single person that ate my food for over two years, I talked to. There's a big difference between doing interesting food from a chef's perspective, and it being interesting and good and satisfying from a customer's perspective."

It also gave him insight into palates and food tastes in the province. "Your average Saskatchewan diner is much more open than they're given credit for."

It's a perspective he carries forward with chefs Michael McKeown and Brian Gibbons at Odla, where the goal is to make people feel comfortable. "We wanted you to feel like you're coming over to our place and we're entertaining you."

Part of the entertainment is savouring Odla's farm ties. Farm One Forty, a small-scale holistic operation outside Saskatoon raising pastured chickens, pigs, sheep, and cattle, owns the restaurant along with Scott and sommelier/general manager Lacey Sellinger.

Scott says by their second year of operation, the restaurant will be self-sufficient on the protein side. "As the years go by, we'll push our produce program. We work with a lot of local farmers and have about twenty-five on the docket for various things."

The Odla experience is a mix between a tasting menu (but without pretentiousness) and family-style dining—but elevated. It's all about reconnecting with Saskatchewan's food system, while allowing the kitchen to cook for you, from small amuse-bouche plates, to shared platters of roasted meats.

"We want to share all the things we've been doing, the beautiful ingredients we get from local farmers and the beautiful meat from Farm One Forty."

Grassroots Restaurant Group

grassrootsrestaurantgroup.ca

The ownership group at Grassroots Restaurant Group.

■ **The Grassroots Restaurant Group** started up after its first baby, the award-winning Ayden Kitchen and Bar, opened in Saskatoon in 2013. The group was founded by Top Chef Canada winner chef Dale Mackay, mixologist Christopher Cho, and chef Nathan Guggenheimer with a goal of providing elevated dining experiences through thoughtfully designed restaurants and sustainable food with nods to Dale's Saskatchewan roots.

After Ayden's opening came Little Grouse on the Prairie (a place serving rustic Italian casual fare along with alla famiglia multicourse tasting menus), Sticks and Stones (modern Asian with craft cocktails), and Avenue in Regina.

Grassroots also holds an annual collaborative dinner series in Saskatoon. "The goal was to make a big splash on the Canadian scene with what we're trying to do in Saskatchewan," says Dale of the not-for-profit Prairie Feast Festival, which donates to the Saskatoon Food Bank and CHEP Good Food. "The idea was to bring Canada to Saskatchewan. We always have chefs from coast to coast coming to show off their food and use Saskatchewan products with their style of cooking."

→ Grassroots Restaurant Group

The festival's theme changes each year—from a carnival-style street party with fire-eaters, to a contemporary event with a local jazz band and ballet dancers—and celebrates the arts in Saskatchewan.

The Ayden Young Chef Scholarship is held alongside Prairie Feast. The competition, open to those under twenty-five, gives aspiring chefs exposure to what others in the industry are doing and helps build a career for the winner, who spends a day in several kitchens in either Calgary or Vancouver.

"I think you need to leave your own home to get a full view of the restaurant industry and what people are doing in other places. It will only benefit you to travel and cook and see other peoples' food," says Dale, adding he's been pleasantly surprised that the majority of young chefs who have competed and applied since 2015 have been women.

As for the future, Dale said Grassroots is done expanding and will keep focusing on Saskatchewan and opening the rest of Canada's eyes to what's possible on the Prairies.

A selection of dishes at Ayden Kitchen and Bar.

Hearth Restaurant
2404 Melrose Ave | 306-664-6677 | hearth.restaurant

Beth Rogers and Thayne Robstad own Hearth Restaurant.

■ **Hearth combines** chefs Beth Rogers and Thayne Robstad's love for Saskatchewan terroir with modern prairie dishes worthy of multiple visits. The seasonal menu features local, wild, and cultivated Saskatchewan bounty while the cozy setting reminds one of a stylish farmhouse living room.

Try Saskatchewan chanterelles, which the couple forages, in the legendary mushrooms with melty cheese and crostini starter, topped with sprigs of reindeer moss. Stand-out entrees include carrot and mascarpone tortellini (so pillowy soft it melts in your mouth) and a seared pork belly served atop a bright coupling of spätzle and root veg. End your meal with a thick slice of homemade pie and ice cream reminiscent of granny's kitchen—right down to the china teacup in which it's served.

The couple grew up in Saskatoon and met in their early twenties. They began cooking in local restaurants before setting out on a culinary journey

126

→ Hearth Restaurant

....

that saw them working in top-notch kitchens in Vancouver and Toronto. They soon tired of metropolitan life. In 2014, they returned home and started a catering company with the end goal of owning a restaurant. "You grow up and you want to leave this place so badly. Then you remember why you love it so much and you find yourself back," recalls Thayne.

Their catering was met with warm support, helping them to build capital for the restaurant they opened in 2018. "We were very lucky. A lot of people loved us," says Beth, referring to businesses like Pine View Farms, which hired them in the early days.

After over a year scouting for the perfect location, the former Crazy Cactus, a spot once home to late night debauchery on Ruth Street, became available. Extensive renovations followed to transform the gaudy Mexican-themed interior into a reflection of the couples' home. "We just want to make this food for the people we love," says Beth, adding a big part of that comes from sourcing Saskatchewan products.

"We talked about the mushroom as a concentration of the forest," says Thayne of a recent chanterelle foraging trip. "Our restaurant is a concentration of this province as far as food goes."

Hearth's decadent carrot cake with homemade ice cream.

Jenni Lessard
Wanuskewin Heritage Park | wanuskewin.com

Jenni Lessard is Wanuskewin's executive chef.

■ **Feeding people for a living** is a special kind of job and not everyone has what it takes. Jenni Lessard is one of those special chefs. Her dishes are works of art and crafted with love.

Jenni, who grew up north of La Ronge in a cabin on a small lake, had free range to experiment in the kitchen. She incorporates her Métis heritage into her cooking and strives to highlight the traditional Indigenous food system.

In 1998, she and her mom opened a café at the farmers' market in Prince Albert. Jenni's son was a baby and rode on her back while she cooked. (Her daughter was a toddler at that time.) She later ran New Ground Café in Birch Hills for seven years, a venture that landed her on *Western Living*'s Top 40 Foodies Under 40 list.

In 2012, she moved to Saskatoon and started Chef Jenni Cuisine, a catering company, along with hosting cooking classes and speaking events through the Local Kitchen.

Jenni shifted to vegetarian catering in 2017 but it wasn't easy as she values local meat producers. However, she found the food waste at large catered events shocking. "What do you do with all this meat? I got tired of having good quality, higher priced meat be part of that overage."

Her food experiences are rich and varied: She's cooked at a wild rice camp in northern Saskatchewan and represented Slow Food Saskatoon at Terra Madre in Turin, Italy. Most recently, she's joined the team at Wanuskewin Heritage Park as the executive chef.

The best way to experience her cooking is at a seasonal Han Wi Moon Dinner held along the Opimihaw Valley at Wanuskewin. Guests cook bannock over an open fire while sipping muskeg tea. The three-course dinner spotlights seasonal foods Jenni foraged from the valley. A Dakota Star storyteller later tells ancient stories against the backdrop of a glorious prairie sunset.

Anthony McCarthy

The Saskatoon Club | 306-652-1780 | saskatoonclub.com

■ **How does one become** an award-winning chef? By watching and learning, says Anthony McCarthy, the Saskatoon Club's executive chef. He grew up near Oxford, England, and it was a home economics class that convinced him of his lifelong pursuit.

Anthony left school at sixteen to study culinary arts in college. At nineteen, he was the head chef at a fine dining restaurant in Oxford. By twenty-five, he was running a high-end country club in Vancouver. It was a great learning period.

"I definitely had kitchen skills and I could manage people well—not being a tyrant and being empathetic." Being a tyrant had become normal behaviour for chefs when he entered the industry in the UK, but it wasn't a path he wanted to follow. "I saw that it didn't get people anywhere. It's not right to treat a human being with such disrespect."

After stints all over Canada and working on yachts in the British Virgin Islands, Anthony put down roots in Saskatoon with his family in 2007. Since then, he's worked tirelessly to promote chefs, ingredients, and local farmers. He's the Canadian Culinary Federation's (CCF) Saskatoon branch president, vice president for the Western Canadian region, and was recognized by the CCF's Honour Society for his work promoting the Canadian culinary scene.

He helps organize events at local soup kitchens, a chef competition at Taste of Saskatchewan, and the annual Chefs' Gala, a collaborative dinner fundraiser that supports local arts groups. For Anthony, it's all about fellowship. "Our chef community is pretty good. We all want to help each other and do better things."

Chef Anthony McCarthy of the Saskatoon Club.

Michael McKeown

Odla | 801 Broadway Ave | 306-955-6352 | odla.ca

Chef Michael McKeown in his kitchen at Odla.

■ **Chef Michael McKeown** is best known in Saskatoon for opening a restaurant that was wholly Saskatchewan. Prairie Harvest Café was a whimsical place that served rustic and delicious comfort food with all Saskatchewan ingredients. (I still dream about the Prairie Harvest lasagna.)

Cooking's instant gratification is what drew Mike. He was working part-time catering banquets while going to university but started skipping classes in favour of more kitchen time. "You can never stop learning. There's infinite possibilities out there and infinite kinds of cuisines. You can always evolve no matter how old you are and how long you've been doing it."

His career took him to various spots around the city before cooking for seven years at northern fishing lodges. His love for prairie ingredients was cemented at those lodges and at places like the Saskatoon Club. "You get to know a few producers and you realize there's a lot more out there in Saskatchewan than you ever thought there was. And especially now, it just gets better every year and more accessible."

Ultimately, Prairie Harvest wasn't economically sustainable and shuttered its doors in 2017. "The location was tough," says Mike. "There were good years and bad years but ultimately the bad outweighed the good."

Still, he says Saskatoon's food scene just keeps getting better. Since Prairie Harvest's closure, he's found a new perfect fit with chef Scott Dicks at Odla, a place where he can cook the food he's best known for and delight all of us who have missed Prairie Harvest since the day it closed.

3

Christie Peters and Kyle Michael

The Hollows | 334 Avenue C S | thehollows.ca
Primal | 423 20th St W | primalpasta.ca

■ **The passion and dedication** that goes into the Hollows and Primal is downright inspiring. Chefs Christie Peters and Kyle Michael helped pioneer a revolution in Saskatoon's Riversdale neighbourhood when they opened the Hollows in 2011. It's a place where nostalgia mixes with modernity, and it's one of the few places in the province offering multi-course tasting menus.

At Primal, the focus is on time-honoured Italian food, whole animal butchery, and handmade pasta made using Saskatchewan-grown ancient grains. (Try the tagliatelle with locally pastured pork and beef heart bolognaise.)

The two chefs and co-owners are crafting contemporary dishes from holistically-raised meat, local and foraged produce at both restaurants. Their food is both modern and reminiscent of hearty prairie fare.

They employ Lisa Taylor and her BiodiverCity Farm (see page 137) to grow produce both in the Hollows' basement and in plots around the city for both restaurants. "She works with me directly," says Christie. "We decide on what seeds to order based on her knowledge and crop rotation."

Christie tans the hides from the animals they butcher and makes soap for the restaurants' bathrooms. The staff preserves and cellars produce in the fall months.

The businesses are run with sustainability at the forefront: All of the restaurants' compost is used in the gardens. Staff also spend time getting out of the kitchens and working in the gardens. "It is in big part to growing up with my grandma who lived through the dirty '30s on a farm in Saskatchewan and the sense of community 'waste not want not' mentality that got them through," says Christie, when explaining why she runs the restaurants the way she does.

Chefs Christie Peters and Kyle Michael own the Hollows and Primal.

131

→ Chefs Christie Peters and Kyle Michael

....

Craft cocktails are an area where sommelier and general manager Adrian Chappell shines. She incorporates foraged ingredients into her cocktail lists which showcase unique spirits. The Wildebeest Room, Adrian's cocktail bar at the Hollows, is the best place to sip one of her creations, paired with a snack menu that's got nothing on your average bar food. Try the boneless dry ribs, made with Farm One Forty pork, or Pine View Farms' buffalo chicken wings with hot sauce made from fermented chili peppers from the Hollows' urban garden.

Christie and Kyle are always evolving. Christie, who got her start under Rob Feenie in Vancouver, did a three-month internship in the fermentation lab at Denmark's Noma in 2019.

Both restaurants are open seven days a week. Come early for the Hollows' weekend brunch and leave time to explore Goldie's General Store, located above the restaurant.

A seasonal dish at the Hollows.

Taste Restaurant Group

tasteyxe.com

The Taste Restaurant Group ownership group: Chris and Courtney Hill, and Carmen and Brad Hamm.

■ **The Taste Restaurant Group** operates four restaurants in Saskatoon, each with a unique concept and each with a commitment to exceeding dining expectations.

Taste's corporate chef is Chris Hill, an award-winning chef who grew up on a farm near Imperial. Chris never had culinary aspirations on his radar until a job washing dishes in the Rocky Mountains changed his mind. His first job after high school was at Moraine Lake Lodge. The experience, helped by chefs who mentored him, convinced him to take up the profession.

"I fell in love with the kitchen world. The food, the pressure, the lifestyle. I think had my first exposure to the industry not gone the way it did, I would not have become a chef." His career has taken him from the Fairmont Chateau Lake Louise to the executive chef position at Elkridge Resort and the Delta Hotels by Marriott Bessborough in Saskatoon.

→ Taste Restaurant Group

A spring risotto
at Bar Gusto.

In 2016, Brad and Carmen Hamm opened Una Pizza + Wine in Saskatoon, a second location for Calgary's restaurant group BMeX, which launched the first Una in that city in 2010. The Una concept builds on popular spots in San Francisco, serving gourmet pizza and wine. Una was one of the first restaurants to bring casual fine dining to Calgary and is still going strong there, as it is in Saskatoon.

Chris and his wife Courtney formed a partnership with the Hamms to create Taste. They opened Picaro, a taqueria-inspired spot in Riversdale that was joined by Cohen's Beer Republic in 2018. Bar Gusto then followed, which is located beside Una, serving upscale Italian food, wine, and cocktails.

Executive chef for Bar Gusto and Una, Alex Stephenson trained in Florence at the 1-Star Michelin restaurant Il Palagio at the Four Seasons Luxury Hotel. Alex builds on Taste's farm-to-table commitment, working closely with local suppliers to showcase seasonal Saskatchewan produce in his dishes. That commitment can be hard for independent restaurants, says Chris. "You have those times balancing cost and quality. We use local products whenever we can. You have to juggle that every day and I think we do a good job of that."

The Local Kitchen

115-123 Ave B S | 306-244-1070 | thelocalkitchenyxe.com

■ **When the Local Kitchen opened** in 2017, it was the only place providing both commercial kitchen space and cooking classes in Saskatoon. It's become a hub for the city's culinary entrepreneurs.

The brainchild of siblings Julie Gryba and Caitlin Olauson, it all began when Caitlin developed the Local Bar (a granola bar made with Saskatchewan pulses), as part of her master's project in food science. The sisters went into production, but it was a difficult task as kitchen rental space was hard to find.

The Local Kitchen is a hub for culinary entrepreneurs.

After researching similar business models and bringing Bailey Gervais with her impressive culinary background on board, the Local Kitchen was born. They wanted an interactive component that would expose the public to what their members were doing. Cooking classes soon became the fastest-growing part of the business. Julie says the classes have helped build the city's culinary community in a way she didn't expect: "We have chefs that now have a way to be a little more creative or build their own brand. A couple of our chefs are amazing, and they work at chain restaurants. It's so nice to be able to show Saskatoon we have some serious talent."

Chefs host pop-up dinners in the space, which includes a demo kitchen and seating for sixteen, along with two other kitchens. Julie also organizes an annual Food Fight Competition to give budding culinary entrepreneurs a leg up. "It's a great way for us to meet those businesses that are perhaps hiding in the shadows and support them in some way."

Simon's Fine Foods

2605 Broadway Ave. | 306-292-6121 | simonsfinefoods.com

■ **Chef Simon Reynolds** is a jovial character, which makes his cooking classes a blast. He's fighting to get people back in the kitchen and learning important skills; skills that ensure self-sufficiency, while keeping food costs in check. "It's helping people cook for themselves rather than eating out. Chain restaurants and takeout food has kind of destroyed peoples' need to cook."

The Norwich, England-born chef was influenced by classically trained French chefs like Gordon Ramsey and Nico Ladenis. "There was a whole bunch of chefs that were ahead of their time back then. And that was the path I took."

That path—cooking from scratch, using seasonal ingredients, and supporting local farms—took Simon on a journey to some of the UK and Australia's best kitchens during a time when the locavore food movement was taking off. "People wanted to know where their food came from and where things were sourced and what they were eating," he says of the late 1990s to early 2000s.

In 2007, he opened a restaurant in Saskatoon, his wife's hometown, and later transitioned to a cooking school. Teaching his children how to eat well has always been a passion. "There are so many things people are rushing around to do but they need to dedicate a couple of hours a week to cooking together—then they'll start to build up real skills."

His advice? Everyone can cook, if they just slow down. "Good food isn't hard. Good food just takes time. People are in a rush to make a gourmet meal in ten minutes."

Chef Simon Reynolds of Simon's Fine Foods.

BiodiverCity Farm

306-280-5225 | biodivercityfarm.wordpress.com
instagram.com/biodivercity_farm

■ **Lisa Taylor's front yard** at her Saskatoon home is overflowing with flowers to keep the bees thriving and pollinating. She and her husband, Jason, run BiodiverCity Farm, a small-scale urban farm located on city boulevards and neighbours' yards.

The farm is aptly named. "Soil biodiversity is important," says Lisa. "It attracts different insects, flowers, plant species, keeps everything healthy, and creates a robust soil microbiome."

She's always been into plants and loves the outdoors. Joining a horticulture club, "gave me my first taste of growing food and what's involved. It turned out, I loved it." She

Lisa Taylor of BiodiverCity Farm.

went on to get her degree in horticulture, which led to her becoming the gardener for the Hollows and Primal, two Saskatoon restaurants that focus on hyper-local ingredients. Pictures on her Instagram feed show the vibrant greens she grows in the Hollows' basement.

Her passion for feeding people is tied to her growing methods. "They know where their food comes from and they know I didn't spray any chemicals on it. A lot of work goes into farming that way. When you can't spray anything to get rid of a pest, there's a lot of problem-solving so I really enjoy that aspect, too."

She began the farm in 2016 with a weekly vegetable subscription. A full-time job in fruit breeding research at the University of Saskatchewan meant she has had to downsize and eliminate the vegetable subscription in recent years.

Contact Lisa for vegetable availability during the growing season. She may offer weekly produce boxes again in the future.

Chain Reaction Urban Farm

434 Ave D S | 306-717-2821 | chainreactionurbanfarm.com

■ **Jared and Rachel Regier** were teachers before they decided to become urban farmers in 2015. The reason was twofold, explains Jared, as they set out to create their ideal small-scale farm. "The unselfish reason was to create a sustainable source of food for people in our community and the selfish reason was that I wanted to have all this food for our family that we couldn't obtain elsewhere."

Jared Regier at Chain Reaction Urban Farm.

The couple sells memberships for weekly vegetable boxes during the growing season. "We have very little waste coming off the farm as long as I keep track of our production numbers really well from year to year," says Jared.

Their urban plots are in yards in the city's core areas and each land owner is compensated with vegetables. Crops that need daily attention are planted in their home garden, whereas root crops are planted in yards further afield. The Regiers use trellises to help intensify production and to keep the vegetables clean. They follow organic practices, such as using netting to keep insects at bay.

Jared makes deliveries by bike. (Customers can also pick up their orders.) "We want to provide sustainable sources of food. And energy is one of the huge resources that is used in our food production."

He even handcrafted wooden boxes for each member. "We couldn't bear to throw our carefully harvested and produced food into a plastic box. We wanted the experience of our members to be special and to show that we value the food that we're giving them."

The couple welcomes visitors to their main site at 434 Avenue D South. Just call ahead to set up a time!

Our Farm

1006 Broadway Avenue | 306-222-6666 | ourfarmyxe.ca

■ **Row after row** of colourful vegetables flourish at Our Farm. Dennis and Karen Skoworodko grow about forty varieties on the two-acre certified organic farm they started in 2015. "If you feed the soil you'll have healthy plants," says Dennis. "If you have healthy plants, they'll taste good. If they taste good, they're probably very nutritious."

Deep purple kale and bright green broccoli thrive under bug netting, while carrot tops line the farm's outer edge. A few rows of sunchokes are enclosed in a fence to keep the deer away. The funky-looking tubers are a prebiotic food, similar in texture to a water chestnut and excellent for the gut microbiome. Growing sunchokes aligns with Dennis's commitment to soil biology: "If you keep your bacteria and your gut healthy, you're going to be healthy. You need to feed your gut bacteria proper food."

Soil fertility is the farm's cornerstone. They work to preserve and enhance the soil's biology through composting and using cover crops.

They run new vegetable trials each year to find varieties with the best flavour. Their criteria doesn't include shipping viability, unlike industrial farming operations.

Our Farm offers annual CSA subscriptions, along with online ordering and is at Dad's Organic Market and on the menu at Calories. The best thing to do, though, is to visit Our Farm's market on Saturday mornings in the St. Joseph Church's parking lot on Broadway to chat farming with Dennis.

"In every teaspoon of soil, there's a million bacteria and they haven't even identified all of them. It's beautiful."

Dennis Skoworodko in his organic vegetable gardens.

Simpkins Market Garden
306-374-0124

Left to right: Jennifer Lockie, her brother Dixon, her mother Audrey, and brother Robert Simpkins.

■ **Dixon Simpkins** is carrying on his family's tradition. He's a fourth-generation vegetable producer in an operation that has been a mainstay at the Saskatoon Farmers' Market since 1976. (His grandfather, uncle, and father were all among the market's founding members.)

His great-grandfather emigrated to the Prairies from England at the turn of the century and began vegetable farming. The operation has not run continuously since then and the farm has moved several times, but the family's commitment to growing good food has remained a constant.

Carrots and potatoes are their staple crops—they keep well through the winter and during years with a bountiful harvest, Dixon has sold carrots right into July. The family makes use of an old-fashioned root cellar, built into a hillside with a breathable straw roof to maintain humidity. "If you get enough product into it, it generates enough heat through respiration that you don't have to add a lot of heat, even in the winter."

Dixon likes to branch out from the root vegetables, trying new varieties, and talking to customers. "Market days are my favourite day of the week—getting to meet people, chatting and talking about the farm."

The sixty-acre garden is on a three-year rotation schedule, which helps eliminate soil diseases. Most all harvesting is done by hand. "And yes, that means a lot of work. It's a bit backbreaking at times," laughs Dixon.

Visit Simpkins Market Garden's year-round stall at the Saskatoon Farmers' Market.

3

Wally's Urban Market Garden

spinfarming.com

■ **Wally Satzewich,** Saskatoon's small plot intensive farming pioneer, devotes much of his time to making agriculture accessible to everyone. In 2000, Wally and Gail Vandersteen launched the SPIN (Small Plot Intensive) farming movement. At that time, Wally's Urban Market Garden was dispersed over twenty-five sub-acre backyard garden plots, rented from homeowners in Saskatoon. "It was nuts, but we managed to make it work," says Wally.

They began farming on a small plot outside the city over twenty years ago. They wanted to expand and bought more farmland, growing vegetables at an idyllic site near the South Saskatchewan River. However, wind and hail, insects, rodents, and deer presented constant challenges. "I thought it was time to look for a different model of farming not based on a large land base and developed SPIN farming over the years," says Wally.

They sold the farm and became urban growers. Growing in the city meant they could shift toward less complicated methods and eliminate mechanization. The SPIN farming method is based on their success in downsizing. Minimal mechanization and maximum fiscal discipline and planning are emphasized in the online guides and training programs Wally teaches.

SPIN farming enables people to start on a small scale and make money growing food. There's little investment needed, and you don't necessarily need to own land. He's taught many people how to turn lawns into profitable food sources. Curtis Stone, who operates a SPIN farm in Kelowna and teaches profitable urban farming, is one of his former students.

"People want to buy local and urban agriculture is about as local as you can get," says Wally.

In 2018, the couple decided to get back to the country and expanded their multi-locational vegetable and flower gardens to the hamlet of Pleasantdale, 200 kilometres northeast of Saskatoon. It will serve as the home base for training programs on sub-acre farming.

Wally's Urban Market Garden has a year-round stall at the Saskatoon Farmers' Market.

Wally Satzewich at the Saskatoon Farmers' Market.

141

Stumbletown Distilling

20-1905 Quebec Ave | 306-952-0691 | stumbletown.ca

Craig Holland of
Stumbletown Distilling.

■ **Saskatchewan's** microdistilling industry has been booming in the province for years. When Stumbletown Distilling opened its doors in 2018, it quickly became famous for its purple wheat vodka—a Canadian first.

The purple wheat is a specialty crop developed and grown in Saskatchewan. It contains high levels of antioxidants (so it must be healthy to drink the vodka then, right?). "We chose it for the sweet, silky characteristics that it imparts on our vodka," says owner Craig Holland. "We love the fact that it's a product developed in Saskatchewan, grown by Saskatchewan farmers, and distributed by a Saskatoon company."

Stumbletown's Maté Amaro is another unique product. It's modelled after the Italian herbal liqueur. They use woodsy yerba mate tea to infuse a flavour that's full of other herbs and botanicals. "We're putting our own spin on it," says Craig of the traditional Italian digestif. "No one in Saskatchewan is making an amaro-style liqueur. And we want to differentiate ourselves with some different products."

Stumbletown also makes gin and has four different types of whisky aging in barrels, but you'll have to wait a few years for a taste of those. They're using alternative grains, like quinoa from the NorQuin plant in Saskatoon, for the whisky.

The distillery is open for tastings and tours and is located in the same building as High Key Brewing, making the area a hotspot for all kinds of craft libations.

○ Lucky Bastard Distillers are Saskatoon's craft-spirit industry. Their free tours of the distillery are excellent (book online), as are their smooth spirits and liqueurs that incorporate different Saskatchewan-grown grains, fruits, and botanicals.

○ Provincial Vodka by Radouga Distilleries is produced near Blaine Lake, just north of Saskatoon and is available for purchase throughout the province.

Farm One Forty

Vanscoy | 306-381-8931 | farmoneforty.ca

■ **When Arlie LaRoche calls,** her sheep and cattle come running. It could be pure affection, but there might be another reason. The animals are on a rotational grazing system, which means that when Arlie whistles, it's time to switch to a new pasture area.

Raising cattle and sheep on grass is standard for Saskatchewan farmers. Arlie differs from the norm because she finishes her animals on grass at home (instead of on grain at a feedlot). Raising chickens and pigs outdoors is not standard in the industrial agriculture industry. Arlie does it because she believes it's better for the animals and the soil. "Pigs especially, they were just born to root and dig. That's why they have trouble with them in hog barns sometimes—because they can't dig. They're on a concrete floor."

Arlie LaRoche in the pasture with her sheep at Farm One Forty.

Leaving chickens and pigs in the same spot too long destroys the soil. "Nothing will grow there except for weeds because it'll be too much of a concentration of manure and urine. If you leave them there for the perfect amount of time and let that spot rest, it grows back like you wouldn't believe."

Arlie, her husband Brett, and their children's farm is near Vanscoy. Farm visits are welcome when you pick up your order. There's also a farmgate store with frozen meats, handmade soap, and candles.

Farm One Forty's meat are on the menu at the Hollows and Primal and select cuts are sold at the Heart of Riversdale Community Market & Café. As of 2019, Farm One Forty's partnership in Odla makes the restaurant one of just a few farm-to-table establishments in Canada owned by farmers.

SaskMade Marketplace

1621 8 St E | 306-955-1832 | saskmade.ca

SaskMade Marketplace stocks a variety of Saskatchewan products.

■ **Stores like SaskMade Marketplace** are the heart and soul of any locally focused food community. Without someone serving as the bridge between the producer and customer, it can be difficult for both parties to come together. In Saskatoon, Emily Li Yan and her knowledgeable staff are that bridge. Emily took over SaskMade in 2017. The Eighth Street store has been open for over a decade, providing everything from fresh produce and frozen meats to canned and dried goods from Saskatchewan producers, along with an inspiring collection of local art and books.

"I have a huge passion in terms of teaching my kids," says Emily, who has two young daughters. "And influencing everyone around us about farmers and telling their stories."

Sales specialists are all highly trained and happy to point customers in the right direction if they're looking for a product not carried in the store. Emily and her staff also assist producers interested in growing their value-added food businesses, directing them to the appropriate channels to meet

→ SaskMade Marketplace

Canadian Food Inspection Agency standards. "We help them build their business and capacity. We give them room to grow. Once everything is ready, we sell their product on the floor."

SaskMade hosts a food sampling day every Saturday, along with a monthly tasting event hosted by different vendors. The website is kept updated with farmer and artisan profiles.

✪ Of course, SaskMade Marketplace is not the only place in Saskatoon bringing together consumers with good, clean, fair food. Other spots that support and promote local producers are Dad's Organic Market, Steep Hill Food Co-operative, Ingredients Artisan Market, and the Bulk Cheese Warehouse, where a master butcher prepares house-smoked bacon and aged steaks.

✪ The Heart of Riversdale Community Market & Café, which includes Soul Foods Conscious Grocers, serves everyone in the neighbourhood by offering pay-what-you-can nourishing food options. They also host weekend farmers' markets.

✪ Ethnic grocers abound in Saskatoon. Check out Pardessi Bazaar, Bistak Groceries, Churchill's British Foods, Petra Market & Jerusalem Butcher Shop, and An An Market. Chatty's Indian Spices is always worth a visit at the Saskatoon Farmers' Market for from-scratch curry kits and homemade naan.

SASKATOON FARMERS' MARKETS

Check the website for current hours prior to your visit.

CHEP **Fresh Food Markets**

Pop-up locations
throughout the city
chep.org/program/
fresh-food-markets

**Community Farmers' Market
of Saskatoon**

London Drugs, 2328 8th Street East
Tuesdays and Fridays
9:00 AM–4:00 PM
Peavey Mart, 820C 51st East
Thursdays, 9:00 AM–4:00 PM

Our Farm Farmers' Market

Broadway and 8th Street
(St. Joseph Church parking lot)
Saturdays, 8:00 AM–Noon
June to September
facebook.com/OurFarmYXE/
306-222-6666

Saskatoon Farmers' Market

2612 Koyl Avenue
Wednesdays, 10:00 AM–3:00 PM
Saturdays, 8:00 AM–3:00 PM
Sundays, 10:00 AM–3:00 PM
saskatoonfarmersmarket.com
306-384-6262

**The U of S Campus
Farmers' Market**

Place Riel Students' Centre
1 Campus Drive North Concourse
Monthly on Fridays
9:00 AM–2:00 PM
September to May
Check website for details:
sustainability.usask.ca

◑ Following spread: **Seasonal produce is in abundance
at Saskatoon's farmers' markets.**

SASKATOON WATERING HOLES

Check the website for current hours prior to your visit.

9 Mile Legacy

229 20th St. W | 306-373-2337
9milelegacy.com

Tours: By request.
Taproom on site.

21st Street Brewery

243 21st St. E | 306-374-7468
hotelsenator.ca/21st-street-brewery

Tours: By request.
Taproom in Winston's Pub's
lower level.

Churchill Brewing Company

839 51st St E | 306-974-0759
churchillbrewing.com

Tours: By request.

Great Western Brewing Company

519 2nd Ave. N | 306-653-4653
greatwesternbeer.com

Tours: By request.

High Key Brewing Co.

1905 Quebec Ave | 306-242-2422
hkbrew.ca

Tours: By request.
Taproom on site.

Lucky Bastard Distillers

814 47th St. E | 306-979-7280
luckybastard.ca

Daily tours, tastings, retail store
and event space on site.

Paddock Wood Brewing Co.

116 103rd St. E B1 | 306-477-5632
paddockwood.com

Tours: By request.
Saskatoon's first microbrewery;
retail store with ready brew kits,
grains and hops.

Parenteau Brothers Meadworks

Saskatoon Farmers' Market
2612 Koyl Avenue | 306-491-8577
(See page 146 for market hours.)

Saskatoon Brewery

610 2nd Ave. N | 306-664-2337

Tours: By request.
Taproom on site.

Shelter Brewing Company

255 2nd Ave. S | 306-979-9249
shelterbrewing.ca

Tours: By request.
Taproom with tacos
from Dylan and Cam's.

East Central Saskatchewan

- Allan
- Annaheim
- Davidson
- Endeavour
- Holdfast
- Hudson Bay
- Humboldt
- Imperial
- Kamsack
- Lac Vert
- Lanigan
- Melfort
- Nokomis
- Porcupine Plain
- Saltcoats
- St. Brieux
- Tisdale
- Viscount
- Vonda
- Wakaw
- Yorkton

4

TRAVEL TIPS

✪ **The Ukrainian Heritage Museum** in Canora depicts all aspects of Ukrainian heritage, arts, and folklore. It's run by a group of volunteers well versed in the region's colourful history. Stop at Canora's visitor information centre (in the CN Museum) for a map of a self-guided walking tour to various historical sites.

✪ **The National Doukhobor Heritage Village** in Veregin holds events during the summer season. Visitors can purchase an ethnic lunch and clay-oven baked bread: **ndhv.ca**

✪ **Duck Mountain Provincial Park** is the highlight for nature lovers thanks to the postcard worthy landscape of hills and boreal forest. There's excellent fishing for pike, walleye, and perch in the lakes in and around the park.

Agriculture is synonymous with Saskatchewan but as you're reading in this book, you'll discover there's more than one way to go about producing food. The east central region is farming territory, to be sure. Vast golden wheat fields sway in the wind, and in the early summer the landscape is coloured by swaths of blue from flowering flax and miles of canary yellow canola. And the humble little bee is vital to it all.

Beekeeping is a profitable industry here thanks to hot, dry summers and a robust agriculture sector that make for impressive honey flows. As of 2016, the province was home to 112,000 colonies—second in Canada only to Alberta. Saskatchewan contributes 25 percent of Canada's honey production.

However, the climate can also drastically impact honey flows, like it did in 2018 when provincial honey flows took a hit after a harsh winter and spring brought a 40 percent kill rate in hives.

East central Saskatchewan is home to several of the province's most respected operations. Polinsky Honey has been at it since 1977 and has a line of beeswax candles, propolis, and body care products in addition to raw honey. Howland's Honey, near Good Spirit Lake, is a regular at the Yorkton Farmers' Market. The family has been making beautiful creamed honey since 1976.

In Humboldt (and in Cochin), Prairie Garden Seeds has been maintaining a large and diverse seed collection since 1986. Gardeners eagerly anticipate getting their hands on the company's annual seed listing catalogue (it's also online). It's owned by seed saving father-daughter duo Jim and Rachelle Ternier, who take part in Seedy Saturday events all over the province.

○ Previous spread: Janeen Covlin with her flock of free-range turkeys at Cool Springs Ranch.

○ Newborn bison calves out with the herd at Qu'Appelle Valley Bison.

Cuisine in this region is heavily influenced by Ukrainian, Polish, and Russian settlers. If you're after a bowl of borscht and a plate of perogies and cabbage rolls, this is the place to enjoy it.

Or try shishliki, a locally prepared specialty at weddings and community events in the Yorkton, Kamsack, and Canora area. Red Barn Family Farm sells shishliki from their farmgate store and makes deliveries in the area, or you can find it at Let's Make Wine in Yorkton. The recipe has been passed down for generations and each family claims to make the best version. Shishliki originated in Russia and consists of meat (lamb is preferred) marinated in salt and onions, then grilled on an open fire on a wooden skewer. New recipe variations include lemon, vinegar, and oil in the marinade.

Family-run bakeries are the heart of many communities here. Places like the Danish Oven in Humboldt are known for from-scratch and preservative-free baking. (Try their homemade white buns.) Yorkton's Wanders Sweet Discoveries does daily pastries and homemade lunch. Likely the best spot for Boston cream doughnuts in the province is at the Wadena Bakery.

Veselka, held annually in Foam Lake, is Western Canada's largest rural Ukrainian festival and features a traditional supper and a paska (Easter bread) workshop. To get your hands on some homemade Ukrainian food any time of year, or classic Saskatchewan squares, like puffed wheat, give Yorkton Bakery's Darlene Lischynski a call (306-563-6252). Darlene doesn't have a storefront but delivers to Yorkton and has a stall at the Regina Farmers' Market.

If pork roasted on an open fire is more your thing, head to Englefeld. The village has held Hogfest every summer since 1972. A dozen hogs are mounted on spits Friday night and continue cooking under watch until Saturday's supper. (Yep, we call the evening meal supper in rural Saskatchewan.) ∎

◑ A perfect spring day at Grovenland Farm.

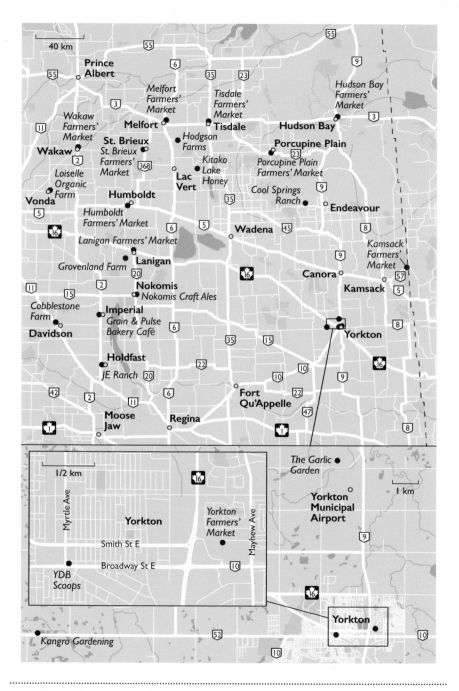

40 km

55

Prince
Albert

6

55

9

55

*Melfort
Farmers'
Market*

*Tisdale
Farmers'
Market*

35

23

*Hudson Bay
Farmers'
Market*

9

3

3

*Wakaw
Farmers'
Market*

Melfort

Tisdale

Hudson Bay

11

St. Brieux

*Hodgson
Farms*

Porcupine Plain

Wakaw

*St. Brieux
Farmers'
Market*

*Kitako
Lake
Honey*

23

*Porcupine Plain
Farmers' Market*

2

368

*Loiselle
Organic
Farm*

**Lac
Vert**

*Cool Springs
Ranch*

9

Vonda

Humboldt

5

Endeavour

35

*Humboldt
Farmers' Market*

6

5

Wadena

45

8

*Kamsack
Farmers'
Market*

16

Lanigan Farmers' Market

9

Grovenland Farm

Lanigan

16

Canora

57

20

11

15

2

Nokomis

Kamsack

5

Nokomis Craft Ales

*Cobblestone
Farm*

Imperial
*Grain & Pulse
Bakery Café*

6

8

Davidson

Yorkton

Holdfast

35

15

JE Ranch

20

10

42

2

6

10

9

11

**Moose
Jaw**

Regina

**Fort
Qu'Appelle**

22

47

22

1

8

1/2 km

*The Garlic
Garden*

16

Yorkton

1 km

**Yorkton
Municipal
Airport**

*Yorkton
Farmers'
Market*

Yorkton

Smith St E

Broadway St E

10

9

*YDB
Scoops*

16

Kangro Gardening

52

Yorkton

10

10

Note: Only artisans and producers who welcome visitors on site are shown on this map.

EAST CENTRAL SASKATCHEWAN ARTISANS

Nvigorate

Kamsack I 306-955-2319 I nvigorate.ca

Betty Forbes at Nvigorate's sea buckthorn orchard.

■ **Sea buckthorn is native** to China, Russia, and Mongolia, and has been used medicinally for centuries. The shrub, which can reach twenty feet tall, is drought tolerant and hardy in extreme cold—ideally suited for Western Canadian growing conditions. Sea buckthorn berries are chock full of vitamins and amino acids, while the leaves are high in antioxidants.

George Strelioss was an early supporter of sea buckthorn in Saskatchewan. In 1998 he planted an orchard of the thorny shrubs that spring forth tangy, tangerine-coloured berries. "He followed new ideas and he didn't mind being the first at something," says his daughter Betty Forbes. An entrepreneur through and through, George was one of the first in Saskatchewan to raise alfalfa leafcutter bees and hosted people from all over the world who came to learn at the farm he shared with his wife Pauline and their children.

George has now passed. Today, Betty and her brother Patrick Bloodoff run the certified organic orchard. Betty left her teaching career in 2007 to develop the thriving business that sells berries and products like tea leaves,

→ **Nvigorate**

....

gelato, jam, syrup, vinegar, and chocolates throughout Saskatchewan, and to restaurants in Vancouver and California.

While she got inquiries from all over the world, it was a lot of work to build a market in Saskatchewan. She opened a stall at the Saskatoon Farmers' Market and said in the beginning, 99.9 percent of people had never heard of sea buckthorn. But stores like SaskMade Marketplace and Dad's Organic Market in Saskatoon and Regina and Alternate Root Organics in Moose Jaw were supportive from the beginning, as were several Saskatoon chefs, such as Christie Peters at the Hollows.

Harvesting berries from the thorny branches is not an easy task. The branches are cut off and placed inside a freezer truck. The frozen berries are then shaken off the next day. "By doing that, it's preserving the nutritional value," says Betty. "My dad was so passionate. The reason he started was he learned about the health benefits. He built a huge sign at the entry to our orchard: Sea buckthorn = Vitamin C+."

If you'd like to visit the orchard, call Betty. Otherwise, visit Nvigorate's stall at the Saskatoon Farmers' Market or find their products at local retailers listed on their website. And watch for Seabuckthorn Days in the fall. The annual fundraiser for the Canadian Mental Health Association includes sampling, chef demos, and educational seminars.

YDB Scoops

37 Broadway St W, Yorkton | 306-782-0263

■ **What could be more fun** than running an ice cream shop in the summer? Not much, says owner Nicole Roy, who bought YDB Scoops with her parents in 2007. "It's turned into a fun and awesome little business that supports my family."

Several years ago, Nicole and her partner Bruce Benneke transitioned into making homemade ice cream and non-dairy fruit sorbets. They rotate between up to twenty-five ice cream flavours. Standard picks include Box of Crayons (five flavours and colours), Saskatoon Cheesecake, Butter Beer, and Minion (banana ice cream with blue raspberry swirl and a white chocolate eyeball on top). They love experimenting with new creations, like dill pickle, maple bacon, peach jalapeño, and mango habanero.

Nicole Roy owns YDB Scoops in Yorkton.

The sky blue and pink building is over a century old and an iconic reminder of Yorkton's past. It was once the office for the Doukhobor settlers' brickyard. Many older buildings in Yorkton still have those original bricks. "The building has a history. It's one of the oldest buildings left in town," says Nicole.

The building was a service station for years and even a fruit stand, but today it's reminiscent of an ice cream cone. After a bad flood in 2010 destroyed the paint, Nicole chose the sky blue and pink colour scheme to match the fun atmosphere she provides her customers and staff. Madison Blackstone, a local artist, painted whimsical murals on the building's walls.

If sweets aren't your thing, there's a small hot-food menu. Nicole's taco in a bag is the best in town, thanks to a secret recipe and fresh ingredients. Nicole also makes custom ice cream cakes; order in advance.

Barefoot Earth Farm
Viscount | 306-231-8303

Rachel Lemke operates Barefoot
Earth Farm outside Viscount.

■ **Rachel Lemke** operates Barefoot Earth Farm outside Viscount where she keeps about a hundred bee hives. It's a small amount compared to commercial operations, averaging two thousand hives. She says one hundred is the perfect amount. "I can focus on the health of every hive."

And she's doing an outstanding job of keeping her bees happy, healthy, and thriving. In 2017, her bees broke the provincial honey flow record. Those one hundred hives each produced an astounding 233 kilograms, all processed in the small honey house she built on her property.

She attributes that record to 2017 beginning in a drought. "A lot of rain will not make for a good beekeeping year because the bees don't get a lot of time to go out and fly." Moisture from previous rainy years was still in the subsoil, meaning the flowers were able to pull up all that moisture and produce a lot of nectar.

Lemke works with a mentor, who bred his bees. She has those genetics in her hives today. "He bred his bees to be a mutt of bees—they'll fly when it's windy, rainy, cloudy."

She sells her prairie wildflower honey at stores in Viscount and Bruno. The Heart of Riversdale Community Market and Café and Three Treasures carry it in Saskatoon. Prairie Bliss Botanicals uses her honey in their organic skincare line. Lucky Bastard Distillers is also a fan—try their Ukrainian honey pepper Horilka Vodka. The distillery also uses Rachel's honey to make a cocktail syrup for parties in their event space.

Kitako Lake Honey

Lac Vert I 306-371-1775 I kitakolakehoney.com

Owner Steve Hawrishok at Kitako Lake Honey.

■ **Kitako Lake Honey** is all about respecting the environment and supporting bees in sustainable ways. The company near Lac Vert makes high-quality, unfiltered raw honey in different floral varieties. Dandelion honey is harvested in late June, while the sweet clover honey comes later in the summer. Hives are moved during the season to be near the best nectar and pollen sources. (Dedicated honey aficionados will want to take a look at Kitako Lake's online honey-tasting guide.)

The raw honey is creamed at low temperatures so as not to damage the health properties. There's the taste of pure Saskatchewan terroir in every spoonful.

Kitako Lake Honey is located in an idyllic spot close to fields, meadows, and forests in the Aspen Parkland—fitting since beekeeping is a calming, meditative career for owner Steve Hawrishok. He said the moments of quietness attract him to beekeeping. "When you're looking at your bees, it can be very peaceful, very present, very relaxing. And then it ceases to become work and that can be a beautiful thing."

Steve's dad began the beekeeping operation and still helps out, along with Steve's mom, at the family farm. Steve took over in 2013; prior to that he lived in Saskatoon and travelled abroad. He never imagined he would end up back on the farm. "I was fairly resistant to the whole thing," he recalls.

"But something changed—I realized I was very lucky to have access to a place like this and that beekeeping is incredibly interesting. It's vital ecologically."

Kitako Lake Honey is sold in Saskatoon stores; visit their website for details.

Nokomis Craft Ales

301 1st Ave E, Nokomis I 306-528-9910 I nokomiscraftales.com

■ **Jeff Allport** opened his microbrewery and taproom smack dab in the middle of Saskatchewan grain farming country and it's a beautiful fit. His four core beers—Golden Ale, Pale Ale, India Pale Ale, and Brown Ale—are made from prairie-grown barley.

He uses Tennessee bourbon barrels for aging the beer. Bourbon generally has a heavy char and that charred oak flavour, along with a bit of the bourbon, permeates into his unfiltered craft beer. A special edition Imperial Stout is first fermented in stainless steel then transferred to bourbon barrels and aged for twelve months.

He also makes sour beers in a rapid, two-stage fermentation process. It's a small part of Nokomis Craft Ales but it's an area of craft production Jeff enjoys. "It's something we would like to grow in the future. It's a centuries-old tradition."

Allport spent most of his adult life on the West Coast. He moved to Saskatchewan nearly a decade ago with his partner. He was surprised at craft beer's virtual non-existence in the province. "It got me thinking ... I was fairly confident in my brewing ability. I wanted a facility that was primarily for production, rather than the brewery/taproom model."

Nokomis was an affordable place to start a business and offered an ideal halfway point between Regina and Saskatoon.

While Jeff says there are easier ways to make a buck—running a brewery can be long, stinky days—there's a reason he does it. "If you're making a product that people enjoy, that's a huge reward." Check the website for retail locations across the province.

Jeff Allport at Nokomis Craft Ales.

Grain & Pulse Bakery Café

207 Royal St, Imperial I 306-963-3287

■ **Imperial** hit the jackpot when Tracy Kelly-Wilcox moved to town. Her training is in both culinary and pastry arts (for which she holds Red Seal certification). Tracy has worked across Canada, at places like Toronto's Bistro 990 and Sooke Harbour House on Vancouver Island.

The menus change daily at Sooke Harbour House and each dish must include items from the garden. "The opportunity to express creativity is totally amazing, but after a while you're thinking, 'I could do Caesar salad and French fries for a year!'"

Caesar salad and French fries hardly describes the food she's making in Imperial, however. While the dishes are approachable, it's a decidedly elevated experience that includes fresh quality ingredients. The menu changes weekly; there's always a grain bowl and a pulse plate. "I didn't want to alienate anybody, but I totally wanted to push the envelope. I wanted to showcase items that everyone around here grows but very few people eat."

Tracy married a cattle rancher when she moved back to Saskatchewan. (She's from Regina but moved away in 1988.) The couple's beef is on the menu at Grain & Pulse, which opened in late 2017. It was the right decision to come home. "Since moving back, all I've seen and experienced is opportunity. It's an exciting time to be in the food scene in Saskatchewan."

Tracy's daily pastry creations are on display in the bakery (try a coconut long john) and locals can sign up for a weekly bread club. And if you call ahead, you might just score a coveted seat at Grain & Pulse's monthly supper club.

Chef Tracy Kelly-Wilcox at her bakery and café in Imperial.

Campbell Greenhouses

Annaheim | 306-598-1200 | campbellgreenhouses.ca

■ **Mary Erickson** is a vibrant, animated woman, especially when she talks about her fish. Tanks full of large koi are helping fuel her farm of the future. Mary and her husband Neil run Campbell Greenhouses with custom-built floating gardens in an aquaponic facility, which combines aquaculture and hydroponic growing techniques. In fact, it's Canada's second commercial aquaponic facility.

Mary Erickson at Campbell Greenhouses.

From their operation in Annaheim, the couple sells microgreens to Safeway and Sobeys stores across Western Canada.

Mary jokingly calls the closed-loop system "the hanging gardens of Babylon."

Up on the second floor, plants line the fish aquarium's ledges, their leaves trailing into the water. The fish produce ammonia which a filtration system converts into a usable nitrogen form for the plants. "That's where the magic happens." she says.

The water system is gravity fed and mimics a waterfall as it comes into the greenhouse. "We want the water to be as turbulent as possible to keep a lot of air and oxygenation in the water because the plants sit in it." The plants take up the nitrogen and any other micronutrients in the water, while also filtering the water for the fish. That clean water returns back up to the three aquariums.

Campbell Greenhouses is an anomaly: an artificial growing environment in the middle of Central Saskatchewan's grain farming country. The plants grow under lights. Everything is indoors in a custom, controllable ecosystem—one reason Mary thinks aquaponics will change farming in the future. "You don't get the benefit of the natural sun ... but we're still growing food," she says.

Country Garden Fresh

Saltcoats | 306-744-2718

Charles and Donna Dyck at the Yorkton Farmers' Market.

■ **A lineup stretching** down the mall aisle is a normal sight at Country Garden Fresh's stand. Charles and Donna Dyck come to the Yorkton Farmers' Market, inside the Parkland Mall, every week to sell their vegetables, baking, and free-range eggs. Seven bread varieties, all made from the Dycks' organic grain which they mill into flour, are always big sellers, as are double chocolate zucchini muffins and poppy rolls.

The couple have been farming for over thirty years, starting with a conventional farm and keeping a garden. About twenty years ago, they got more serious about the farmers' market, switched to organic growing methods, and expanded their market garden's size to a few acres.

Charles says they moved to organic farming when he saw what chemicals were doing to his soil. He also didn't like working with chemicals and the involved risks. More recently, permaculture has caught the couple's interest, so they've begun using cover crops and making compost for fertilization. "We take the approach that if you feed your soil, your soil will feed you. We feed the microorganisms in the soil and the life in the soil—then that will in turn provide you with healthy plants and crops," says Charles.

Their grain crops are certified organic but not the vegetables. "We used to certify but most of our customers, if they want to see what we're doing, they can come out to the farm."

The farm is forty-three kilometres from Yorkton. Call ahead to organize a visit—the Dycks would be happy to show you their operation. "I just like growing things and seeing new life every spring," says Charles.

The Garlic Garden

Yorkton I 306-786-3377 I yorktongarlic.com

■ **One of Western Canada's** premier suppliers of quality garlic is located on a farm just outside Yorkton. Darrel and Anna Schaab planted their first garlic crop in 2005. "We weren't sure what we were doing or if [it] would be marketable," says Darrel. They ended up with four thousand heads of garlic and sold it all within a few weeks from the farmgate. And so, they planted more the next year and the next year after that, learning as they went.

The planting runs from mid-September until October and is all done by hand—the only way to ensure a uniform head of garlic. They hope for ample snow to insulate the crop and wait for April when it begins to emerge. Scape season hits in June. (Scapes are snapped off and sold so the plant's energy goes into making garlic.) About two weeks later, it's garlic harvesting time, a hot, dirty, methodical job.

Anna says meeting people who enjoy their garlic is the best reward: "It's the people that come around and say, 'Your garlic is the best garlic!' We've had customers since 2005—it's awesome."

She's particular about who helps with the harvest since all the garlic must be gently sorted and cleaned by hand. And the heads that go to farmers' markets must be aesthetically perfect. "It's a matter of pride," says Anna with one of her trademark grins.

The Garlic Garden is at the Regina and Saskatoon Farmers' Markets and usually does farmgate sales in the summer. The garlic is also in stores throughout Saskatchewan, Alberta, and Manitoba.

Darrel and Anna Schaab at their farm outside Yorkton.

Grovenland Farm
Lanigan | 306-365-3037 | grovenlandfarm.ca

■ **Grovenland Farm** is a place where both ecological and health benefits are key. Lisa and Ben Martens Bartel believe the relationship between animals and native prairie grasses is a productive biological system. Their goal is to help the soil microbiology and perennial polyculture thrive. "We try to mimic the sort of disturbance that bison would have represented. And

Ben and Lisa Martens Bartel of Grovenland Farm.

get healthier and healthier pastures every year that way," explains Ben.

Their chickens, cattle, and pigs are all raised on pasture as much as possible, which means a better end product for humans. "The health profile in terms of the balance of fatty acids that you get from having fresh greens in your diet is much healthier. The omega 3s and 6s are better balanced."

In 2011, the couple had careers in Winnipeg. They weren't planning to return to Saskatchewan, but after becoming more aware of the benefits of locally sourced foods, they had a change of heart. "We were concerned about where our food came from and realized we had the skills to do it," says Ben. "And we wanted to be sustainable for ourselves," says Lisa. It turned out Ben's parents were on a parallel local food journey and were happy to help the couple and their three children with the farm.

During garden season, they sell CSA vegetable subscriptions (full farm shares are also available). Winter meat and eggs are sold from November to June. They deliver to Saskatoon, or better yet: Load up the kids and head out to the farm to pick up your order.

Hodgson Farms

Melfort | 306-921-7584 | facebook.com/HodgsonFarms

■ **If you didn't think** cantaloupe could grow in Saskatchewan, you're not alone—the orange melons aren't a common sight. Susan and Mark Hodgson began growing cantaloupes several years ago in high tunnel greenhouses. Susan said that once they figured out how to grow the Halona variety, it's been an "amazing" endeavour. Some weigh up to three kilograms.

"We didn't know how to tell when they were ready, so we were out there knocking cantaloupes," she says with a laugh. But that's not how you tell if a cantaloupe is ripe, they later learned. "If you pick it up and it releases itself, they're vine-ripened," says Mark.

The Hodgsons even grow the cantaloupes outdoors now. As long as the frost stays away, the cantaloupes are happy. And if your only experience with cantaloupe is the bland, watery grocery store variety, you're in for a treat. Hodgson cantaloupes are bursting with flavour.

So too are their oversized strawberries, thanks to Mark's fertilization methods. "Over the years, we found easier methods to farm and grow our fruits and control our weeds." At one time they had forty thousand strawberry plants but have downsized to five thousand. They also grow raspberries, potatoes, rhubarb, and horseradish.

"I like the fact that there's no chemicals in our food right now. I'm eating real food. And so is our family," adds Susan about feeding their three children.

Mark also operates a licensed abattoir on the farm where he does his own butchering.

Hodgson Farms is at the Melfort Farmers' Market every Thursday. Give them a call for U-pick strawberries and raspberries or if you'd like a tour of the farm.

Mark and Susan Hodgson
in their cantaloupe field.

Kangro Gardening

Hwy 52, Yorkton | 306-620-8335 | kangro.ca

■ **Another popular stand** at the Yorkton Farmers' Market belongs to Kangro Gardening. It's conveniently situated beside a large grocery store's entrance, subtly making people think about buying locally before they enter the store. Plus, it's hard not to be attracted to Brendon Purton's overflowing baskets of vibrant, fresh vegetables all grown without herbicides or pesticides.

Brendon's dad Bob began the market garden two decades ago on their property just outside Yorkton. The two now run the operation together. It consists of six greenhouses and a five-acre outdoor garden. "Gardening's always been a big passion of my dad's. I'm happy that I ended up really liking it too and am fortunate I can take things over eventually," says Brendon.

The Purtons grow their vegetables in pots in the greenhouse, everything from beefsteak tomatoes, cucumbers, eggplants, and peppers to lettuce, Swiss chard, and kale. The outdoor garden is full of cabbage, a popular stable in Ukrainian and German households in the Yorkton area. Kangro grows all that cabbage for the fall supper season (a time in Saskatchewan ubiquitous with celebrating the harvest in community halls and churches). Some churches will order several hundred-kilograms to make cabbage rolls, sauerkraut, and the like.

Brendon says the Yorkton community has been supportive. "Although it's quite busy, it's not stressful. It doesn't feel like work to me. As busy as I am in the summer months, I always know there will be time off later in the year."

Visit Kangro's website for the farm store's hours.

Brendon Purton at the Yorkton Farmers' Market.

Loiselle Organic Family Farm

Vonda | 306-227-5825

■ **The Loiselle family's** agricultural roots run deep. Marc and his wife Anita, along with their children, farm land near Vonda that's been in Marc's family for well over a century. In 1985, they began working with certified organic and biodynamic agricultural practices.

While the Loiselles grow a range of cereal, pulse, hay, and oilseed crops, they are best known for their heritage Red Fife wheat. Thanks to their efforts, Canada's oldest wheat is enjoying a renaissance. The Loiselles began growing Red Fife in 2001, at a time when the wheat was nearing extinction. "Red Fife is more difficult to grow agronomically, but it has that great taste and Slow Food story behind it," says Marc, who is also a long-time advocate for organic farming in Saskatchewan.

Anita Loiselle delivers a load of Red Fife wheat to Bryn Rawlyk at the Night Oven Bakery in Saskatoon.

His Slow Food connection began in 2004, when he attended Terra Madre in Turin, Italy. It was an experience that left an "indelible mark." That was also the year he became the sole grain supplier for Victoria's Fol Epi bakery (under a different name at that time).

He and Fol Epi's owner lugged sacks of flour onto the plane for their booth at Terra Madre's Hall of Tastes, where they gave out samples of freshly baked Red Fife bread each morning. "There wasn't much being grown. We got this huge exposure through Slow Food. It took off from there. We're still going strong with it and it's become the mainstay for our farm."

→ Loiselle Organic Family Farm

The Loiselles' grains, like Musketeer rye, Red Fife, and Rouge De Bordeaux wheat, have been mainstays at Saskatoon's Night Oven Bakery, (page 114) which stone mills their grain on site. Marc ships Red Fife to Flourist, a stone-ground mill making flour fresh to order in Vancouver. "It's exciting, especially to be working with people that are so interesting and dynamic."

The family are staunch supporters of eating well and self-sufficiency. Being able to share that experience, while dealing directly with their customers, is a bonus. "It's that human connection, actually sharing with people their experience of eating healthy, organic food. It's a passion to be able to do what I do as a farmer," says Marc.

They also raise rare breed Dexter cattle, and offer beef along with pork and egg sales. You're welcome to visit the farm (just call ahead) or Saskatoon delivery is easily organized.

Cobblestone Farm

Davidson | 306-715-2042 | berkshirepork.net

■ **Cobblestone Farm** is one of just a few farms in Saskatchewan raising heritage Berkshire pigs—both for meat animals and for breeding stock to sell. But raising the pigs is far beyond a business for Joanna Shepherd. "My pigs are my passion," she says with a big smile.

She and her husband Carl emigrated to Manitoba from England. When a customer at the butcher shop where they both worked told them she couldn't find Berkshire pigs in Saskatchewan, it got the wheels turning. They bought a farm near Davidson in 2010 and now have about a hundred pastured pigs, along with laying hens. Joanna always wanted to keep pigs, especially the breed her family used to raise back home.

They've raised other breeds over the years but prefer the Berkshires. They're a hardy breed, well-suited to winter climes, and have superb meat quality. "They're way friendlier, way calmer. I do spend a lot of time with them but they're not as noisy as some of the other breeds." Since Joanna sells breeding stock to family farm operations, her pigs' temperament is important. "Anything we have that's aggressive, we don't keep."

Joanna Shepherd feeding her heritage Berkshire pigs.

The pigs' diet is supplemented with fruit and vegetables from a program organized by Loop Resources. The program partners with Western Canadian grocery stores to help small farms get animal feed while reducing food waste. Joanna picks up the produce, which expires the day of pickup, once a week for her pigs from Save-On-Foods in Saskatoon.

Order pork and eggs through the farm website—a range of delivery options are available. Email or call Joanna if you'd like to visit the farm.

Cool Springs Ranch

Endeavour I 306-547-4252 I coolspringsranch.ca

The cattle at Cool Springs Ranch near Endeavour.

■ **Janeen and Sam Covlin's kitchen** is what every good farm kitchen should be: a gathering place overflowing with buckets of garden produce, freshly creamed butter, bulbs of garlic, and links of home-made sausage. An oversized wooden dining table sits smack dab in the middle of all the action, a necessity for the Covlins and their five children.

Cool Springs Ranch uses holistic animal management techniques for its cattle, pigs, turkeys, and chickens. The animals are raised on grass and are rotated to new grazing areas often to ensure their own health and that of the soil. (Overgrazing quickly kills pasture land and makes it easy for weeds to invade.)

The couple moved to the farm, which they now run with Janeen's parents, after they were married in 2001. The following year, the BSE crisis (mad cow disease) hit, forcing them to take jobs off the farm. "We paid good money for stuff and then it went to nothing for a long time, so we really struggled to make ends meet," says Janeen.

Janeen had always been a fan of Joel Salatin and knew she wanted to run her farm more in line with his teachings, while developing a direct-to-consumer market. A course through the Weston A. Price Foundation taught her the ground rules and, "has been the framework for everything we do since then."

Cool Springs Ranch delivers each month to Saskatoon and Regina. The farm has a market store (directions are on the website), along with an abattoir for on-site butchering and animal processing.

JE Ranch

Holdfast | 306-488-4408 | jeranch.ca

■ **Michelle was a born and raised city gal.** Then she met Jacob Ehmann. The farm boy from Holdfast swept her off her feet. She soon left a downtown office job and headed for the country. "I moved to the farm and traded my heels in for shovelling shit!" she says with a laugh.

Three kids later, Jacob and Michelle are happier than ever as their direct-to-consumer business grows alongside their holistic animal management at the ranch. The couple and Jacob's father Ken raise grass-finished cattle and goats on the original quarter of land homesteaded by Ken's grandfather. They're working to create a market for goat meat in Saskatchewan. They decided the best way to do that was by substituting goat meat in their already popular beef recipes.

The Ehmanns' cattle, goats, and horses are pastured together in a rotational grazing system. "Comingling the animals really cleans up the pasture. It uses all the plants that are on the land and helps out with parasites," says Jacob.

When winter hits, the animals are fed hay (it's tested annually for nutrient levels) in the pasture—another technique that builds grass and soil health. "From all the work that's done in the wintertime feeding out there, the pasture in those areas will be double the depth in colour."

Find JE Ranch's meat on Local & Fresh's website or visit the Ehmanns at their Regina Farmers' Market stall. Online ordering (with pickup at the farm if you like) is on their website along with a list of restaurants carrying their products.

The Ehmann family raises grass-finished cattle and goats on their ranch near Holdfast.

Lost River Permaculture

Allan | lostriverpermaculture.com

■ **A craft distillery and cattle ranch** are nestled in the picturesque countryside bordering the south Allan Hills near Dundurn and the fabled Lost River. Lost River Distillery is family owned, small batch, and artisanal. The family crafts premium vodka from prairie grains and naturally pure artesian spring water.

Shawn Ward and Lisa Landrie-Ward and their children.

"Our neighbour related a story to us how the CPR rail line used to source water from our farm to use for their steam engine locomotives. The aquifer at the source was preferred for its remarkable purity and seemingly endless supply of crystal-clean, fresh water," says Shawn Ward.

The family began their ranch in 2008 when they purchased the cattle grazing land southeast of Saskatoon. A distillery on the ranch followed in 2015. "It brought a unique twist to the farm. Who doesn't love beef and liquor?" says Lisa Landrie-Ward.

Cattle are grazed throughout the summer, raised without hormones or antibiotics, and finished on a grain and barley ration. The beef, which is aged a minimum of twenty-eight days, is sold by the side and by various cuts on Lost River's website. "Restaurant owners also love the fact that we're local and we produce a fantastic tasting product," says Lisa.

Order Lost River's vodka through their website or find it in Saskatoon at Ingredients Artisan Market, Metro Liquor, Urban Cellars, and Sobeys Liquor. Beef delivery is available to Saskatoon and the surrounding area.

➲ **The elevators in Liberty.**

EAST CENTRAL SASKATCHEWAN FARMERS' MARKETS

Check the website for current hours prior to your visit.

Hudson Bay Farmers' Market

Legion Hall, 303 Main St
Thursdays, 11:00 AM–3:00 PM
July to September
facebook.com/
groups/880432388662837/
306-865-3677 or 306-865-4136

Humboldt Farmers' Market

Misty Gardens, 534 Bruce Street
Dates and times updated on Facebook
facebook.com/pages/category/
Farmers-Market/Humboldt-
Farmers-Market-769968709843186/
306-366-2140

Kamsack Farmers' Market

Lodge parking lot
Saturdays, Noon–3:00 PM
July and August

Duck Mountain Provincial Park
Wednesdays, 11:00 AM–3:30 PM
June to September

Lanigan Farmers' Market

In front of the Lanigan
Heritage Centre
Wednesdays, 3:00 PM–6:00 PM
July to September

Melfort Farmers' Market

Melfort Mall, 1121 Main Street
Thursdays, Noon–5:00 PM
306-752-5394

Porcupine Plain Farmers' Market

Fisherman's Cove, just outside
Greenwater Park
Saturdays, 11:00 AM–2:00 PM
April to end of July
306-278-3123

Porcupine Plain Community Hall
Fridays, 10:00 AM–2:00 PM
August to December

St. Brieux Farmers' Market

Behind Insync Hair F/X
615 Main Street
Fridays, 3:00 PM–6:00 PM
June to September

Tisdale Farmers' Market

Tisdale Town Square
Tuesdays, 8:30 AM–Noon
Mid-July to October

Wakaw Farmers' Market

Wakaw Curling Rink
Saturdays, 10:00 AM–2:00 PM
Mid-May to October
wakaw.ca/live/farmers-market
306-864-2632

Yorkton Farmers' Market

Yorkton's Parkland Mall
277 Broadway St. E
Thursdays and Saturdays
9:00 AM–2:00 PM
March to December
yorktonfarmersmarket.ca

CHANTERELLE
MUSHROOMS

Jewels from northern
Saskatchewan forests

Chefs the world over know about Saskatchewan's wild chanterelle mushrooms. That's because the province's unique climate and terroir helps to produce some of the world's most vibrantly coloured and robustly flavoured chanterelles.

Beth Rogers and Thayne Robstad have been foraging mushrooms for years. The couple opened Hearth Restaurant in Saskatoon in 2018, a place that highlights the province's unique local food bounty in chef-focused dishes, often with ingredients they foraged.

To find the highest quality chanterelles, it's best to go picking at the beginning of the season. On a picking trip, the chefs were happy to share the tricks of the trade but were strict about one thing: Their spot in a jack pine forest northeast of Prince Albert must be kept secret.

An old growth forest is key to finding the best chanterelles, says Thayne. Speaking from personal experience, he attributes it to nutrients from dying and rotting trees leaching into the ground. "You can walk 200 metres where it's been logged, and you won't find a single mushroom." Gnarled trees with twisted branches signal an old

◔ A wild chanterelle mushroom, Saskatchewan's forest jewel.

growth forest. So too does a forest floor littered with trees, fallen so long ago they've become part of the ground. The mushrooms live in symbiosis with the trees—their health helps determine the mushrooms' health. A varied terrain that helps capture moisture is also ideal for chanterelles.

In the couple's prized picking spot, it feels spongy underfoot from reindeer moss blanketing the ground. Crispy on the outer edges and cushy soft underneath, the moss has silvery tips that descend into earthen colours at the root. Chanterelles burst through the moss, often in the small spaces between fallen logs. Thanks to the moss's texture, the chanterelles stay clean as they grow through it. The mushrooms' colour is similar to that of an apricot and easy to spot if you keep your eyes trained on the ground.

A starter on Hearth's seasonal menu features these wild mushrooms and is served with melty cheese and topped with sprigs of reindeer moss. The moss doesn't have a ton of flavour, but it carries acidity well. It's tossed with a vinaigrette and used as a garnish to balance the rich cheese. Chanterelles also add a pop of colour and an earthy flavour to Hearth's seared pork belly dish.

The couple grew up in Saskatoon and met in their early twenties. They began cooking in local restaurants before setting out, like

many young chefs do, on a culinary journey that saw them working in top-notch kitchens.

Travelling North America in a camper van later followed, along with jobs picking mushrooms for the commercial market. They've picked mushrooms across the country, but Saskatchewan's forest jewels are particularly special. "They should probably be on our flag," Beth says with a laugh. "We love food that is naturally from the land. These mushrooms taste like how the forest smells."

⊙ Chanterelles have prominent gills attached to a dense stem.

Sharing that expression of Saskatchewan terroir is the couple's focus at Hearth. "The way we look at it, these mushrooms are a concentration of this [forest]," says Thayne. "And then when we cook them, we concentrate them again. It's like a punch in the face of forest. I've had chanterelles from all over the country, but these are the ones that taste like Saskatchewan."

A FORAGERS' GUIDEBOOK

Saskatchewan chanterelles are compact, dry, clean, and full of flavour. The colour is "wicked orange ... almost unnatural it's so beautiful," says Thayne.

Chanterelles generally have a vase shape which becomes more pronounced in older mushrooms. Another sure way to tell it's a chanterelle is by turning it over. The prominent gills on the underside are thick and attached to a dense stem. The smell is a mixture of moss, damp wood, and, oddly, peaches.

Walk slowly and methodically, paying close attention to the ground beneath your feet. Chanterelles are small—look for little orange hats peeking out of the reindeer moss.

⊙ Beth Rogers and Thayne Robstad foraging for wild mushrooms in the boreal forest.

Timing is everything with chanterelles. Mushroom season varies. For chanterelles, it begins in early to mid-August and continues until the first freeze. The earlier in the season, the better, especially if it's a dry year. Without enough rain, the mushrooms will only flourish for a few weeks at best.

Usually, when you find one, you'll find many more in the same area. Think of chanterelles as apples growing on a tree—except this tree, called the mycelia, is growing under the ground.

There are two schools of thought when it comes to picking. Some pluck the mushrooms out of the ground, while others use a knife to cut the stem. Thayne and Beth believe in the latter method as they think it's healthier for the mycelia to leave the chanterelle stems in the ground. "We feel that if you pluck, you disrupt that system. We're just doing our best," says Beth with a smile.

They don't clear cut an area either, instead leaving behind large mushrooms to reproduce and repopulate. "They need to live their whole life and their spores need to fall to the ground and grow more mushrooms," she adds.

WHY THE SECRECY?

The jack pine forest is a hobby spot for Thayne and Beth. The mushrooms they pick there are "something we can bring back to share at the restaurant." However, the spot helps support others' livelihoods, so the couple doesn't reveal the location.

After a morning of picking, the two like to picnic in the forest, a thermos of coffee at the ready. It's a relaxing place, a nice afternoon picking spot.

Commercial picking in remote areas of northern Saskatchewan is a different story. The secrecy among pickers comes from the competitive nature of the business. "Everyone wants to have the best spots and the biggest hauls and make the most money," says Beth.

It's those spots, with highly concentrated fungi, where people from all over come to make their living on the "mushroom flush," as they move across North America throughout the growing season. Rustic bush camps, without running water or cell service, pop up. The mushrooms are sold to buyers who package the product and sell to stores or exporters.

⊙ The wild mushroom appetizer at Hearth Restaurant.

What began as a little orange treasure poking up through the moss can later become a coveted delicacy on international grocers' shelves and on world-renowned restaurants' menus. In Thayne and Beth's case, the chanterelles they pick travel south just a few hours and spend life in Hearth's cooler before tantalizing diners' tastebuds.

Saskatchewan chanterelles are truly unique. Chanterelles thrive in other parts of the country, but often grow much larger than in Saskatchewan. "And then you cook them and they're just full of water—which is fun. But these ... they punch above their weight class for chanterelles," says Beth.

Saskatchewan's drier climate means the chanterelles are small and the flavour is concentrated, making the province's forest jewels in demand globally. "Chefs all over the world know how to say Saskatchewan because of these mushrooms," says Thayne. It's just one more reason to be proud of Saskatchewan's diverse food bounty. ∎

⊙ Following spread: Unloading bee hives at Barefoot Earth Farm.

Southeast Saskatchewan

5

TRAVEL TIPS

✪ **Over the Hill Orchards** offers tours, tastings of their fruit wines, a retail store, and pop-up Supper in the Orchard events in partnership with the Regina Chefs' Association.

✪ Take the kids to **Motherwell Homestead National Historic Site** to learn about Saskatchewan's pioneer history. Early Saskatchewan settler and community leader W.R. Motherwell became the minister of agriculture thanks to his passion for scientific farming methods.

5

When it comes to restaurants, a few of Saskatchewan's best hidden gems are in the southeast region. The Grotto is in Vibank, the Happy Nun is in Forget, and Carnduff is home to the Olive Branch Bistro. Find authentic Neapolitan pizza in Ogema at Solo Italia. And in North Portal, Daybreak Mill processes crops of cereals and ancient grains, many of which the mill's owner grows on her farm.

Some of Saskatchewan's best food festivals are in the southeastern region, too. Take the Great Saskatchewan Bacon Festival for example—who doesn't love bacon? Saskatchewan chefs and home cooks travel to Kipling to compete in the ultimate bacon taste test in sweet and savoury categories. Savour the Southeast festival celebrates Saskatchewan-made food and spirits in a cabaret-style event in Estevan. Sample local food and spirits during the tasting event at Weyburn's Flavours of Fall Food and Beverage Expo.

This is agriculture country; grain farms and cattle ranches stretch as far as the eye can see. Driving through the region gives you a sense of expansiveness as the golden fields of wheat wave in the wind right up to the horizon line.

The Qu'Appelle Valley runs through the northwestern tip of the region. The North West Company established Fort Qu'Appelle as a fur trading post in the early 1800s, later followed by the Hudson's Bay Company. In 1874 the Cree and the Salteaux bands of the Ojibwa people and the Assiniboine signed Treaty 4 in Fort Qu'Appelle, ceding Indigenous territory to the federal government in exchange for payments, provisions, and rights to reserve lands. Today, Fort Qu'Appelle is home to the All Nations Healing Hospital, one of the first health care facilities owned and operated by a First Nations government in Canada.

⊕ Previous spread: **A cattle herd in Saskatchewan's ranching country.**
⊕ **Taking the crop off the field in southeast Saskatchewan.**

Lumsden and Craven are also in the Qu'Appelle Valley. Both towns are picturesque and have some wonderful places to stop in for a bite to eat. Vegetable producers abound in the valley. You can plan an afternoon visiting their farms, then head to 641 Grill in Craven or Free Bird in Lumsden to end the day.

Regina Beach gets busy in the summer. The lakeside community has a lively farmers' market and in August, the Regina Beach & District Lions Club holds a pit beef barbeque: seasoned, marinated beef slow-roasted in a deep earthed pit for twelve hours. ■

↑ Stunning autumn colours abound in the valley near Lumsden.
↪ Saskatchewan's bees adore the Canada thistle's flowers.

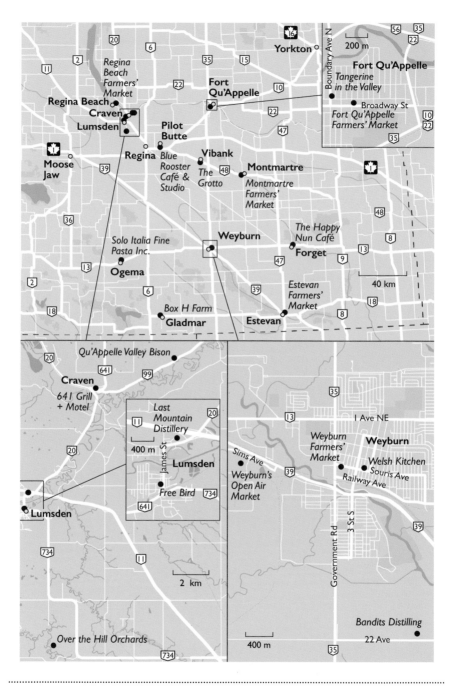

Yorkton

Fort Qu'Appelle
Tangerine in the Valley

200 m

Fort Qu'Appelle

Boundary Ave N

Broadway St
Fort Qu'Appelle Farmers' Market

Regina Beach
Regina Beach Farmers' Market

Fort Qu'Appelle

Craven
Lumsden

Pilot Butte

Regina

Blue Rooster Café & Studio

Vibank

The Grotto

Montmartre
Montmartre Farmers' Market

Moose Jaw

Solo Italia Fine Pasta Inc.

Ogema

Weyburn

The Happy Nun Café

Forget

Estevan Farmers' Market

40 km

Box H Farm
Gladmar

Estevan

Qu'Appelle Valley Bison

Craven

641 Grill + Motel

Last Mountain Distillery

400 m

James St

Lumsden

Free Bird

Lumsden

Sims Ave

Weyburn's Open Air Market

Weyburn Farmers' Market

Weyburn

Welsh Kitchen
Souris Ave
Railway Ave

3 St S

Government Rd

Over the Hill Orchards

2 km

400 m

Bandits Distilling
22 Ave

Note: Only artisans and producers who welcome visitors on site are shown on this map.

194

SOUTHEAST SASKATCHEWAN ARTISANS

Solo Italia Fine Pasta Inc.

202 Main St, Ogema | 306-459-7747 | soloitalia.ca

Marco De Michele at Solo Italia in Ogema.

■ **For Marco De Michele,** pizza is synonymous with Naples, the home of Italy's only "real" pizza. After moving here in 2012, he knew he had to bring his traditional food culture to Saskatchewan.

He began by making pasta and cannelloni with his wife Tracey Johnson. (They met in Costa Rica and lived in Italy before moving to her hometown, Ogema.) "At one time, we were producing pasta for three days in a row without sleeping, without sitting. It was incredible," he says.

An old butcher shop in Ogema had been destroyed by a fire. The municipality gave it to Marco, who along with his father-in-law, rebuilt the now iconic red and yellow Quonset on Ogema's main street.

It soon became apparent pizza would be a hit, but Marco didn't want to make it in an electric oven. After two years of research and a garage project, he built Solo Italia's wood-fired oven. "Everybody fell in love," he says, both with the soft dough made using a long fermentation, and the quality Italian ingredients, like San Marzano tomato sauce.

And if the pizza is a little softer than what you're used to, that's because it's authentic Neapolitan. "The name 'pizza' in Italian means something soft," explains Marco. "Pizza that is like crackers—don't call it pizza! Please call it brick because it's heavy—heavy and crunchy."

Solo Italia's products are in retail locations across the province along with Safeway and Sobeys. Your best bet, though, is to head to Ogema for a fresh, wood-fired takeout pizza. Grab a spot at the outdoor picnic tables and pretend you're at an Italian sidewalk café. And, if you're lucky, the ice cream stand down the street will be open for dessert.

Three Farmers

1-877-295-1551 | threefarmers.ca

Siblings Natasha (left) and Elysia Vandenhurk co-own Three Farmers.

■ **Plant-based protein** is all the rage these days and people are looking for foods that deliver. Three Farmers makes some of the province's most recognizable value-added foods, using products grown on family farms. The company is owned by Elysia and Natasha Vandenhurk, along with their father and two neighbouring farmers in southeast Saskatchewan.

In 2011, Three Farmers started out with cold-pressed camelina oil, made from the ancient oilseed crop that's relatively new to the Prairies. In the beginning the original three farmers grew the camelina for the company. They've since contracted outside farmers who also follow holistic land management practices to grow for them.

The company expanded rapidly and rolled out a popular chickpea snack line in 2014, later followed by roasted green peas and lentils. Of course, the journey hasn't been easy but prairie people have never been afraid of a hard day's work.

→ **Three Farmers**

Canada's snack market is booming, says Elysia. "And that's where the fastest, most significant growth in our company has been felt. Our focus is a plant-based pulse snack manufacturer."

The company's marketing tells a story that takes buyers from the farmer's field to their snack bag. (Traceability bar codes on the products allow consumers to find out who made the product and where.) Keeping the business wholly in Saskatchewan was a no-brainer for Three Farmers. "We want to stick with products that are sustainably grown around us," says Elysia. "We've really noticed that people don't understand how much Saskatchewan produces food-wise for the whole world. We like putting that story out there."

Their products are sold across Canada in major and natural food grocers and in the American market via Amazon.com. But with growth came new challenges. "What was really hard in the beginning isn't our biggest challenge now. Challenges change over time."

A manufacturing problem was solved by working with partners. There was no one in Canada that could roast chickpeas for Three Farmers at the capacity they needed, and in an allergen-free facility. "We had to take it upon ourselves to get into that manufacturing piece." They partnered with Prairie Berries, which already had a food safe facility that was only in use six weeks of the year.

"Everything is very hard and it's even harder if you try to do it by yourself. As long as it's a win-win you'll get to where you're going that much quicker and easier if you work together," says Elysia.

Visit their website for store locations where their products are sold.

Blue Rooster Café & Studio

505 Aaron Dr, Pilot Butte | 306-337-4555 | cafebluerooster.ca

■ **The Blue Rooster Café & Studio** is a vibrant community gathering spot in Pilot Butte, just east of Regina. Sisters Kelly Haas and Wendy Erratt opened their café and art studio in 2014. Kelly takes care of the cooking side, while Wendy handles the art studio.

In a burgeoning town, the sisters have created a space that combines their passions. The food is homemade, right down to the ketchup and dressings, and you won't find a microwave or deep fryer in the little kitchen. The eggs, ground pork, and beef are from local organic farmers, as are the garden vegetables in the summer.

Serving made-from-scratch food was important for the sisters. They are both cancer survivors. "That's the kind of food we wanted to provide and eat ourselves," says Wendy. "We just do our best," adds Kelly.

While there is daily baking available (try the Zehnammon Roll, an old family recipe that combines a cinnamon roll and local Zee-Bee honey), the café's focus is on the savoury side. The Studio Burger, served on a brioche bun, is out of this world, juicy and delicious (get it with Smashed Potato Poutine), while the Thankful Blue Rooster

Sisters Kelly Haas and Wendy Erratt own Blue Rooster Café & Studio.

is a flavourful combo of grilled chicken, homemade stuffing, cranberry chutney, and thyme aioli.

A range of arts and crafts classes are geared toward different age groups and include family art nights, watercolour workshops, youth paint nights, crocheting, and even children's cooking classes.

The Cookie Lady's baking is also for sale at the café, along with specialty cookies from another baker in the area. Note: As of September 2019 the café is under new ownership but still serves great homemade food.

Welsh Kitchen
405 Souris Avenue, Weyburn | 306-842-7687

■ **In a city** with a plethora of chain restaurants, it can be tough to find a home-cooked meal. That's why the lunchtime lineup at Weyburn's Welsh Kitchen stretches out the door.

Vicki Leas and her mom started the business in 2009. (Vicki now runs it with her husband and sister-in-law.) The two didn't have any experience running a bakery or restaurant but they jumped in, wanting to provide Weyburn with healthy, homemade food. Vicki and her staff bake up to ten different kinds of bread each day, along with burger and hot dog buns, and treats that fill a brightly lit dessert cooler. "The first day we opened, I look back and I can't believe it, that was the first day I made bread," recalls Vicki, who continued doing all the baking for years before hiring a second baker.

The lunchtime lineups are for the $11 feature of a homemade soup and sandwich on freshly baked bread. Turkey and beef are roasted in the tiny kitchen. For an extra dollar, diners can add on dessert, like Saskatchewan favourites such as matrimonial cake or a Nanaimo bar.

On the first Thursday of the month, Vicki features a roast turkey dinner with all the fixings over the noon hour. Breakfast is served until eleven and all day on the weekends. In April, the bakery puts out hot cross buns. Homemade cheesecake and sugar cookies are always in the display cooler.

"I cannot believe how busy it is," says Vicki. "I'm so blessed that we've done well. Weyburn needs something [else]. There are so many fast food restaurants here."

Vicki, Chelsey, and Dan Leas operate the Welsh Kitchen in Weyburn.

641 Grill + Motel
2 Fraser Ave, Craven | 306-731-2223

■ **Farm-to-table** is a misused concept in the culinary world and true farm-to-table restaurants are few and far between. In Saskatchewan, 641 Grill in the Qu'Appelle Valley is one of the few restaurants owned by ranchers. And their beef is, of course, on the menu!

Kali and Mathew Eddy, who bought the restaurant after it sat vacant in their hometown for six months, live on a ranch near Craven with their three children. The name came from the 641 grid that used to run in front of the property.

"The valley has so much to offer in terms of local produce and suppliers. We are probably most proud that we serve our very own family farm-raised

Left to right, the Eddy family: Vann, Kali, Wit, Mathew, and Dax.

beef and pork. When you bite into the Eddy burger, it doesn't get more local than that," says Kali. An extensive list of local suppliers is included on the menu full of elevated comfort food and ranges from potatoes (for the hand-cut fries) from Craven Riverside Gardens to Leaning Maple Meats in Strasbourg. Staff grow herbs and vegetables in garden boxes on the property.

The restaurant epitomizes rural Saskatchewan life outside and in, with scenic valley views and an eclectic antique-filled décor. The barn-board walls even came from the family's old corrals and barn. Vintage licence plates and deer antlers decorate the walls and succulents planted in old oil cans sit atop the bar which stocks Last Mountain Distillery spirits and Saskatchewan craft beer.

"We thought small towns deserve great food and funky décor," says Kali.

The Grotto

101 2nd Ave, Vibank | 306-762-2010

....

■ **The Grotto** is one of the best places in Saskatchewan to eat authentic, homemade Mexican food. Kevin and Cecilia Zimmerman own the lively little spot located inside a former Ursuline convent built in 1923. Much of the history has been preserved, including the altar area in the former chapel, which now houses the main dining room. The original grotto is behind the building in an area where Cecilia keeps garden boxes, brimming with fresh produce and herbs.

Kevin explains the name for the restaurant they opened in 2007 came naturally. "A grotto is a place of sanctuary, a place where friends gather and meet."

Both are self-taught culinary wizards. Cecilia honed her skills after moving to Vibank with Kevin. (They've been married close to thirty years.) She was missing food from Oaxaca, the region where she grew up in southern Mexico. She went back, learning the recipes and tricks of the trade from people in small communities. And those authentic tastes are what she brings to the Grotto. "She's a natural," says Kevin. "She just has that flair for it."

The Grotto is open Friday and Saturday nights. One night is for Cecilia's Mexican dinners, the other for Kevin's southern BBQ. Reservations generally need to be made weeks in advance, as there's just one seating per night. Guests are encouraged to linger and enjoy the space after their meal. Trust me, it's worth the wait and worth the drive.

"We're just cooking for who's coming, so it's personal," says Kevin.

Cecilia also offers weekly Mexican cooking classes; call to register.

Cecilia and Kevin Zimmerman with their son Javier.

The Happy Nun Café

357 Main St, Forget | 306-457-7780

Gayla Gilbertson and her husband Leon own the Happy Nun in Forget.

■ **In a restaurant** that's as much a part of the landscape as the endless golden wheat fields, friendships are made over homecooked food and live music. Don and Shannon Shakotko opened the Happy Nun Café in 2006. The couple were strong proponents of the arts, including live music, and wanted a venue to bring people together in southeastern Saskatchewan.

When the Shakotkos retired, Riley Riddell and Katie Vinge-Riddell bought the café and continued the tradition. After Katie's untimely death, the Nun's closure left a gaping hole in the community. Friend and former employee Gayla Gilbertson decided "to follow what my heart said to do" and purchased the café in 2018. Her husband Leon helps out— the couple even had their first date there.

"It's the heart of the community. It means so much to so many people in southeastern Saskatchewan. There's been weddings, engagements, anniversaries there."

Gayla's son describes the food as "grandma's cooking but jacked up." Gayla says, "it's comfort food with a little twist. I want people to feel comfortable and have a positive experience."

Her menu changes monthly and may include favourites, like Cats Got the Cream short ribs, which uses craft beer from Rebellion Brewing, a pan-fried pickerel, watermelon, and feta salad, or perhaps Moroccan lamb kabobs.

Kids are welcome at the Nun. Call ahead to reserve a table nearest the kids' reading section against bookcase-lined walls, or a cozy corner near a big armchair, perfect for nursing. Tables aren't flipped so just relax and enjoy the full Nun experience.

✪ While you're in the area, stop at the Stoughton Meat Market. The family-owned grocer has an in-store smokehouse and butcher.

Tangerine in the Valley

121 Boundary Ave N, Fort Qu'Appelle | 306-332-0100

tangerineregina.ca/in-the-valley

■ **A seasonal restaurant** in historic Fort Qu'Appelle serves up a small menu of affordable and high-quality eats. It was a new venture in 2018 for Aimee Schulhauser, the owner of Tangerine, a popular Regina café. "Fort Qu'Appelle has a soft spot in my heart. It's a beautiful valley and the meeting point of four different lakes."

She proudly recognizes her restaurant operates on Treaty 4 Territory, traditional lands for Cree, Saulteaux, and Assiniboine people. Treaty 4's first signings were in Fort Qu'Appelle in 1874. "We're surrounded with an Indigenous history that we really appreciate."

To pay homage to the area, Aimee found a 1981 Fort Qu'Appelle map and had it blown up for wallpaper. She'd found an older map, from 1891, during her

search into the town's history, but that one showed residential school locations. "That was really eye-opening. I had to be a bit more sensitive."

The menu stays the same for the season (it operates May to September) and features homemade pasta, curry bowls, salads, and gourmet sandwiches on freshly baked bread. "The flavour of it is similar to Tangerine. We wanted to make it light and a nice alternative to some of the chains in town."

Portuguese and Spanish wines are available and coffee beans come freshly roasted from Caliber in Regina.

If you're looking for French fries, though, you're out of luck—there's no deep fryer. "We had a lot of pushback on that," says Aimee. "But the people who know our brand know that we wouldn't have one."

Owner Aimee Schulhauser's Tangerine in the Valley is open seasonally in Fort Qu'Appelle.

JP Vives

Free Bird | 240 James Street, Lumsden | 639-392-7132 | freebirdeats.com

■ **Chef JP Vives** was puzzled as to why Lumsden didn't have a thriving local food scene. The picturesque prairie town is surrounded by vegetable growers, beekeepers, a distillery, a fruit orchard/winery, and a local butcher. He decided to shake things up in 2019 and opened his first restaurant, Free Bird.

JP grew up in Lumsden and got his first job at a café in town. After high school, he headed to Victoria, BC, for culinary training. He apprenticed at the Fairmont Empress Hotel before coming home and joining the team that made La Bodega a Regina culinary destination.

JP worked at the now-closed Flip Eatery and Drink under Dave Straub (a gifted chef and leader who tragically passed away in 2018) before moving to Saskatoon. When a friend opened Congress Beer House, JP managed the kitchen, presenting unique takes on prairie comfort food that helped cement the gastropub as a popular downtown spot in Saskatoon.

His new venture promises to be just as successful. The rotating menu features a daily cut, burger, pasta, and fish, plus brunch on Sundays. There's an evening menu featuring shareable dishes, where JP further stretches his creative muscles. Think elevated vegetarian dishes with an Indian focus, chicken karaage, and a cheeseboard with local honey. "It's common food done uncommonly well. I love hearty food, but I throw my twist on things."

✿ While in Lumsden, stop for an excellent cup of coffee at Fourth & James, visit Frontier Gardens' farmgate store for fresh produce, and head to Over the Hill Orchards for a tour (book ahead).

Chef JP Vives
opened Free Bird
in Lumsden in 2019.

Acre 10 Gourmet Greens
Pilot Butte | 306-581-7703

Allisha Grigg dropping off a vegetable order at Avenue Restaurant and Bar.

■ **Allisha Grigg's childhood** was one influenced by nature and agriculture. She grew up on a Saskatchewan grain farm, before the family moved to Lumsden. Her first job was at a vegetable garden near Craven, whetting her appetite for growing food. "That's where I got my hands in the dirt. For my entire life, that smell of raw dirt and being with the seeds and the plants was just something that I needed."

After twelve years in the corporate world, she got back to her roots. "I just decided it wasn't good for my soul anymore. I needed to get back to growing." By that time, she was living on an acreage east of Regina with her partner and their four boys. She started the business small with microgreens in the basement. Next came a larger heated growing facility, followed by a greenhouse. Similar to the barn-raising days of yore, the whole family helped build the greenhouse. A three-acre garden full of heirloom tomatoes, carrots, beans, and lettuce, and a new orchard round out the operation.

Her first customer was Regina chef Milton Rebello, "which made me feel like I made the right move. It unfurled from there and we've worked really hard to get where we are now." Along with selling at Italian Star Deli's seasonal market, Allisha delivers to a range of local restaurants (and her products are in Italian Star's cooler year-round). Chefs help influence her growing decisions.

Everything is grown as organically as she can, right down to the seeds, which Allisha buys from Mumm's Sprouting Seeds, an organic seed company in Parkside (see profile on page 72).

Heliotrope Organic Farm

Craven | heliotropefarm.com

■ **Heliotrope's stand** at the Regina Farmers' Market has always been my favourite. It's a beautiful sight to behold: wooden baskets overflowing with vibrantly coloured and unique heirloom vegetables.

Rick Letwinka and Hayley Lawford grow for flavour, not appearance or quantity, and use biodynamic practices. They also grow many of their own seeds, using greenhouses to start the plants. "We plant by the calendar as far as germinating the different crops at different times. Certain days are better for fruits or leaf or root crops, and so we try to start all of our plants off on the right foot in that way," explains Rick.

The farm makes its own biodynamic compost teas for all the fields. "We have a two-year cycle where all of our waste product from this year will be put into our seedlings two years from now."

Heliotrope began life as a farm-to-fork restaurant in Regina. It later became clear the farming aspect was the more attractive in the equation. They sold the restaurant and bought the organic farm in the Qu'Appelle Valley in 2004.

Rick Letwinka and Hayley Lawford of Heliotrope.

Rick is an advocate for good, clean, fair food. He has brought in the same five agricultural workers from Mexico every season for the last decade. "For them to do the same job, working twelve or fourteen hours a day, in Mexico, they get paid $8 day." That doesn't buy much, especially if you're supporting a family. It's a scenario Rick calls "modern-day slavery."

There's always a cost behind cheap food. "There is a reason things cost more and why they can ship it from Mexico and it's cheaper at the store. Someone is having to work as a slave so you can get it for cheap."

Visit Heliotrope's stand on market days in Regina and Regina Beach. Their produce is on the menu at Bar Willow and Crave Kitchen + Wine Bar. Sign up for a seasonal vegetable bin service on their website.

Last Mountain Distillery

70 Hwy 20, Lumsden | 306-731-3930 | lastmountaindistillery.com

■ **In a province** where dill pickles are revered, it's no surprise Last Mountain Distillery's naturally infused dill pickle vodka is the company's top selling spirit. Last Mountain, the province's first micro-distillery, opened in 2010.

Owners Meredith and Colin Schmidt started out in their two-car garage. "We put everything we had at the time into converting that garage into a distillery," says Meredith. A friend of Colin's started one of the first microdistilleries in the United States and encouraged the couple to follow suit. A little over a year after opening, they'd graduated to the current building in Lumsden.

Last Mountain's product line includes moonshine made from Canadian apples and a private reserve whisky. Wheat comes from a farm near Earl Grey, delivered to a bin outside the distillery. Products like Prairie Cherry Whisky are geared for those with fond memories drinking paralyzers around the campfire. It's a combo of Last Mountain's wheat whisky barrel aged with organic sour cherries from nearby Over the Hill Orchards. Vodka coolers are a recent addition and are all made with Last Mountain's naturally flavoured vodka, water or soda, and sugar—with no sulphites or preservatives.

The distillery's tasting room is open year-round; visit their website for hours and for distillery tour times. If you take a tour, don't be surprised to

see bags of cucumbers, garlic, and dill about, just waiting to take on life as that famous vodka.

Last Mountain's products are in SLGA stores, Sobeys Liquor stores, and at the farmers' markets in Regina and Saskatoon.

Meredith Schmidt owns Last Mountain Distillery with her husband, Colin.

Daybreak Mill

North Portal | 306-927-2695 | daybreakmill.com

■ **In 1963,** a farmer named Alvin Scheresky went against the trend. Instead of adding chemical inputs to his Oxbow-area farm, he bought cleaning equipment and a mill, and was one of the first organic farmers in North America to do so. He helped found the first provincial chapter of the Organic Crop Improvement Association and operated Saskatchewan's first organic flour mill.

"He was really inspirational," says Nicole Davis Huriet of her mentor. He owned the mill until the early 2000s before selling to a couple who moved it to North Portal. In 2012, Nicole bought the company which included 540 acres of organic land. She share farms with her dad on a few thousand acres of land that's been in their family since 1892.

Nicole Davis Huriet of Daybreak Mill.

The two grow almost everything for Daybreak; what they don't grow is sourced from other organic Saskatchewan farmers. Daybreak sells whole grains and legumes, stone-ground flours, and cereals. The biggest sellers are the ancient and heritage grains, especially popular with customers with gluten intolerances. "I think ancient grains are healthier for people and they're better for the soil," says Nicole.

She uses a series of three stone mills, the same ones Alvin built in 1963. "It is a slower process, which makes our flours a little bit more expensive. There's no heat or steam used. The whole nutrition of the grain is kept throughout the process."

After the flour is milled, it's put through a sifter to emulsify the oil and germ back into the product, which gives it an eight-month shelf life or up to two years if kept frozen. "It's really important to me to provide a nutritious product that I feel good about eating myself. If we switched to a hammer mill, we could mill a lot more flour, but it doesn't fit with the direction I want to go with the business. I don't want to sacrifice quality for growth."

Daybreak's website lists all Saskatchewan retail locations and offers online ordering with shipping options.

98 Ranch Inc.

Lake Alma | 306-447-4600

■ **At Ross MacDonald and Christine Peters's 98 Ranch,** the focus has always been on the grasslands. Encouraging the health and functioning of the grassland ecosystem is a long-time passion for Ross; he even attended university in Montana to study that very thing, along with low-stress stocksmanship and animal behaviour.

Over time, the operation has evolved "into trying to produce a grass-based product that gets the consumer closer to the ranch level." Ross does that by matching animals to available resources while trying to make as small an industrial footprint as possible. It also means valuing the wildlife habitat and the landscape's ecological function. "I think that's the best story that livestock agriculture has to tell. We can be complimentary to a lot of those other demands."

Cattle are grazed longer into the winter and graze earlier in the spring. Ten years ago, Ross began using genetics from cattle producers in the United States pushing grassland health alongside animal selection. "The cattle are smaller in general and hold their condition under the harsher condition with way fewer inputs. So that's been nice to see."

He's also proving that grass-finished cattle can produce beef just as good as their grain-finished counterparts. "I know you can develop a product that will take a large percentage or all of its diet in forage and provide a really marbled, desirable beef product. When you add onto that the nutrient density in terms of the fatty acid profile coming out of a forage-finishing system, it's pretty exciting."

98 Ranch's cattle are not yet 100 percent grass-finished; Ross is taking his time to develop a quality product. "We want to make sure we've done our due diligence to make sure we know which animals work and which animals don't."

98 Ranch offers ranchgate beef sales. Just give Ross or Christine a call to arrange a pickup and/or a tour of the farm.

Ross MacDonald and Christine Peters out checking their herd at 98 Ranch.

Box H Farm

Gladmar | 306-815-7191 | boxhfarm.ca

Mark Hoimyr of Box H Farm.

■ **At Box H Farm,** the Hoimyr family (Mark, Laura, and their two children) works with nature to raise healthy livestock while keeping the land just as healthy. What began as a conventional mixed farm later transitioned into a cattle operation.

The Hoimyrs have studied soil health and cattle's positive effect on grasslands when properly managed. "We're starting to get things right," says Mark. Since they moved to a rotational grazing system, "we're seeing improvements in the soil."

It led to finishing some of their Angus cattle on grass, a successful venture that's helped Box H Farm's direct-to-consumer products stand out in Saskatchewan. (They sell beef from fifteen grass-finished cows each year through their own markets.) "It was just a perfect fit. The animals best suited for being finished on grass are the type of animals we want to raise: low maintenance, walk past a thistle and get fat kind of cattle." To finish a cow on grass takes more time than conventional methods, but the Hoimyrs believe it's worth the effort for an end product that's nutritionally dense.

"They have to be completely full-grown before we can use the grass to put fat into the meat, into the marbling," says Mark. "We test our hay in the fall and the highest quality feed goes to the bunch we are finishing. Being in good condition first thing in the spring sets us up well for an easier finish on grass."

Box H Farm's grass-fed beef and pastured pork are available via online orders, on Local and Fresh's website, and at the Local Market in Regina and the Estevan Farmers' Market (grab a tub of their honey, too).

Qu'Appelle Valley Bison

Craven | 306-540-7007

Patrick O'Ryan at Qu'Appelle Valley Bison.

■ **Patrick O'Ryan** never pictured himself a bison rancher but when the real estate developer met his sister's herd his mind was forever changed. "I had a very strong bond immediately ... so I decided to go ahead with it."

About a decade ago, Patrick's sister and her husband began bison ranching on the O'Ryan family's grain farm. When they were ready to retire, Patrick took over the herd. Part of his learning curve was learning how to raise bison, which are essentially wild animals. "I don't force them to do anything. I read their energy very quickly which helps keep me alive," he says with a laugh.

He keeps his herd all together in one pasture. "That's their nature—that's how they spent several thousand years on these prairies evolving. When they're allowed to operate as an organic unit, they feel more at ease and less stressed."

He tries to mimic nature as closely as possible. The bison only eat prairie grasses (and hay in the winter). He feeds them a supplement to provide the vitamins and minerals missing from the native grasses in the area. "The land is pretty much tapped out in this area for copper and selenium."

Patrick does farmgate sales of his grass-finished bison and makes deliveries to customers in Regina. "For me, it's very rewarding for one's connection with nature, especially a majestic animal like the bison—how iconic is that?"

Patrick also provides hides and skulls to Tatanka Boutique and the Buffalo People Arts Institute in Regina; both organizations are working to revitalize traditional connections for Indigenous people.

◑ **The view from Seven Bridges Road near Lumsden.**

SOUTHEAST SASKATCHEWAN FARMERS' MARKETS

Check the website for current hours prior to your visit.

Estevan Farmers' Market

Estevan Shoppers Mall parking lot
Saturdays, 9:00 AM–1:00 PM
May to October
facebook.com/Estevan-Farmers-Market-113475595345218/
306-634-3521

Fort Qu'Appelle Farmers' Market

310 Broadway St, across
from Co-op Food Store
Saturdays, 9:00 AM–1:00 PM
May to September
facebook.com/fortfarmersmarket/
306-450-2652

Montmartre Farmers' Market

Curling Rink, Main Street
Fridays 10:00 AM–Noon
May to September

Regina Beach Farmers' Market

115 Centre Street,
in the parking lot of Rudy's
Every second Sunday
11:00 AM–3:00 PM
May long weekend to end of June

Sundays, 11:00 AM–3:00 PM
July to Labour Day weekend
reginabeachfarmersmarket.com

Weyburn Farmers' Market

Weyburn Mall
Saturdays, 9:00 AM–2:00 PM
May to December
facebook.com/
weyburnfarmersmarket/
306-870-0125

Weyburn's Open Air Market

2nd St and Souris Ave.
Canadian Tire parking lot
Saturdays, 9:00 AM–2:00 PM
Mid-May to October
facebook.com/
weyburnopenairmarket/

SOUTHEAST SASKATCHEWAN WATERING HOLES

Check the website for current hours prior to your visit.

Bandits Distilling

#3 22nd Avenue SE, Weyburn
306-559-4753
banditsdistilling.ca

Tours: By request.
Visit website for retail locations.

Last Mountain Distillery

70 Highway 20, Lumsden
306-731-3930
lastmountaindistillery.com

Tours: Every Saturday
Retail store on site.

Over the Hill Orchards

Lumsden
(visit website for directions)
306-535-1278
overthehillorchards.ca

Tours: By request.
Retail store, pop-up dining events on site.

HARVEST
ON THE FARM

———

The harvest season is always a special time of year on the farm. This is the time to reap the rewards from seeding, get the crop in the bin, and secure income for the year to come. It's satisfying to get out in the field and see a year's worth of work and planning come to fruition.

It's a time to celebrate and it's also a time to make haste before winter's cold sets in. That means early mornings getting the combines ready and working as late into the night as possible before the crop gets tough. The weather's hot during harvest—the air is dry but with a brisk edge. Farmers have a sense of urgency as the days grow shorter, threats of hail and rain on their mind. It takes a team to get the harvest off, both out in the fields and in the kitchen, preparing enough food to keep everyone going.

I spent a good chunk of my childhood riding along with my dad (and sometimes grandpa—we all farmed together) in the tractor during seeding and in the combine during harvest. When I was younger, there was space for me to curl up on a big ledge in the tractor cab, bouncing over the rough miles, which often lulled me to sleep in the afternoons. I set up camp on the combine floor, mesmerized by the header reel methodically pushing row after row of golden wheat into the feeder house. I'll always remember the day Dad brought home a newer model. It had a small seat, made just for me! Sitting up on that seat beside him made me feel quite grown up. I pictured driving that massive machine all by myself one day.

◉ **Gordon Sharp taking the crop off at Sharpland Farms.**

I also remember many meals shared during harvest, often in the back of a pickup truck with the tailgate down. Everyone would gather round for a break, relishing my mom's hearty stew and apple pie. The hustle and bustle never ceased in either my grandma's or mom's kitchens during harvest. As important as it is to get the crop off, it's just as (if not more) important to have nourishing food to fuel you through those long days. "Feeding the men" was a task both women took seriously and their homemade, from-scratch cooking was a source of pride. Fast food or microwave meals didn't exist in my childhood home. I didn't realize until I was much older the values that were instilled in me by watching my mom and grandma find joy in making food—food that would carry their husbands through the long, hot days.

There's a distinct smell in the air during the autumn harvest months. It's a smell of dust, mingled with dirt and the sweat of physical labour that comes from fixing broken parts in the field or climbing out of the grain truck to unload. It's the smell of tears and happiness, worry and hope. And it's the smell of my childhood. The moment I climb into the combine with my dad, that smell transports me.

The light is different during harvest. The landscape takes on a golden glow as the sun shines through the yellow swath churned out by combines in the field and grain augers back at the yard. At sunset, the red and golden tones filter through that dust for an image that's pure Saskatchewan, the world's breadbasket.

Dad is in his early seventies and still loves harvest time the most. He farms with my brother Dane Sharp and his wife Tanya at Sharpland Farms in southeastern Saskatchewan. Over the past seven years, they've been transitioning their approach to regenerative agriculture methods, which focus on natural growing systems to produce healthier, more nutrient-dense plants.

"We were growing tired of the high artificial inputs and the low diversity system that seems to be the norm in conventional agriculture," says Dane. Dane and Tanya have studied extensively with pioneers in regenerative agriculture and are always learning from several who use these methods in Saskatchewan, such as Axten Farms (axtenfarms.ca) and Wecker Farms (weckerfarms.com).

They eliminated chemical seed treatments and vastly reduced fungicide usage. They do extensive tissue, sap, and soil tests to determine what their crops are lacking and then apply the needed

⊙ **A golden wheat field at Sharpland Farms.**

⊘ Following spread: **Going for a ride at Box H Farm.**

micronutrients, along with kelp, fish, humic, and fluvic acid. "We have found that by doing this and trying to correct the root causes, our crops have not had as many disease and pest issues."

They grow up to eight different crops each year and add in as much diversity as possible through intercropping. Intercropping helps reduce chemical inputs by helping provide the soil and plants with greater microbial diversity.

Sharpland Farms also grows Camelina for Three Farmers (profile on page 197) using these regenerative methods. "My hope is to collaborate with more food companies who have the same values for healthy soil, healthy plants, and better food, and to learn from others headed in this direction," says Dane.

As of 2019, they're also farming land that's certified organic. It's this combination of knowledge and experience that will help Sharpland Farms create a thriving ecosystem in their area of Saskatchewan. "I feel that being able to have all the tools available, drawing from the conventional and organic systems and everything in-between, will allow us to succeed." ∎

Regina

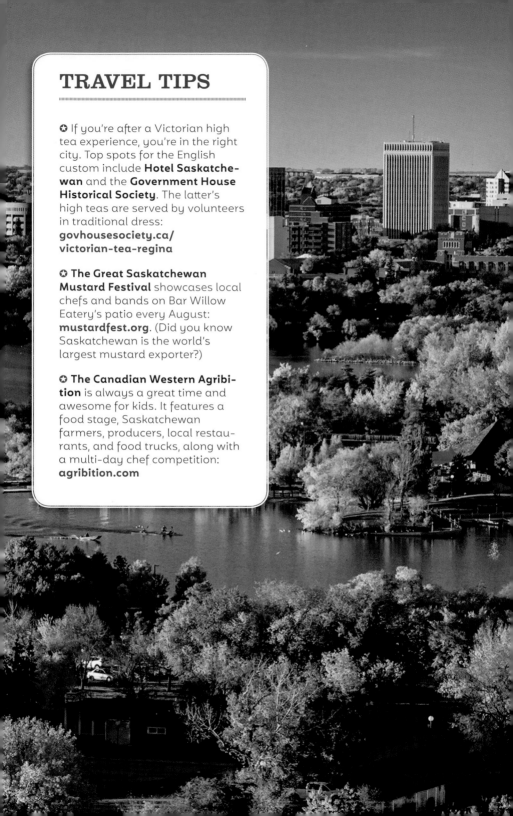

TRAVEL TIPS

✪ If you're after a Victorian high tea experience, you're in the right city. Top spots for the English custom include **Hotel Saskatchewan** and the **Government House Historical Society**. The latter's high teas are served by volunteers in traditional dress: **govhousesociety.ca/victorian-tea-regina**

✪ **The Great Saskatchewan Mustard Festival** showcases local chefs and bands on Bar Willow Eatery's patio every August: **mustardfest.org**. (Did you know Saskatchewan is the world's largest mustard exporter?)

✪ **The Canadian Western Agribition** is always a great time and awesome for kids. It features a food stage, Saskatchewan farmers, producers, local restaurants, and food trucks, along with a multi-day chef competition: **agribition.com**

Regina, Saskatchewan's crown jewel, was renamed after Queen Victoria in 1882. (Cree hunters called it Oskana-Ka-asateki or "the place where bones are piled.") And the city's food community is proving itself fit for a queen, too. In 1883, Regina became the capital of the Northwest Territories and remained the capital when the new province of Saskatchewan was established in 1905.

Arts and culture are everywhere in the Queen City. The Royal Saskatchewan Museum began here in 1906. The Saskatchewan Arts Board and Creative Saskatchewan are also based here. It's home to the MacKenzie Art Gallery, the largest public gallery in the province.

Regina is Saskatchewan's agriculture industry hub, hosting a range of large trade shows and events. The Canadian Western Agribition is held here each year and is the country's largest livestock show. Protein Industries Canada, a newly formed supercluster that aims to make Canada a leading global source of sustainable, high-quality plant protein and plant-based co-products, is also headquartered in Regina.

Food security initiatives abound and are an excellent example of Regina residents' community spirit. Regina Education and Action on Child Hunger (REACH) was formed as a community response in 1990 after reports identified children in the city were vulnerable to hunger and malnutrition. REACH operates a community mobile store selling affordable, fresh food.

The Regina Food Bank is actively engaged in not only distributing, but growing food for people in the community. A 2016 grant from Federated Co-operatives Ltd. (which stocks Saskatchewan-grown produce in its grocery stores) made the food bank's Four Seasons Agriculture Project a reality. The centre has vertical composting garden towers, aeroponic tower gardens, and even a Farm Bot, a robotic farming machine. Employees work with food bank clients

○ Previous spread: **The Saskatchewan Legislative Building.**
○ **Regina's Wascana Lake bursting with fall colours.**

and school groups teaching people how to grow their own food year-round in small spaces in their homes.

Other volunteer-driven organizations, like Food Regina and Regina Food for Learning, work to improve food security, sustainability, and resiliency in the city's food system.

If you're a craft beer lover, Regina is your city. In addition to several excellent local breweries, the Saskatchewan Craft Brewers Week is held here every year.

One of those local breweries is likely one of Canada's best. Bushwakker has been around since 1991, and its first owner, the late Beverly Robertson, is known as the founding father of Saskatchewan's craft beer industry. He was the chairman of the Saskatchewan Health Research Board between 1988 and 1992, and suggested a policy idea to the Saskatchewan government that resulted in legislation allowing brew pubs in the province in 1989.

Bushwakker is as relevant as ever in Regina and hosts all kinds of events, like Oktoberfest Week, to engage local craft beer lovers. People line up for hours (sometimes even overnight) for the annual blackberry mead release in December.

Regina loves to celebrate multiculturalism and the best summer festival to experience all the food is Mosaic.

Chefs here are more engaged now than ever to elevate the city's culinary scene and highlight the local food bounty. At the Capitol, Joel Williams features products like Saskatchewan Snow Beef on the menu. Caraway Grill is the best spot in the province for elevated Indian fare (try the matar paneer). For sushi, head to Enso or Orange Izakaya Fusion Café & Bar.

The city's café culture is thriving, too. From homemade shortbread at Naked Bean, to vegan chocolate cookies at Brewed Awakening and overflowing vegetarian bowls at 13th Avenue Food & Coffee House, there's something for everyone.

Chefs Milton Rebello and Louise Lu, owners of Skye Café & Bistro, are leading the charge in sourcing ingredients from organic farmers near Regina. They take those ingredients and craft exquisite, delectable dishes to delight all the senses, served in equally exquisite surroundings. ∎

⊘ **Skye Café & Bistro's brunch menu includes this delectable Shakshuka.**

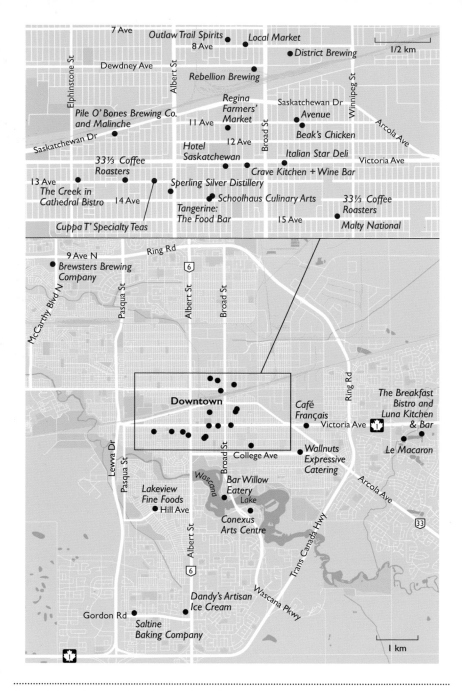

Note: Only artisans and producers who welcome visitors on site are shown on this map.

REGINA ARTISANS

Dandy's Artisan Ice Cream

4570 Albert St | 306-543-1200 | dandysartisanicecream.com

....

■ **There isn't much that compares** to hand-churned ice cream. All the better if that ice cream comes in flavours reminiscent of a fine pâtisserie. Daniela Mintenko launched Dandy's Artisan Ice Cream in 2019. One bite of the handcrafted and decadent triple chocolate brownie will forever change your taste for ice cream.

Daniela, who was born in Colombia, was working in Vancouver after attending fashion school when she knew she needed a change. "I didn't really feel like it was something I was feeling passionate about," she says of the fashion industry. "I strongly believe if you don't have any passion you can't keep doing that because you will be miserable."

One thing she did feel passionate about was ice cream, a favourite childhood dessert. She took a course in small-scale ice cream production at Penn State— one of the world's best places for teaching the craft.

She wanted to open a store in Regina, her husband's hometown, but didn't have a culinary background. "You need to learn how to bake in order to make the perfect ice cream," she says of her decision to attend pastry school.

Dandy's has twelve signature flavours, with an additional five that change monthly. There are gluten-free and vegan options, along with a small espresso menu, using beans from Regina's Caliber Coffee Roasters.

My recommendation: a scoop of strawberry honeycomb, made with Over the Hill Orchards' strawberries that are roasted, spiced, and made into jam. Crunchy, homemade honeycomb candy tops it all off.

Daniela Mintenko at Dandy's Artisan Ice Cream.

✪ If you're an ice cream lover, be sure to visit Milky Way. It's a Regina tradition to line up on opening day in March or April. (Pack a toque though; sometimes opening day coincides with unexpected -20°c temps!)

Fancy Pants Kitchen

fancypantskitchen.com

■ **Karen Morley's career** has taken her from living in San Francisco to travelling the world. The former photogrammetrist for the United States Air Force is now turning out artisanal chocolates in Regina. "I've always had this fascination about the intersection of food and geography and why you eat what you eat."

Karen Morley in her happy place—making chocolate.

It was a cancer diagnosis, with only a 30 percent chance of survival, that set Karen on the chocolate route. While battling cancer, she got into chocolate. The chemistry of making it reeled her in. She soon realized that to make artisanal quality and to develop her own recipes, she'd need further training. The professional chocolatier attended both Vancouver's Ecole Chocolate and the Chocolate Academy in Montreal.

"You have to understand about moisture migration, fat migration, and crystallization. People don't think of it that way. They think of the pretty stuff you decorate. But to me it was the confluence of those things that was pretty amazing."

She uses chocolate from Barry Callebaut, a company whose Forever Chocolate program is targeting 100 percent sustainable chocolate by 2025. "The big chocolate companies are just buying up stuff and the plantations are getting denuded," explains Karen, adding that Barry Callebaut works with farmers on becoming more sustainable. The company doesn't buy from plantations that use child labour either.

In the future, she'd love to open her own shop. She's wary, though; it's expensive to get small scale chocolate-making equipment and supplies shipped to Regina.

For now, you can find her luxury, hand-painted chocolates at Italian Star Deli. Custom orders are available through her website. Watch for pop-up events.

33 ⅓ Coffee Roasters

1130 15th Ave and 3008 13th Ave | 306-525-5001 | 3313coffeeroasters.com

Eric Galbraith, owner of 33 ⅓ Coffee Roasters at his new café, Craft Services in the MacKenzie Art Gallery.

■ **Eric Galbraith** started roasting coffee in his backyard with the goal of making great coffee for himself and his friends. "I just thought I would source some of the best coffees I could find and that's what I did. I've kept with that motto," he says. Some of the best he can find includes sourcing beans on coffee origin trips, like the one he took to La Chumeca Micromill in Costa Rica.

Eric graduated from the early days, learning how to roast beans on his barbecue, to a large commercial roaster and founding 33 ⅓ in 2012. The first neighbourhood café soon followed, in a funky space it shares with Malty National Brewing. 33 ⅓ later expanded again, turning their roasting facility in the Cathedral neighbourhood into a café.

In 2018, Galbraith and his team opened Craft Services at the MacKenzie Art Gallery. In a thoughtfully planned spot meant to mimic a film set's social scene, the café is a place where art, coffee, and good food collide. Unlike 33 ⅓'s other spots, where the focus is on coffee, Craft Services employs a head chef and a pastry chef. "It's a modern café but we're also treating it like an old school cafeteria," says Eric of the menu, which features fresh pastries and a bread program.

33 ⅓'s freshly roasted beans are for sale at several spots in Regina, along with Fourth and James Bakery in Lumsden and Museo in Saskatoon. Check the website for updated locations or for wholesale orders.

✪ Caliber Coffee Roasters is another outstanding Regina roaster. Visit their website calibercoffee.ca for retail locations.

Café Français
1-425 Victoria Ave E | 306-757-2233

■ **With its artisanal pastries** and the black and white Parisian cityscape gracing one wall, Café Français is a perfect spot to escape life's stresses.

Chef Inyoung Chang prepares French cakes and pastries, like palmiers and croissants, from scratch every day. The ever-changing selection is guaranteed to enchant the eyes as well as the palate. Try the Pear Charlotte—pear mousse with vanilla chiffon cake and poached pear in red wine.

Inyoung is from South Korea, and she studied French cuisine at Le Cordon Bleu's Seoul campus. She was a fashion designer before that but realized cooking was her calling. She ran her own restaurant in South Korea before moving to Canada. She lived in Vancouver for a time before bringing her talents to Regina.

She and business partner Ranjan Arora met while working at the Hotel Saskatchewan. They opened the café in 2014 and have been expanding their offerings and Inyoung's creativity ever since. Weekend brunch, monthly multi-course dinners, and high tea service, complete with fine china, are all available, along with daily light lunches and artisan breads. The traditional high tea tier includes finger sandwiches, tea biscuits, petite fours, and macarons.

Inyoung designs the dinner menus based on what's in season and available from her local food suppliers. The dinners, which sell out months in advance, are served with optional wine pairings. "She has so much potential and things she wants to do," explains Ranjan of the decision to hold the multi-course dinners. And anyone who visits the café is grateful for that creativity.

Chef Inyoung Chang and Ranjan Arora
own Café Français.

Cuppa T' Specialty Teas

2732 13th Ave | 306-352-4411 | cuppatteas.com

■ **If an ethically sourced,** clean product is your cup of tea, there's a shop in Regina you must visit. Jule Gilchrist's Cathedral neighbourhood store serves as a tea room and meditation studio—the two go hand in hand, after all.

She serves a smoky Lapsang that's a perfect combination with Earl Grey in the winter months. When the temperatures rise, the Butterfly Pea Blue-flower tea is popular. Made from Thai blue flowers, the tea is vibrant indigo that turns to a pink/purple colour when citrus is added.

If you're an adventurous type, Jule carries pu'erh, a fermented tea typically from China. Pu'erh is fermented for a minimum of a year and some for up to forty or even fifty years. "I quite like it but it's a funky taste," says Jule. "It's really earthy."

Jule Gilchrist of Cuppa T'.

Jule sources only from fair-trade tea markets that specialize in clean teas. Clean teas differ from organic teas because of more rigid testing standards. Organic tea needs to be grown without chemicals but can become contaminated during storage, handling, or when other ingredients are added. "Clean tea is tested for five hundred items. If [contamination] shows up, it gets sent back to the country of origin. A lot of times people drink tea for health benefits, so you're going to want it as good as you can get."

Cuppa T' has a sign-up board for classes in tea tasting and meditation. In the summer, Jule makes tea-infused ice cream.

Le Macaron

2705 Quance St E | 306-779-2253 | lemacaronregina.com

■ **In 2010,** Regina was in need. The café options were slim, and the places serving decent lattes coupled with decadent desserts slimmer still. Gilles Gobin had been quietly doing his pastry chef thing at the Hotel Saskatchewan for ten years. Then, he and his wife Jacqueline opened Le Macaron, an artisanal pâtisserie, where almost everything, right down to the striking garnishes, is made in-house.

Gilles's macarons quickly became famous; it wasn't uncommon to see weekend cookie lineups. His light little French cookies are still the café's biggest sellers (ten thousand each month!). He's perfected the macaron art: A slightly crisp outer layer gives way to a chewy inner layer. The buttercream filling borders on overly sweet but doesn't cross the line.

The crêperie offers a choice of breakfast, savoury, and dessert crêpes. A twenty-one-foot dessert cooler is devoted to an array of pastries and cakes, like petits fours, almond croissants, and caramel cheesecake. The top shelf houses the showstoppers: French tortes. The three-layer mousse-based cakes are finished with a mirror glaze and have delicate finishing elements, like gold-flecked letters.

Gilles has moved into a mentorship role with his staff. He hired one chef right after her graduation from the Culinary Institute of Canada. "She's learned a lot. Sometimes the student surpasses the teacher," he says, laughing.

He laments the modern prefab baking culture, hoping to pass along his love for true pastry arts. "Nowadays, everything is out of a box. I want to impart something ... the tricks of the trade. The craft."

✪ Be sure to also visit Kneaded, Regina's first dedicated gluten-free bakery.

Pastry chef Gilles Gobin at Le Macaron.

Saltine Baking Company

3902 Gordon Road | 306-525-1527 | saltinebakingco.com

A fresh loaf of sourdough, hot out of the oven at Saltine Baking Company.

■ **There are few foods** as comforting as a warm slice of buttered homemade bread. And Ashley Schmalenberg's bread is about as good as it gets.

Her culture is about a year older than Saltine Baking Company, the business she launched in 2014 with a stall at the Regina Farmers' Market. "I fermented it myself, just at home, and it's been on the counter ever since. It's a fermentation of flour and water. It allows the bread to leaven naturally without the use of commercial yeast."

It's a slow, patient process to make bread without commercial yeast. Saturday bread begins Thursday night when she mixes the starter. Friday morning, she turns the dough (rather than kneading it) every thirty minutes. It's left to bulk rise for a few hours before it gets shaped and divided. The dough continues to rise overnight and then is baked fresh in the morning.

Saltine's three main breads, Parmesan pepper, raisin pecan, and three seed, are supplemented with a country whole wheat loaf and those made from various heritage grains, like Einkorn. Ashley uses organic local grains from mills in southern Saskatchewan for the breads and savoury pastries for which she's become famous in Regina.

Saltine Baking Company opened its bricks and mortar location in 2018. Along with bread, croissants and pastries are always available—try one with homemade ricotta cheese filling.

Visit the website for hours of operation and an updated list of where to find Saltine's products elsewhere in the city.

Rebellion Brewing
1901 Dewdney Ave | 306-522-4666 | rebellionbrewing.ca

■ **As Mark Heise puts it,** "You gotta come to Saskatchewan if you want to enjoy all the good things in life." And one of those good things is his craft brewery's Lentil Cream Ale. You heard right—a beer made from lentils. And it's really, really good. So good, in fact, that when Mark attends beer conferences, people from all over the world have heard of Rebellion's lentil beer.

Mark Heise and his three partners (Evan Hunchak, Jamie Singer, and Neil Braun) founded Rebellion Brewing in 2014. Mark, an award-winning home brewer and certified beer judge, said the craft beer industry is about so much more than just beer. "It's a catalyst for culture, and for community, and for basically raising the profile and drive of Saskatchewan." Rebellion, like the province's craft beer industry in general, is grassroots and authentic.

As for that lentil beer, it wasn't Mark's idea but that of his cousin who works for AGT Food and Ingredients. (The Saskatchewan company is one of the world's largest suppliers of value-added pulses and staple foods.) "He asked about making beer with lentils at some point. I said, 'Well, that sounds really terrible,'" Mark says, laughing.

But his cousin was persistent. AGT would provide the lentils; Mark just had to brew it. "I thought to get him off my back, I'd brew it once and he'd see that it didn't taste very good. We brewed it and it tasted great," he says of the bestselling beer. It's a beer that resonates with people in Saskatchewan, where the majority of Canada's lentils are grown.

Mark Heise, owner of Rebellion Brewing.

6

Greg Reid

Lakeview Fine Foods | 3404 Hill Ave | 306-586-5221

■ **Greg Reid** made a name for himself in Regina with an artisanal butchery business, slinging some of the best beef around at the Regina Farmers' Market. He's now Lakeview Fine Foods' in-house butcher. He began his grassroots venture by renting kitchen space at Best Food Forward, which offers a weekly meal delivery service and also rents kitchen space to culinary entrepreneurs.

Greg works tirelessly with area producers to build products he's proud to share with his customers. Some of those producers are Mark and Laura Hoimyr of Box H Farms, who have been experimenting with grass-finishing. "Grass-finished beef is something that's really different. It's hard to do in Saskatchewan. So that's why Mark and Laura are special in what they do," says Greg.

"Even grass-finished animals need a coating of fat and internal fat. If not, they're not going to taste right. You notice with their grass-finished beef, they have a nice fat coating. It's dense, hard fat, which is what you want to see. The structure of the meat holds up."

Greg's from Newfoundland—he moved to Regina for love—and his background is as a chef. He owns a French-inspired catering company called Between Dog and Wolf with his business partner. But craft butchery is his main passion.

Lakeview Fine Foods is a wonderful local grocer that stocks Lockwood Sourdough bread, Koko Pâtisserie products, produce from Novictus Gardens, cheese from Coteau Hills Creamery, and even sustainably grown flowers from Lark Farm.

Find butcher Greg Reid at Lakeview Fine Foods.

Avenue Restaurant and Bar

100-2201 11th Ave | 306-525-1919 | avenuerestaurantandbar.com

■ **Avenue serves elevated dishes** using prairie ingredients reminiscent of comfort food but with a modern edge. It's owned by the Grassroots Restaurant Group and incorporates the same concept Ayden made popular in Saskatoon. Avenue was named for good reason in 2019 to Canada's Best New Restaurants Top 10 list published by Air Canada's *enRoute* magazine.

Executive chef and co-owner Nathan Guggenheimer says the name comes from a way to access a destination, an experience, or a memory. "An avenue is always chang-

Executive chef Nathan Guggenheimer at Avenue.

ing and becoming something new." And by sourcing from a variety of Saskatchewan farmers and producers, Nathan's providing an avenue for diners to have new culinary experiences while learning about the local food trail.

One of those producers, Allisha Grigg, operates Acre 10 Gourmet Greens (see page 206). While they were in season, her heirloom tomatoes stole the show in a starter that combined housemade goat cheese, fresh plums, smoked tomato coulis, and pistachios. "I love that I can tell her tomatoes are grown with love," says Nathan. "There's a lot of care taken. And it smells great. It tastes great. It's fresh. You can just see Allisha in her ingredients."

Mixologist and co-owner Christopher Cho ensures Avenue's cocktail menu and wine list are up to snuff. He's worked at a range of top-notch spots throughout the country and is known both for his commitment to craft methods and exceptional service.

Avenue, on 11th Avenue in the heart of Regina's downtown, is in a tastefully remodelled space that maintains the 1914 heritage building's character. It's a place to see and be seen in Saskatchewan's capital, thanks to a modern aesthetic that mixes warm wooden tones with grey and pops of deep plum and lime green.

At press time, Nathan had moved on to a new opportunity (as chefs tend to do) but remains an owner in the restaurant group.

Mariana Brito

Malinche | 1808 Cameron St.

■ **Tijuana-born chef Mariana Brito** creates authentic Mexican dishes from scratch using prairie ingredients for her wildly popular food truck, Malinche, which sets up shop beside Malty National. Mariana strives to showcase seasonal products and works closely with Saskatchewan farmers.

Chef Mariana Brito (middle) and her team at the Malinche food truck.

Her talent extends far beyond Latin cuisine, too. She's trained in the pastry arts in Spain, taken whole animal butchery courses in the United States, and worked in New York City.

Her commitment to building a thriving independent restaurant industry in Regina shows: She helped start Le Macaron and Homestead Bar A Vin, along with 641 Grill in Craven. She was also the lead instructor at Schoolhaus Culinary Arts.

In 2014, she founded Backyard Enterprises, a culinary company for pop-up dinners. A few years later, she began holding events at Over the Hill Orchards, which she soon turned into a seasonal restaurant. (The orchard now hosts weekend dinner events in partnership with the Regina Chefs' Association.)

At the time, she was called crazy for starting something in Lumsden. "I thought there was an opportunity. If there's good food, people will come." And come they did. Mariana and her team did a mailing list and handed out postcards to advertise the dinners. Soon, every Saturday night was booked, and they had expanded to Fridays.

As for the future, we have much to look forward to as long as Mariana's around. "I am determined to keep contributing to the culinary growth and development of Regina through real food." She's doing that through a new restaurant located inside Pile O' Bones Brewing Co.

✪ If pop-up dinners are your thing, Stalk Fine Dining hosts one delectable event per month. Visit stalkyqr.com for reservations.

The Creek in Cathedral Bistro

3414 13th Ave | 306-352-4448

The Creek's chef Ricardo Rodriguez and former chef Martin Snow.

■ **The Creek in Cathedral** has not one but two head chefs, both equally talented and creative, who play off each other's strengths in creating seasonal menus that explore new tastes at every turn. Ricardo Rodriguez takes care of the daytime shift, while Martin Snow handles the evening. Anything happening on one chef's menu is incorporated into the other's—they need to keep things fresh. Their talents shine when they get to work side by side. "Some of the plates that have come out of this kitchen on nights that we're working together … I still get that feeling … Oh, that was amazing. Like that was just amazing where we've taken it," says Martin.

Martin has been with the Creek since it opened in 2000. His signature dishes feature kicked-up comfort food, like truffle mac and cheese or braised lamb shank panzottis.

Ricardo hails from Patagonia, on the southern tip of Argentina, and brings a South American flair and flavour to the bistro and to his catering company, Patagonia Kitchen. He's lived in Saskatchewan since 2001 and during that time has fallen in love with local ingredients. He says the trend toward using more of those ingredients was slow to catch on, but he's happy to see where things are at now. "We can bring in everything from around the world but what makes us special is our own prairie products."

The Creek is one of a handful of restaurants taking a more farm-to-table approach in the province. Owner Jasmine Godenir and her parents both grow large gardens for the bistro.

At press time, Martin Snow had moved on from the bistro.

Tim Davies

Bar Willow Eatery | 3000 Wascana Dr | 306-585-3663 | barwillow.ca

■ **When the Willow on Wascana** opened in 2004, the restaurant (which also has some of the best views in the city) pioneered Regina's local, seasonal food movement. It was rebranded in 2019 as Bar Willow Eatery. Cheeky cocktails are served alongside local beer and edgy small and shared plates.

The Wascana Lake restaurant has been chef Tim Davies's home for over a decade. "I'm very unlimited in what I'm allowed to do, which doesn't happen very often. And that's kind of nice. I can just work directly with suppliers."

Tim grew up in Ottawa, studied culinary arts in Victoria, and worked in the mountains before returning to Vancouver Island to run a brunch restaurant where he met his wife. After Tim left to train in Europe for a year, she convinced him to move to Regina and introduced him to the Willow's owners, which included chef Moe Mathieu at that time.

After over a decade cooking in Regina, Tim says small scale and urban farming has really taken off. Heliotrope Organic Farm (see page 207) is one of his biggest vegetable suppliers. "They got it figured out. They have a great belief system that we share with them."

Tim's protégés are helping shape Regina's culinary community. Ashley Schmalenberg runs Saltine Baking Co. (see page 236) and Greg Reid is an artisanal butcher at Lakeview Fine Foods (see page 238).

Bar Willow carries on the Willow Wine Club tradition by hosting tasting events. The eatery also offers small tasting pours to make for fabulous evenings out on that big wooden patio overlooking the lake.

At press time, Tim had left Bar Willow for different opportunities. The restaurant he helped cement as a Regina institution is well-worth your patronage.

Chef Tim Davies.

✪ Beer Bros. Gastropub is another excellent eatery started by the Willow's founding ownership group.

Niki Haritos

The Breakfast Bistro, Luna Kitchen & Bar | 3215 E Quance St
306-206-1811 | breakfastbistro.ca | lunakitchenbar.ca

Chef Niki Haritos at Luna Kitchen & Bar.

■ **Niki Haritos** grew up working in her family's restaurants, but when she was younger she didn't particularly like the familial obligation. However, when the family left Greece and settled in Regina, Niki came to love making food for people.

Niki; her parents, Dina and Bill; and head chef Tiffani McBee opened the Breakfast Bistro in 2014. "Tiffani was so creative and ambitious. I learned so much from her and it took off from there," recalls Niki. The bistro was so popular, they opened an evening concept, Luna Kitchen & Bar.

After Tiffani left to pursue a pastry career, Niki took over the kitchen. It came with challenges, to be sure. "I tried doing Tiff's menu, but I had no idea how to do it because that menu was all about her." At that time, besides Dina's homemade Greek desserts, the family's background didn't come into play on the menu.

On the advice of a friend, Niki began trying features closer to her roots. "I sat down and thought about how I can start introducing myself as a chef to customers. I got rid of [the old menu] and changed everything." While Luna isn't a full-blown Greek restaurant, it is a place to experience the Haritoses' heritage in beautifully executed dishes with Mediterranean flair. And Bill's hospitality will make you feel like an old friend.

Everything, from Dina's tomato sauce to the hollandaise, is made from scratch. "You get what you pay for," says Niki. "I don't believe in anything packaged. If you can't make it, don't put it on the menu."

6

Moe Mathieu

Chef Moe Mathieu at a pop-up dinner event at Over the Hill Orchards.

■ **Chef Moe Mathieu** is a true pioneer in Saskatchewan's culinary scene. Close to twenty years ago, he and four partners (Greg Hanwell, Darren Carter, James Taylor, and Dave Burke) opened the Willow on Wascana, the first restaurant in Regina with a seasonal menu, serving local food sourced from Saskatchewan producers.

Their ethos went far deeper than eating a local diet, a trend that's been embraced in more recent years. For the Willow crew (who later opened Beer Bros. Gastropub & Deli together), it was about supporting an agricultural system that benefited the province.

But twenty years ago, people thought they were crazy. "We got told we were going to be shut down in a month and that we were stupid for trying to open up a restaurant that had all Saskatchewan products," recalls Moe. "I don't know why we didn't do that before—sourcing locally—but we didn't. And it took a really long time."

Moe rejects the food pioneer title, saying it should be shared with Remi Cousyn (see page 119), who opened Calories in Saskatoon around the same time. (Remi has since retired and sold Calories to two long-time employees.) He remembers trying to find local suppliers—a "nightmare" at the time—and sharing what he found with Remi. "One guy sold leeks. I'd take twenty-five pounds one week, Remi would take twenty-five the next week. It was hilarious."

Pine View Farms (see page 85) was launching at that time, too. "I said, 'I'll take all your stuff. I want to know what you feed, and I want to know that the birds are taken care of. I want to see your facility.' It was a really different way of thinking at that time in Saskatchewan."

Moe spent several years teaching at Luther College. "When I go through any dinner that I've done, there's an opportunity. With almost every situation, you can teach. It's our responsibility to do that."

He's now the director of Nutrition, Retail, and Production for the Saskatchewan Health Authority in Saskatoon.

Leo Pantel

Conexus Arts Centre | 200 Lakeshore Drive

■ **Leo Pantel** has been the Conexus Arts Centre's executive chef for over thirty years. It's a role that sees him putting on community dinners for Regina's homeless one day and executing a prestigious event for world leaders the next.

He got his start at small-town restaurants before taking a sous chef position at what was then the Saskatchewan Centre of the Arts. During his first week, he helped cater an event for French president François Mitterrand. "It really opened things up for me and got me into unique catering functions."

He says that ability to constantly innovate is what's kept him at Conexus for over three decades. Leo has also been on the Canadian Culinary Federation Regina Branch's board since the mid-1990s, and attends the Canadian Culinary Federation National Conference every year to learn from and connect with other chefs from across the country.

Chef Leo Pantel of the Conexus Arts Centre.

Those national connections have helped open up international opportunities, such as the World Heritage Cuisine Summit & Food Festival, where Leo and fellow Regina chefs Jonathan Thauberger and Milton Rebello represented Canada in 2018.

Leo says his commitment to the culinary arts must keep apace with the city's evolving food culture. "The culinary knowledge of our patrons has greatly increased over the years. We like to take it to another level. It's been exciting that way. It keeps me motivated."

While black-tie events demand unique menus, most also offer the chance to pay homage to prairie ingredients. "We're a large facility but we're still able to work with a lot of local suppliers and highlight what we have here in Saskatchewan."

Paul Rogers

Beak's Chicken | 1511 11th Ave | beakschicken.com

■ **Paul Rogers** is an anomaly in Saskatchewan: one of the few to turn a popular food truck into a profitable bricks and mortar restaurant. He started Beak's Chicken in 2013. His fried chicken quickly became a hit, probably because, as Paul says, "from start to finish, we put twenty-four hours of love into it."

The process begins with an overnight brine. The meat is cooked sous vide to keep it moist and then hand dredged and fried. "Nothing is pre-made. We start from scratch," says Paul. "We put a lot of time and effort into it."

He's expanded on the food truck's menu since opening up shop on 11th Avenue in 2018. The menu is relatively simple; Paul sticks to what he does best.

Paul was born in Ottawa but grew up in Regina. He cut his teeth working in kitchens in Regina, Vancouver, and Europe before returning home. The food truck trend had hit Regina full force and Paul saw an op-portunity. Running the food truck allowed him to build a client base and

come up with a fried chicken recipe for success, but it wasn't ideal in the long-term: "The biggest challenge was the climate—you get about three months out of it realistically."

The recipe for Beak's most popular dish hasn't changed since 2013 and likely never will. Chicken and Waffles consists of two strips of fried chicken, topped with homemade gravy and bacon jam, nestled between two made-from-scratch Belgian waffles.

Paul Rogers, owner of Beak's Chicken.

Jonathan Thauberger

Crave Kitchen + Wine Bar | 1925 Victoria Ave | 306-525-8777

cravekwb.com

■ **Chef Jonathan Thauberger** wholeheartedly embodies the characteristics that make a good chef: passion for the ingredients and a willingness to explore. He earned his chops in his thirty-plus year career out on the West Coast, working in Vancouver restaurants before heading to the Okanagan. That's where the award-winning chef's love affair with ingredients really began. "It wasn't until moving to the Okanagan and tasting that tree-ripened peach, still warm from the sun ... it ruined peaches for me really," he says with a smile.

Chef Jonathan Thauberger of Crave Kitchen + Wine Bar.

He's been the executive chef at Crave Kitchen + Wine Bar since 2012 and more recently a partner in the restaurant housed in the former Assiniboia Club's historic building. It's a place with continually evolving and tight menus, based on what's in season and what Jon has been creating in the kitchen.

The focus at dinner is on the sharing slabs, served overflowing with his housemade charcuterie, like Saskatchewan Snow Beef pemmican, preserves, and spreads.

He goes above and beyond to source quality cheese from small, artisanal Canadian companies. "They do it more for love than they do it for anything else, especially on the cheese side."

While creating an elevated dining experience is always foremost, Jon is humble about Crave's aspirations. "All we're trying to do here is have good product and serve good, solid food. We're not trying to be fancy or cutting edge. We just try to do solid things that people enjoy."

6

Curtis Toth
Hotel Saskatchewan | 2125 Victoria Ave | hotelsaskatchewan.ca

■ **The Hotel Saskatchewan** is one of two historic hotels built by the Canadian Pacific Railroad in the province (the other, the Bessborough, is in Saskatoon). It's a regal hotel, befitting a queen, and, in fact, she has stayed there.

Curtis Toth has been the executive chef since 2017. He and his talented staff exceed hotel food expectations. Curtis was born and raised in Regina, where he got his first restaurant job in high school. "That's where I developed a love for cooking. I like organized chaos."

The Hotel Saskatchewan's executive chef Curtis Toth.

He took culinary training at the Southern Alberta Institute of Technology (SAIT) in Calgary and worked under Michael Noble at Catch. His career took him to Ireland, then back to Calgary to the Hyatt Regency before transferring to the hotel group's Huntington Beach location in California. There he helped transition the hotel's restaurant to Watertable, a Spanish-themed concept that has won numerous awards.

Curtis follows a rustic and refined ethos with his menus. "I've always been successful at that: simple, quality food that's prepared well, while trying to support local producers in the process."

He also likes to have fun. Prohibition Tea (Last Mountain Distillery's vodka with the hotel's house tea in a china teacup) is served weekdays at five in the Circa 27 lounge. The ritual pays homage to Saskatchewan's Prohibition past. In keeping with the English tea tradition, gourmet toasties (like citrus chicken salad with sun-dried cranberries from Prairie Berries in Keeler on toasted sourdough) complete the spread.

"I think people can taste love in food. If you don't care about what you do, it'll come through in your food and you won't be successful."

Wallnuts Expressive Catering

232A College Ave E | 306-543-9255 | wallnuts.ca

Laurie Wall at Wallnuts Expressive Catering.

■ **Laurie Wall's catering company** was born out of a desire to do better. At a networking event she attended over fifteen years ago, she remembered the food was "horrible. I just thought, 'My God I could do way better than this.'" And she did, arranging her first catering contract with the event organizer. "I was in my element and got tons of positive feedback."

What began as a side gig soon became the single mother of two's bread and butter. Laurie established Wallnuts at a time when there weren't a lot of independent, off-site catering services in Regina. "I travel a lot and get inspired with food that way for sure," says Laurie of her globally inspired menus. "And I just brought something different to the table."

Six years in, the space beside Laurie's commercial kitchen was for sale. It now houses Eatable – Wicked Food to Go where her hearty takeaway meals are sold, along with baking and preserves. Everything is made from scratch in the Wallnuts Kitchen—it's how Laurie was raised on the family farm—and what's not used in the kitchen is composted on a worm farm.

Produce comes from Laurie's farming friends' and her parents' gardens. Her egg lady drops off twenty dozen each week.

She's delving into artisanal cheesemaking after attending David Asher's Black Sheep School of Cheesemaking. And in 2018, Laurie took a course in traditional butchery and charcuterie in southern Italy, which has helped further Wallnuts' nose-to-tail philosophy.

Aimee Schulhauser

Schoolhaus Culinary Arts | 2171 Lorne St | 306-543-2665
schoolhausculinaryarts.ca
Tangerine: The Food Bar | 2234 14th Ave | tangerineregina.ca

Tangerine's menu changes daily and always features a hot lunch option.

■ **"Made from scratch today"** is the ethos behind Tangerine: The Food Bar and Schoolhaus Culinary Arts. Tangerine, with its gourmet coffee, decadent baking, and rotating menu with plenty of vegetarian options, has been operating for over a decade.

After training at SAIT in Calgary, owner Aimee Schulhauser got her start in the Queen City with a catering company (now called Catering by Tangerine). At her clients' insistence, she opened Tangerine and, because she believes there's a chef inside all of us, started Schoolhaus Culinary Arts in 2014. Tangerine in the Valley, her newest endeavour, is a seasonal restaurant in Fort Qu'Appelle (see page 204).

→ Aimee Schulhauser

Tangerine's menu has changed every single day since it opened. There's always a soup, sandwich, hot lunch, crustless quiche, and vegetarian option. Winter calls for a cozy combo; during summer, a portable picnic. "We wanted to make sure we could make the best out of what was in season and fresh. We also wanted to stretch our creative muscles," says Aimee who encourages her staff's culinary imagination.

Opening Schoolhaus and teaching people how to cook has been the most gratifying thing she's done. "I'll say at the beginning of class, 'I'm going to show you a skill that will change your life. Here's how to hold a knife.'"

She says learning how to cook is transformational and when she's teaching people, she's at her best. "We socialize and come together over food. There's satisfaction in creating it together and then eating it."

Schoolhaus started with just six types of cooking classes and now offers over three hundred, taught by both professional chefs and self-taught cooks. "We don't think that chefs are the sole keepers of knowledge in the food world," says Aimee with a smile.

Enjoy a latte in the sun at Tangerine.

✪ CJ's Cooking Studio also offers hands-on cooking classes in Regina. Email cj.katz@sasktel.net for info and look for her line of Be a Kitchen Hero spices sold throughout the city.

Outlaw Trail Spirits
1360 Scarth St | 306-527-6533 | outlawtrailspirits.com

■ **Ever heard of the Outlaw Trail?** It's a cool piece of Saskatchewan history, but not one many of us know about. Outlaw Trail Spirits pays tribute to Saskatchewan's Wild West history through aptly named artisan spirits, like Big Muddy Outpost vodka, using locally sourced ingredients.

Charmaine and John Styles, Ken Balius, and Stella Dechaine founded the distillery in 2016 in Regina's thriving Warehouse District. John is a Scotch lover thanks to his family history. (They're from Scotland's Orkney Islands.) "I felt it was a need for me to try and produce something that a Scotch lover would enjoy. It boils down to selection of ingredients, creating the mash bill, and experimenting around small batch production."

Outlaw Trail gets creative with different grains to produce flavours whisky lovers will appreciate. They use ancient grains, old-fashioned two-row malted barley, and specialty malts from England, like a chocolate malt (traditionally used in porters) that does interesting things to whisky flavour profiles.

While it may work in Scotland, one cannot build a business on Scotch alone in Saskatchewan. "You've gotta have cash flow while it's aging," says Charmaine. To that end, they also make vodkas and liqueurs, like a limoncello-style Lady Luck Lemon Vodka and Calamity Jane Ginger Vodka, which has a sharp, hot ginger flavour.

John is most proud of their Old Foggy Bottom single malt. In 2018, the American Distilling Institute gave it a bronze medal and best in category for an international specialty spirit at its Craft Spirits Awards in Portland.

The distillery is open for tours and tastings; it's best to book ahead.

Be sure to ask staff about a self-guided walking tour to Rebellion Brewing, District Brewing Co., Bushwakker Brewpub, Pile O' Bones Brewing Company, and Malty National Brewing Corp.

Charmaine and John Styles own Outlaw Trail Spirits with Ken Balius and Stella Dechaine.

✪ Visit coronach.ca to arrange a tour of the Badlands and Butch Cassidy's Outlaw Trail.

Italian Star Deli

1611 Victoria Ave | 306-757-6733 | italianstardeli.com

Siblings Gino and Marina Giambattista are the third generation running Italian Star Deli.

■ **Regina's iconic Italian Star Deli** started in 1966 as a confectionary selling everything from chandeliers to cigarettes, and, of course, cured meats. Siblings Gino and Marina Giambattista now run the business their grandparents Frank and Gina started, the place where their father has worked since high school.

Italian Star has become known for more than just its impressive assortment of imported European goods. It's also a place to find local food products from those without a bricks and mortar location. "We just want to get people's names out there," says Marina. "We want to make sure that they have a chance—it helps us, it helps them, it's great for the Regina area." They also host pop-up farmers' markets in front of the building, open to whomever would like to sell their products.

Marina takes care of the deli, while Gino handles the dry goods side. "I'm in the front, she's in the back. Distance makes the heart grow fonder," says Gino, with a smile, of working with his sister. "Without Gino doing the front, I don't know how anybody could do it alone," says Marina.

6

→ Italian Star Deli

....

"Nonna did it alone for many years when Nonno worked for the City of Regina."

While it's undoubtedly the best place to find olive oil and gourmet cheese, Italian Star's claim to fame is their paninis—it's a recipe that hasn't changed over the years. Other things have changed, though, as the business has evolved with its customer base, offering more Eastern European and South African imports, and custom meat and cheese trays.

○ Regina has plenty of independent grocers that support and promote local producers: Dad's Organic Market, Takeaway Gourmet, Lakeview Fine Foods, and Body Fuel Organics, which also sells Chef Malcolm's Handmade Pies—worth a visit to the store in their own right!

○ Head to Recharge Café for vegetarian takeaway meals.

○ The city has several full-service ethnic grocers, like Ngoy Hoa Asian Foods, India Food Centre, Regina Ukrainian Co-op and Boutique, and Seoul Mart.

Local and Fresh, The Local Market

1377 Hamilton Street | 306-861-0487 | localandfresh.ca

■ **Tim and Carla Shultz** had a dream for a more accessible local food system in southern Saskatchewan. Their goal of bringing a farmers' market to people through an online platform expanded in 2019 when they opened the Local Market in Regina's Warehouse District.

It all began from their first-hand experience gained running a market garden operation for over a decade and learning how difficult it is to make a living selling directly to consumers. "It was a vision for a better market for producers," says Tim. "We felt there was a place to create a platform for producers to market their products, to help them elevate their business, and let producers focus on producing."

It was also a way to bring together local food options and make it easy for year-round consumer access. Local and Fresh launched in 2014 with fifteen producers. It's grown to include over one hundred producers on the website along with delivery and pickup options six days a week. There's also a restaurant food service division.

The couple knew the best way to really connect consumers with local food was through a bricks and mortar location. "Consumers want to be able to touch and feel and learn and see with their own eyes." The Local Market, housed in the former Weston Bakery Building, includes a grocery store where the online platform has been transformed into a retail setting.

The artisan food court combines a commercial kitchen with kiosks which chefs can rent to host pop-up events. "Our vision for Local and Fresh was to create a platform for entrepreneurs to succeed in the food business. The Local Market takes it one step further."

An event space completes the building and also serves as a weekly farmers' and artisans' market venue. "I'm so passionate about this. It's been a vision for so long," says Tim.

Tim Shultz at the Local Market in Regina.

REGINA FARMERS' MARKETS

Check the website for current hours prior to your visit.

Regina Farmers' Market
200-1822 Scarth Street
Wednesdays, 9:00 AM–1:00 PM
Saturdays 9:00 AM–1:00 PM
reginafarmersmarket.ca

REGINA WATERING HOLES

Check the website for current hours prior to your visit.

Brewsters Brewing Company
480 McCarthy Blvd N
306-522-2739

1832 Victoria Avenue East
306-761-1500

Tours: By request.
Taproom on site.

District Brewing Co.
1555 8th Ave | 306-790-2337
districtbrewing.ca

Tours: By request.
Visit website for retail locations.

Malty National Brewing Corp.
1130 15th Ave | 306-525-5001
maltynational.com

Tours: By request.
Taproom on site.

Pile O' Bones Brewing Co.
1808 Cameron Street
306-559-6444
pileobonesbrewing.com

Tours: By request.
Taproom on site.

Sperling Silver Distillery
2124 Albert St
306-751-0000
sperlingsilver.com

Tours: By request.
Retail store on site.

◔ A seasonal dish featuring ingredients from local producers at the Hotel Saskatchewan in Regina.
◑ Following spread: The charcuterie board at Luna Kitchen & Bar.

Southwest Saskatchewan

7

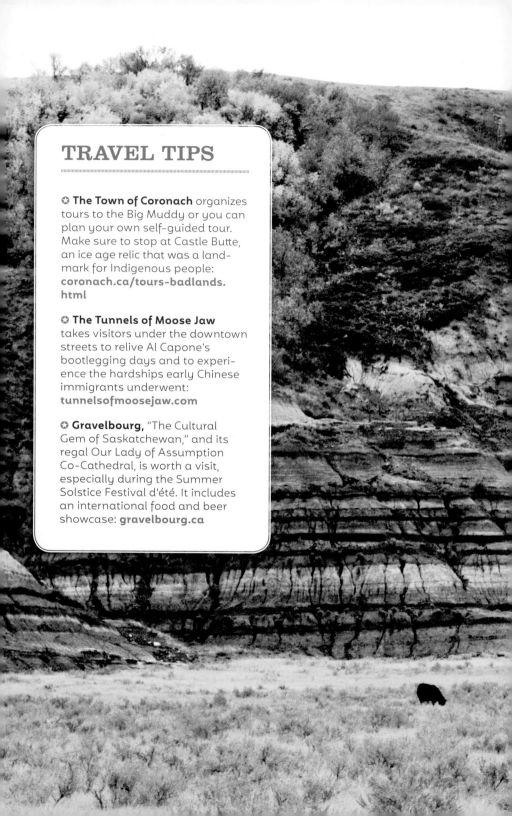

TRAVEL TIPS

✪ **The Town of Coronach** organizes tours to the Big Muddy or you can plan your own self-guided tour. Make sure to stop at Castle Butte, an ice age relic that was a landmark for Indigenous people: **coronach.ca/tours-badlands.html**

✪ **The Tunnels of Moose Jaw** takes visitors under the downtown streets to relive Al Capone's bootlegging days and to experience the hardships early Chinese immigrants underwent: **tunnelsofmoosejaw.com**

✪ **Gravelbourg,** "The Cultural Gem of Saskatchewan," and its regal Our Lady of Assumption Co-Cathedral, is worth a visit, especially during the Summer Solstice Festival d'été. It includes an international food and beer showcase: **gravelbourg.ca**

Saskatchewan's southwest region is ruggedly beautiful and diverse. The Big Muddy Badlands and its eroded buttes, cone-shaped hills, and steep cliffs are at the southern tip of the province. In the 1890s, the Outlaw Trail ran from the Big Beaver/Coronach area, through the United States, ending in Mexico. It was a time when police patrols were infrequent; the closest North-West Mounted Police post was several days' ride away. It made an ideal situation for outlaws who used the caves in the Big Muddy Valley to their advantage.

The Badlands give way to native prairie grasslands. Grasslands National Park is in the west, where bison roam free. If you're camping, check out the Fireside Chats at Grasslands Park: share stories around the campfire with park interpreters, while you roast marshmallows or cook bannock. Cowboy Coffee, brewed over the campfire, is held on Sunday mornings.

The Great Sand Hills Ecological Reserve is also in the southwest. The sand hills are one of Canada's largest areas of active sand dunes.

The region is generally warmer and drier than the rest of the province, making it ideal for cattle ranching. Many of Saskatchewan's largest cattle operations are in the southwest, carrying on a ranching tradition that began over a century ago.

Cypress Hills Interprovincial Park's lush valleys and streams are an oasis. The forest-covered hills are the highest point between the Canadian Rockies and the Labrador Peninsula. The area was once a giant plateau surrounded by glaciers and was a sacred gathering place for Saskatchewan's Indigenous people for centuries.

Several communities have thriving local food systems. Swift Current is a real gem, with a bustling, vibrant farmers' market and

↻ Previous spread: **Wide load indeed; a not uncommon sight on rural Saskatchewan roads.**
↻ **The buttes in the Big Muddy Badlands in southwest Saskatchewan.**

an excellent craft brewery, Black Bridge. The Nightjar Diner is worth a stop, too. The community's Mennonite Heritage Village celebrates summer each year with its Watermelon Festival. The fruit is served cold alongside traditional roll kuchen (deep-fried pastry). Mortlach is home to the Little Red Market Cafe, chef Chad Forrest's eclectic spot serving up Louisiana Creole cuisine with locally sourced ingredients.

Shaunavon has Harvest Eatery, one of the province's best restaurants. Mortlach celebrates the province's famous fruit at an annual Saskatoon Berry Festival while Kindersley plays host to the Grilledcheesapolooza Music Festival.

The Taste of Maple Creek Food Festival happens every August. Visit during July for the town's heritage festival or in June to attend the Maple Creek Canadian Cowboys Association Rodeo. Head to the Historic Reesor Ranch for a barn dance or suppertime cowboy poetry readings throughout the season.

Eastend holds a food and drink festival combined with a street dance during its annual Dino Days, a celebration of the region's paleontology. Saskatchewan's famous Scotty, a Tyrannosaurus Rex, found in Eastend's badlands in 1991, is the heaviest and oldest fossil of its kind ever discovered.

Consul is in the far southwestern corner of Saskatchewan and Manley Bread & Honey makes it worth the trip. It's run by the town's pastor and his wife, who buy their eggs and honey from three young farmers in the area. In 2019, brothers Cam (age fifteen) and Will Blakley (twelve), along with their friend Jon Rutkowski (fourteen), began the Southwest Growing Cooperative in Consul to sell their honey, pastured eggs, and organic vegetables. ■

⊙ **Life gets messy on the farm sometimes, as the youngest member of the Pearl family discovers. The family owns Prairie Pearl's Homestead near Imperial.**

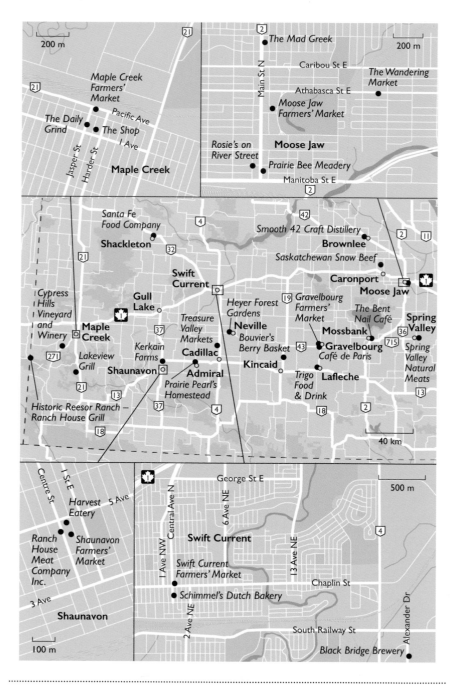

Maple Creek

200 m

[21]

Maple Creek Farmers' Market

The Daily Grind

The Shop

Pacific Ave

I Ave

Jasper St

Harder St

[21]

Moose Jaw

200 m

[2]

The Mad Greek

Main St N

Caribou St E

The Wandering Market

Athabasca St E

Moose Jaw Farmers' Market

Rosie's on River Street

Prairie Bee Meadery

Manitoba St E

[2]

Santa Fe Food Company

[4]

[42]

Smooth 42 Craft Distillery

Brownlee

[2]

[11]

Shackleton

[32]

Saskatchewan Snow Beef

[21]

Swift Current

Caronport

Moose Jaw

Cypress Hills Vineyard and Winery

Gull Lake

Heyer Forest Gardens

[19] Gravelbourg Farmers' Market

The Bent Nail Café

Spring Valley

[36]

Maple Creek

Treasure Valley Markets

[37]

Neville

Bouvier's Berry Basket

[43]

Mossbank

[715]

Spring Valley Natural Meats

Lakeview Grill

[271]

Kerkain Farms

Cadillac

Gravelbourg
Café de Paris

Kincaid

Shaunavon

[21]

Admiral

Prairie Pearl's Homestead

Trigo Food & Drink

Lafleche

[13]

[13]

[37]

[4]

[18]

[2]

Historic Reesor Ranch – Ranch House Grill

[18]

40 km

Shaunavon

100 m

Centre St

I St E

Harvest Eatery

5 Ave

Ranch House Meat Company Inc.

Shaunavon Farmers' Market

3 Ave

[1]

George St E

Central Ave N

6 Ave NE

500 m

I Ave NW

Swift Current

Swift Current Farmers' Market

13 Ave NE

[4]

Chaplin St

2 Ave NE

Schimmel's Dutch Bakery

South Railway St

Alexander Dr

Black Bridge Brewery

Note: Only artisans and producers who welcome visitors on site are shown on this map.

266

SOUTHWEST SASKATCHEWAN ARTISANS

Culture Mother

Gravelbourg | 306-650-7420 | culturemother.ca

Keirsten Eva with her homemade sourdough.

■ **After fermented foods** changed Keirsten Eva's poor health, she knew she had to share the wealth. In 2011, the new mom had asthma, allergies, fibromyalgia, irritable bowel syndrome, and depression. A friend gave her a kombucha SCOBY and taught her about fermentation, the oldest form of preservation. Eva said her symptoms disappeared within three months of daily sips of the fizzy probiotic drink.

She, her partner, and their three children now eat a variety of cultured foods. "Fermented foods helped heal my gut and helped heal my entire body."

Eva ships live cultures throughout Canada. She's heard a range of powerful testimonials from clients. "And so that's why I feel like screaming it from the rooftops. Everybody needs to know how to make these foods. This is what speaks to our DNA, these life-giving foods," says Eva.

Her website has detailed instructions for making fermented foods at home, along with ample photos, additional resources, and even bread, waffle, and pancake recipes for the sourdough starters. If you're of the gluten-free persuasion, don't knock sourdough bread until you've tried it. The bacterial culture helps consume and break down the naturally occurring sugars in bread. That makes it easier to digest those nutrients. Plus, sourdough has a taste depth unlike grocery store bread. Allow it a long rise (overnight or longer) for the ultimate flavour.

Eva also sells her homemade sourdough bread at the Gravelbourg Farmers' Market.

Gravelbourg Mustard

Gravelbourg | gravelbourgmustard.ca

Gravelbourg Mustard's Val Michaud.

■ **Val Michaud** was a newbie to the food industry but in under a decade she has put Saskatchewan mustard, a.k.a. "prairie gold," on the map. Her gourmet, European-style mustards are so good, in fact, that they scored her a deal on the Dragon's Den in 2017. Since then, she's had interest from across the country. Over 135 businesses carry her products which include rubs, dressings, dry mustard, and mustard seeds.

Val's nine flavours are all stars in their own right. It just depends on what kind of taste you're after. Perhaps it's a sturdy German- or French-style mustard, a kicked-up jalapeño, or a delicious honey dill.

Saskatchewan produces about 80 percent of Canada's mustard but much of that is exported for processing and packaging, then imported back to Canada for sale. Val wanted to change that when she bought the company in 2011. Gravelbourg Mustard is the only prepared mustard that's grown, processed, and packaged in Saskatchewan using local talent, resources, and labour. Val is from Gravelbourg and rents space at Saskatoon's Food Centre to make the mustard.

"With a passion for food and making every day a little more gourmet, we are always looking for new ways to show you how to use our mustard." One of those ways is through cocktails. Gravelbourg Mustard's signature cocktails include a stirred cranberry mustard martini that won over the Dragons when Val made it for them on air.

A full list of retailers is on Val's website, along with a free mustard recipe book.

Santa Fe Food Company

306 Franklin Street, Shackleton | 306-587-7710 | santafefoodcompany.com

■ **In 1999,** Cam McLeod was one of the first in the province to plant an orchard of Carmine Jewel sour cherries, which were developed at the University of Saskatchewan. Carmine Jewels, with their cold hardiness, excellent quality, and potential for mechanical harvesting, are now the most widely grown commercial cherry crop in the province. They're also a Saskatchewan superfood. The deep purple cherry's flavour is tart and intense. They're chock full of antioxidants and anti-inflammatory properties, plus they naturally contain sleep-aiding melatonin.

Cam's two orchards, one in Shackleton and the other near Cabri, supply him with enough cherries to sell to processors and to make his own line of products. He began Santa Fe Food Company to make simple, healthy, and delicious products. The name came from Santa Fe locomotives, which were the first to use the former CP Railway lines bordering his property after the lines were privatized.

The company began with sour cherry juice (a shot at bedtime will cure all that ails you). Next came cherry-based sauces and Cherry Chelish (like a sweet onion relish but with cherries and rhubarb) in 2011.

The Cherry Chertney combines cinnamon, cloves, cherries, and gooseberries. It pairs well with pork, chicken, wild game, or sweeter dishes. His bestselling Rib N Wing Sauce, spiced up with a dash of cayenne and red bell peppers, can be used as a marinade, salsa, or dip.

Santa Fe products can be purchased online and are for sale at retail locations throughout Saskatchewan.

Cam McLeod owns the Santa Fe Food Company in Shackleton.

Zak Organics Food Co.

Moose Jaw | 1-800-897-4803 | zakorganics.com

■ **Transitioning into the snack food industry** was a natural progression for the Zak family. Allen, his wife Marilyn, their two sons, and Allen's father run the family's 7,000-acre organic farm in southern Saskatchewan. The couple started their company making snack foods from green peas, with business partner Daena McMurdo in 2015.

Allen recalled trying to find convenient snacks when their boys were growing up: "It was either high fat, high salt, loaded with monosodium glutamate or it had added colours. We've got to be able to do better." And do better they have, by taking a crop they grow and turning it into an organic snack line without additives, fillers, or preservatives.

Today, Zak Organics Crunchy Peas are sold all over Saskatchewan and into Alberta, BC, Ontario, and Quebec, and the family is trying out international markets.

To get there, Allen started by testing green peas. He grew twenty different varieties to find a suitable crop. A BBQ rotisserie for roasting followed, along with many a burnt batch, before they approached the Food Centre in Saskatoon for development guidance and processing in 2014.

Allen also went back to school for an MBA. "I knew I needed more business experience in order to do something like this."

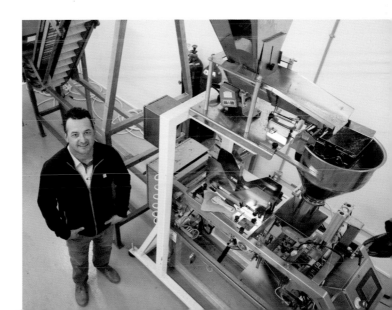

Allen Zak of
Zak Organics
in Moose Jaw.

→ **Zak Organics Food Co.**

They got hailed out and lost the pea crop one year, which set them back considerably, "but we just kept at it." By 2015, the company was incorporated and the following spring, the first product was on the market. The processing centre is in Moose Jaw, two hours northeast of the farm near Fir Mountain.

Allen is a fourth-generation farmer, growing wheat, kamut, lentils, peas, and flax on the same land his great-grandpa homesteaded in 1911. He bought the farm in 1997 from his dad and farmed conventionally for the next decade. A trip to England awakened him to how big the organic industry was overseas and its potential here at home. "This is where people are going. They're concerned about what's being put in their food and organic is definitely the answer."

"You need to have more patience," says Allen of organic farming. "You have to work with Mother Nature. Sometimes it just works awesome and you hope those fields are right next to the road! Sometimes it goes against you."

Café de Paris
306 Main St, Gravelbourg | 306-648-2223

■ **Gravelbourg's rich heritage** is immediately evident in the architecture. Our Lady of Assumption Co-Cathedral is the town's claim to fame. A national historic site, the 1919 cathedral combines Roman and Italian architecture. It sits in a park at the end of Main Street, a reminder of the town's French Catholic roots.

The European-style Café de Paris in Gravelbourg.

It was only fitting then that Toos Giesen Stefiuk opened Café de Paris just up the street from the statuesque cathedral. The café's décor, the chandeliers, white tablecloths, and an Eiffel tower on the chalkboard menu, are all decidedly Parisian. So too is the sidewalk café in the back garden where ivy grows up mural-painted walls.

Gravelbourg is a small-town kinda place. Everyone knows each other, and you may get a few interested stares from coffee row if you're new in town. It was a hard sell for Toos when she opened the café in 2005 with the help of a young chef. At that time, few in town were willing to pay for a latte and forget explaining that it didn't come with free refills. "It took a while to establish but after two years, I started to make some money. And then, it suddenly started to grow and grow," she says.

Toos sold the café several years ago, but under new ownership it has remained much the same. And Toos, now a town councillor, can often be found there, a cup of the town's best coffee in hand.

The Daily Grind

132 Jasper St, Maple Creek | 306-662-3133

Long-time baker Val Leppke at the Daily Grind.

■ **Established in 2005,** the Daily Grind in Maple Creek is known for homemade soup and biscuits, home-style baking, and more recently, freshly ground coffee. Owners Tina Cresswell and Dave Turner bought a coffee roaster from Stephen Girard, a pottery artist in Eastend. Stephen had been roasting coffee for several cafés and restaurants in the area prior to selling his roaster. He was kind enough to share his recipes with Dave, who does the roasting for the Daily Grind.

"I'm excited about it," says Tina of their organic, fair-trade beans. "I'm happy with who we're getting our beans from. They don't have a middle man. They buy the beans direct from the growers."

The Daily Grind is an eclectic café, with seating amid the attached gift shop that reveals Tina's passion for antiques. Her commitment to quality ingredients and home-cooked food is what ensures a loyal customer base. "I was brought up to believe that you grow your own food or you buy from people who grow their own," she says. "My mom was farm-to-table before farm-to-table was popular. She grew most all of our food and what she didn't grow, came to us in the back of pickup trucks from farmers."

Long-time baker Val Leppke makes everything fresh each morning and Tina credits her with much of the café's success: "She's a really, really good baker."

FoodCraft By Sarah
Swift Current | 306-774-9514

■ **Life in the big city's** not for everyone—sometimes a prairie girl craves the open skies. Sarah Galvin grew up in rural Saskatchewan. She moved to Calgary to pursue a career in real estate. Then, about a decade ago, she came back home, settled in Swift Current, and created FoodCraft by Sarah.

She bakes rustic sourdough on a stone in her backyard oven, using a blend of organic Saskatchewan flours: Red Fife, spelt, rye, or seven grain are mixed with white flour. Local sprouted lentils and wild rice from the north also make an appearance.

When she first moved to Swift Current, it was hard to find good, local food. "I called it a desert in every sense of the word. Because most other bakers were not focused on local, I was able to use ingredients that people enjoyed, like wild blueberries from the north." Sarah's also known for her scones and her handcrafted marshmallows. Her most recent challenge was learning how to make croissants.

She's helped the seasonal farmers' market evolve over the years and has become a profitable business model for the vendors. It's held Saturdays under big tents in downtown's Market Square. "It has now become who I am and what I do. People are very appreciative of my products. Everyone is happy on market day and we visit and have fun."

Sarah Galvin with her homemade bread at the Swift Current Farmers' Market.

Schimmel's Dutch Bakery

139 Central Ave N, Swift Current | 306-773-9596

■ **Cinnamon buns** are a staple in Saskatchewan, but the ones from Schimmel's Dutch Bakery stand out in a crowd. Phyllis and Jack Schimmel operate their easily recognizable shop in downtown Swift Current. It's the only place in town with a windmill out front.

Jack was born into pastries. The third-generation baker opened his own shop at just nineteen, next door to his current location. Over forty years later, he still loves the early mornings and the lingering smell of fresh bread on his clothes.

The baking is a mixture of Saskatchewan favourites, along with those from Jack's Dutch roots. "I have a long line of recipes. I blend in Mennonite recipes as well," he says, which come from Phyllis's background.

In the summer, Jack makes mini-doughnuts on Saturdays at the Swift Current Farmers' Market. And he's passed on the doughnut gene. His son Jimmy runs Hobo Donuts in Regina. "He's doing very well—better than Dad!"

It's easy to find their stall at the farmers' market. Just follow the aroma of freshly baked cinnamon buns. The Schimmels bring an impressive mobile oven to the market. Inside, racks house sheet after sheet of baking—cinnamon buns, pies, and beaver tails—before they're served up to anxiously waiting customers.

Savoury picks include bacon wraps and fergassa (chive, garlic, and cheese) buns. No matter what you choose, you won't be disappointed. "That's the one thing we've always stood by: the quality and freshness," says Jack.

The bakery is open Tuesday through Friday and also serves lunch.

Phyllis Schimmel pulling hot cinnamon buns out of the oven at the Swift Current Farmers' Market.

The Shop

113 Harder St, Maple Creek | 306-662-2253 | theshopmc.com

■ **The Shop** has lived many lives in Maple Creek. It started as a tractor dealership, and when Jordyn Winzer bought the building it was an abandoned Chinese restaurant. Everything's been redone but the building's roots remain—a testament to the town's agricultural roots.

The Shop opened in 2016. The bakery and deli are in a high-ceilinged space full of natural light, all the better to show off a bursting display case. Try the Callebaut Brownies, edible cookie dough (sans eggs, of course), or Saskatchewan staples like Nanaimo bars and date squares (with added ginger and orange zest).

Homemade cookies, like bacon oatmeal, buttered popcorn, coconut, and butterscotch are popular, as are macarons and Millionaire bars—a sinful shortbread, salted caramel, cookie dough,

Jordyn Winzer owns the Shop in Maple Creek.

and dark chocolate combo. The croissants and scones are baked fresh every morning. Eggs and veggies come from farmers near Maple Creek.

The sweets are just one side of the business, however. The Shop is a popular caterer in town. And the fresh bread (sourdough, baguettes. and flatbread) always sells out.

Winzer began baking as a kid. Her dad was allergic to eggs, so she tried out different recipes for him. She attended SAIT in Calgary, studying baking and pastry arts, then professional cooking. After working for a catering company there, she came back home to the Prairies and opened the Shop.

✪ **Stop by Howard's Bakery** in Maple Creek, too. Founded in 2009, it's a favourite place in town for homemade baking, custom cakes, and light lunches. The Rockin' Horse Cookhouse & Bar is a great dinner option.

Prairie Field Honey
Swift Current | 306-778-0880

■ **It's a family affair** at Prairie Field Honey. Brenda and Kevin Epp run the business with their teenage sons Michael and Matthew. Grandparents often help out in the extraction room.

Located in Swift Current, they have partnerships with area farmers—honey or beeswax candles in exchange for putting hives in fields. Brenda says the alfalfa on a field with their hives is so thick the farmer can barely cut it. "The bees really do make a difference."

Brenda Epp at the Swift Current Farmers' Market.

Attracted by honey's health benefits, the Epps started out with a hundred hives eight years ago. At that time, the boys were children. Brenda and Kevin wanted to teach their sons the value of a hard day's work.

The business has grown to two hundred hives. And the Eppses' sons are capable of running the operation alone. "They have an appreciation of where their food comes from and what it takes to get that honey off the field," says Brenda.

Their hives are all within fifteen minutes of Swift Current. The combination of knowing the farmers and honey's health benefits makes it a worthwhile endeavour. "It's not an easy process. It's heavy and you've got to wear your suit. It's hot out there and you get stung. But I love it that we can do it as a family."

Prairie Field Honey has a booth at the Swift Current Farmers' Market on Saturdays from June to September. The Epps sell honey and Kevin's beeswax candles from their home in the winter.

Ranch House Meat Company Inc.

473 Centre St, Shaunavon | 306-297-4050 | ranchmeats.ca

■ **The Stevenson family** opened Ranch House Meat Company in 2011 for two reasons: to sell people quality animal proteins and to create value-added products using their beef. Beef from several different ranchers in the area, along with the Stevensons', is on the shelves in their shop. So too is locally raised pork, bison, lamb, and goat.

Vince developed his pasture-to-plate protocol to give people a different option from commercially raised animals. He wants customers to know where their meat comes from. "My animals, and the ones we butcher for the shop, are raised out here on grass. Then, we finish them on barley, but they're not congested. I see them every day so I know how they're raised."

Stevenson brought in a retired butcher when they opened Ranch House. He shared his recipes and expertise and got them started on the right path. They've since experimented and branched out over the years.

The beef is all dry-aged in Ranch House's cooler. The shop is full of homemade jams, pickles, sauces, and local baking. "We're just as natural as we can be. That's what I want to do."

Vince is building a fully modernized slaughtering facility at his ranch, Kerkain Farms (profile on page 298), where the offal and bones will be composted. His challenge now is to get Ranch House's products to a wider marketplace so more people in Saskatchewan can eat high-quality meat from animals that have lived a good life.

Vince Stevenson in the meat cooler at Ranch House Meat Co.

Coteau Hills Creamery

Moose Jaw | coteauhillscreamery.com

■ **Until recently,** Kirby Froese was Saskatchewan's only artisanal cheese-maker. (He was joined by Saskatoon Spruce in late 2018.) He and his wife Crystal launched Coteau Hills Creamery in 2016.

Their milk, purchased through SaskMilk, all comes from Caroncrest Farms Dairy in nearby Caronport. The dairy's owners, the McLeod family, are also partners in the creamery. The milk is then pasteurized at Coteau Hillses' shop.

Kirby is a commercial winemaker by trade. The couple lived in BC for close to twenty years before moving to Saskatchewan. Making cheese was a natural progression for him. "It's all about time, temperature, hygiene. All of the things that are critical in creating really good wine are exactly the same for cheese. However, cheese has quite a few more variables to it."

Those variables keep Kirby on his toes in a new career he thoroughly enjoys. "With wine, I had one chance every year to make it. With cheese, I could be getting milk in every other day if I wanted to experiment."

Coteau Hills' small batch cheese is all handcrafted and doesn't contain yield-increasing powder or stretchers. His main type is a Balkan-style feta, but he's experimented with bloomy rind, Brie, and Reblochon recipes. His first blue cheese was released in mid-2019.

A sage-infused farmer's cheese has done well in the past. "It's just a simple cheese. It's very straightforward, quick to make, and then I infuse it with the sage grown here in town." Sometimes, simple is best.

Kirby Froese at Coteau Hills Creamery.

The Bent Nail Café
411 Main St, Mossbank | 306-354-7737

■ **The heart of any Saskatchewan small town** is always the local restaurant or coffee shop and the Bent Nail Café in Mossbank fits the bill perfectly. The building started off as a hotel in the early 1900s and has housed a number of eateries over the years, including a Chinese food diner, that ubiquitous sight in many prairie small towns.

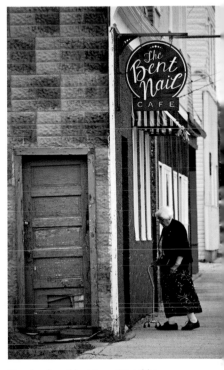

In 2012, Doug and Holly Hutchinson bought the building with a vision to open a restaurant serving quality locally focused food. After an extensive renovation process that exposed and restored the original tin ceiling, the café was given a fresh modern look while upholding a sense of the building's history.

The café was more popular than they anticipated, and the stress of running a bustling restaurant soon took a toll. In 2013, they sold the business to Joel and Cheryl Mowchenko, who farm in the area. "We added some of our own touches but we

Mossbank resident Irene Wuschke entering the Bent Nail Café.

tried to carry on with the vision they had because it lined up with what we had always envisioned for the restaurant we wanted to run," says Joel.

One of those personal touches is a burger made from the Mowchenkos' own grass-finished beef and served on a homemade bun. It's a succulent, delightful affair, especially when accompanied by a salad made with in-season local greens.

Harvest Eatery

492 Centre St, Shaunavon | 306-297-3315 | eatharvest.ca

Husband and wife duo chef Garret "Rusty" (right) and Kristy Thienes opened Harvest Eatery in 2013.

■ **Shaunavon has got it going on.** Apart from being the home of country music's Hunter Brothers, the southwestern town is a Saskatchewan culinary destination. Husband and wife duo chef Garret "Rusty" and Kristy Thienes opened Harvest Eatery in 2013, a welcoming place where they offer an eclectic mix of sustainable Saskatchewan comfort food.

"We know who's growing the food, how they're taking care of it, what their methods are. That is what's going to keep the restaurant and our food system functioning," says Rusty.

Think roasted carrots with pulses, bison tartare, wild boar ravioli, and Lake Diefenbaker trout gravlax. A carefully curated wine list is made to pair with the rotating menu where you'll sometimes find Perigord truffles and pigeon. A Moroccan-spiced lamb sirloin plate has a mixture of rich lamb and cassoulet, topped with rejuvenating orange slices.

Nine-course holiday tasting menus are mostly unheard of in rural Saskatchewan, but not at Harvest Eatery. That's the kind of place the Thieneses wanted to create. It's a place where one feels equally comfortable in a cocktail dress, champagne in hand, or grabbing a pint with pals.

While Rusty controls the kitchen, Kristy runs the front of the house like a well-oiled machine. They both had long careers in the industry before opening their own place.

Kristy, who drives a '58 Chevy Bel Air and gives elderly customers a ride home from time to time, explains they've always made it a point to support the farmers, ranchers, and artists in the area. The restaurant doubles

→ **Harvest Eatery**

as an art gallery for local artists to display and sell their work at no cost. "We feel that visual, performing, and culinary arts go hand in hand and are so proud of all the talented people in our community."

You must always leave room for dessert at Harvest Eatery, especially if the Nanaimo bar is on the menu. It's the same chocolate graham base your grandma made but elevated, with maple crémeux filling in the place of traditional custard and a chocolate ganache topping, sourced from a town in Ecuador where Rusty once lived. It's finished with a sprinkling of burnt maple sponge toffee, raw cacao nibs, and a maple foam.

"It's always important to me that it's not about your first bite," says Rusty. "It's your last bite." Those last bites at Harvest Eatery come with a mixture of regret and joy—joy in the flavour and regret that it's all over, until the next time, that is.

Chef Rusty's take on the classic Saskatchewan square: the Nanaimo bar.

✪ While you're in Shaunavon, visit the Meeting Grounds Coffee House for a crêpe or homemade baking.

Historic Reesor Ranch – Ranch House Grill

Cypress Hills | 306-662-3498

■ **The Historic Reesor Ranch** is a southwestern treasure, made all the more so by the Ranch Hall Grill serving up hearty daily buffets. It's Saskatchewan's first provincially designated heritage ranch and has been in the Reesor family since 1904. It's a wonderful place to explore ranch life in Cypress Hills. Scott and Theresa Reesor offer various guided tours—on ATV and horseback—and carry on the family tradition of cattle ranching.

The steak supper features an eight-ounce bacon-wrapped sirloin from Deerview Meats.

They opened the grill five years ago to cater to overnight guests. "It's always been something we wanted to offer," says Theresa, who takes care of the from-scratch cooking. (Scott's in charge of barbecuing.)

A hearty ranch-style breakfast buffet begins at nine every morning. "It's not fancy but it's certainly filling," says Theresa. "And there's enough there for everybody from vegetarians to people who love their meat."

Dinner is at six—just don't call it dinner. "Some people like to call it dinner, but we stick with supper. It's more ranchy," says Scott with a grin. Scott's barbecued sirloin steak is your best bet. Deerview Meats, an abattoir just across the Alberta border, supplies the steaks wrapped in their house-cured bacon.

Lunches are served picnic style—healthy, portable, and with your choice of a drink.

The couple prefers people to call ahead but walk-ins are always welcome. Grab a beer or a glass of Cypress Hills wine and a snack if you arrive earlier than six; then settle in and wait for Scott's cowboy poetry reading to begin.

❂ While you're in the area, stop in at Grotto Gardens Country Market. The kids will love the goats, while parents will enjoy from-scratch baking on a cheerful patio overlooking the gardens.

Joel Fitzpatrick

Lakeview Grill | Cypress Hills Interprovincial Park | 306-662-4381

■ **Chef Joel Fitzpatrick** was born in Guyana but when his catering business there wasn't taking off, he decided to try his luck in Canada. Two friends he'd met travelling sang the country's praises, so he applied to restaurants in Canada. One of the responses came from Tina Cresswell, the owner of Maple Creek's Star Café. (Tina has since sold the restaurant.) "It felt right, so I took the risk and flew out to Saskatchewan in 2013," says Joel. "It's been one of the best decisions I've made. I wouldn't take it back for anything."

Joel studied international business but hated it and always worked in restaurants during university. He later moved to Europe to train in the culinary arts, which kicked off a lifelong love affair with good food. "I've been doing my thing ever since then," he says with his trademark ear-to-ear grin.

His thing included being part of the team that opened Jamie's Italian, part of Jamie Oliver's UK franchise, in Oxford. Gennaro Contaldo, Jamie's mentor, trained Joel in Italian cuisine.

Joel's now the proud owner of the Lakeview Grill at Cypress Hills Interprovincial Park. It's a seasonal, family-friendly restaurant with a big wooden patio looking out on Loch Leven. The food isn't the pre-made, frozen fare one might expect at such a place, however. Joel has worked tirelessly to find a balance between the from-scratch cooking he's known for and the demands of a quick service restaurant. There are bison sliders, sun-dried tomato and chicken paninis, fresh soup, and baguettes. And hot dogs for the kids.

Chef Joel Fitzpatrick of Lakeview Grill.

The Mad Greek

925 Main St, Moose Jaw | 306-693-4333 | themadgreekeatery.com

■ **The Mad Greek** has been a Moose Jaw favourite since 2002 when John Iatridis followed in his restaurateur father's footsteps and opened the doors to his own place. The Mad Greek is famous for its classic dishes and boneless Greek ribs. Dry pork ribs, which aren't ribs at all but rather chunks of breaded and deep-fried pork loin, are a Saskatchewan institution.

John cuts the "ribs" from pork sourced from Fellinger & Sons Meats in Moose Jaw (he buys all of his meat from the family-owned butcher shop) before egg washing, breading, and deep frying them. A Greek dressing John and his dad developed over twenty-five years ago is tossed on the hot-from-the-fryer ribs before serving. It's a hugely popular menu item; John figures he goes through 650 pounds each week.

He remembers getting requests for boneless dry ribs when he first opened the Mad Greek. "We were trying to be very Greek, with the exception of pizza and lasagna. In Moose Jaw at that time, it was tough. You had to really conform. The idea of someone eating Greek food back then would be throwing feta on a pizza," he says with a laugh. Pizza is another bestseller. John makes the dough and sauce from scratch and buys quality cheese to make his own blend.

After his family immigrated from Greece, his dad and uncle opened the Ambassador Restaurant in 1963. They later founded the family-run Rodos Pizza chain, known for thick crust pizza. (The Moose Jaw location remains today.)

John Iatridis and a plate of his boneless Greek ribs at the Mad Greek.

✪ Moose Jaw has several independent restaurants worth a visit. Bobby's Place Olde World Tavern has good British pub food while Hopkins Dining Parlour offers a more traditional experience in a (reportedly) haunted historic mansion.

Rosie's on River Street
11 River St W, Moose Jaw | 306-693-2229

Chris Schubert at Rosie's on River Street.

■ **For the best burger in Moose Jaw,** head to Rosie's on River Street. The juicy flat top burgers are home-made and mouth-wateringly good. You've got your pick of an aloha burger (with mango BBQ sauce and grilled pineapple), a gorgonzola and onion burger, or a Greek Freak (with feta and tzatziki). Don't worry, there's good ol' fashioned bacon cheese-burgers, too.

But don't take it from me; Rosie's burgers have also been voted best in the city by a Discover Moose Jaw online poll.

The eclectic sports-bar spot is decorated with a mishmash of collect-ibles, including Saskatchewan and Canadian paraphernalia, records, and vintage movie posters. There's a giant moose head, mounted behind the bar, which wears different hats depending on the game being broadcast.

Chris Schubert, who opened Rosie's in 2016 with his dad and a few friends, explains they named the place after River Street's infamous madam Rosie Dale. A painting in the entrance pays homage to her and the city's bootlegging past. "She didn't pay her protection money to the police chief so she got kicked off of River Street. She trained unmanned horses to pick up the johns and take them to just outside town where she moved. She was very entrepreneurial for the time."

While not every menu item is made from scratch—they just don't have the kitchen space for it—they do as much as possible in-house. "I wanted it done right," says Chris. "People just seem to appreciate simple food made right."

287

The Table Catering Company
Moose Jaw | 306-631-2820

Corina Riley at a winemaker dinner hosted by the Table Catering Company.

■ **Corina Riley** believes wholeheartedly food is an experience that brings people together. Her vision with the Table is to create culinary memories that satisfy more than hunger. "When there is intention behind the food that is prepared, it truly creates an experience."

She grew up in the kitchens of her family's small-town restaurants on the west coast of BC. "After having my children, I was really motivated to pass on my love and appreciation of food. I believe it's never too early to instill a love of quality, nourishing foods that appeal to all of our senses."

The family left Vancouver for Moose Jaw and Corina fulfilled her desire to cook professionally. "It was as if the vastness of this place opened something up in me. Living life at a slower pace allowed me to really tap into my passion for food." She began experimenting in the kitchen, her creativity helped along by what she grew in her large garden.

She made it to MasterChef Canada's final rounds in 2014. The next year, she took over the interim head chef position at Little Red Market Café. She launched the Table in 2019, offering high-quality catering services and custom menus. She also hosts pop-up brunches and winemaker dinners in Moose Jaw.

Corina works closely with the Wandering Market to source ingredients from farmers in the area. "I am in love with the quality and range of ingredients Saskatchewan has to offer. I love being able to connect with the people who grow and produce the ingredients."

Trigo Food & Drink

132 Main St, Lafleche | 306-472-3663

■ **What does it take** to convince a Calgary lawyer to move out to rural Saskatchewan and open a restaurant? In Adam Henwood's case it was a lifelong culinary passion that prompted him to leave his career and move to Lafleche. "I was growing dissatisfied with the practice of law, getting burnt out and seeing some colleagues have heart attacks at an early age."

After extensive renovations, he opened Trigo in 2018, and is establishing a place in the community that celebrates seasonal food sourced from Saskatchewan producers.

His cooking skills come from yearly month-long vacations spent at a friend's cooking school in Cambodia. "I really developed a passion for cooking with fresh ingredients ... that are local to Cambodia."

Henwood heads up Trigo's kitchen, where he does old standbys a little differently. On wing nights at Trigo, expect baked wings that have been flour-dredged with spices. "We put a lot of effort behind it. We don't just open up a frozen bag and drop it in the deep fryer. And the town seems to be quite supportive."

Adam would like to see Trigo as the heart of the community. To that end, he hosts live music nights and themed food weekends, like the yearly Festival du Voyageur when tourtière, poutine, bannock, and maple syrup pie are served inside followed by maple syrup taffy pulling outdoors.

Adam Henwood in the kitchen at Trigo Food & Drink.

✪ If you're looking for another unique dining option in the area, head to Nash's Restaurant and Lounge in Assiniboia and try the traditional roast lamb or Greek platter, made using family recipes handed down over generations.

Bouvier's Berry Basket
Hwy 19, Kincaid | 306-264-3691

■ **When Elaine and Ronald Bouvier** started a small berry U-pick back in 1996, they expected a few neighbours and people from nearby Kincaid as customers. "I never expected the way things went. People come from all over," says Elaine.

Elaine's orchard has grown to over five acres. Saskatoon berries are her biggest and most popular crop. She also grows sour cherries, haskaps, apples, raspberries, strawberries, and even watermelon and grapes. A large dugout on the property provides irrigation.

"We've made a lot of great friends over the years from it and people that we look forward to seeing every year." Picnic tables are sprawled throughout the manicured yard, flanked by towering poplars, weeping willows, and fir trees. There's even a Biffy Bin, an old grain bin the couple converted into a wheelchair-accessible washroom decorated with antiques like an old branding iron.

Treasure the haskaps if you can get your hands on them; it's a constant battle against nature to grow the berries. The bushes are all netted or else birds will decimate the harvest.

The Bouviers host a music festival in July to kick off the saskatoon-berry season. People come from all over for a slice of Elaine's homemade cherry pie and for a lounge under one of those big poplars.

Elaine Bouvier with the first grapes of the season.

Clean Spade Urban Farm

Swift Current | 306-774-8411 | wholecaroline.com

Caroline Barrington sharing a laugh with customers at the Swift Current Farmers' Market.

■ **The Swift Current Farmers' Market** is a bustling, vibrant place. Caroline Barrington's laugh carries over the din as her customers patiently wait in a long line to buy her veggies. Caroline, a holistic health coach, launched Clean Spade Urban Farm in 2013 with one small garden plot. She grows everything organically (but is not certified due to the cost and paperwork involved).

Urban farms are popular in Saskatoon but Clean Spade is the only one in Swift Current. Caroline's main crops are lettuce mixes and microgreens. Her garden also brims with heritage carrots, beets, potatoes, Swiss chard, garlic, and zucchini.

During her day job, she coaches people about healing foods. "I know that they're going to feel like a million bucks if they eat my food." Everything is harvested a maximum of two days before each week's market. "If it's so fresh it actually tastes good, people buy it, and feel good!"

Along with helping people in her community eat healthier, setting an example for her children also motivates her. "I wanted to teach them about growing food, about business and work ethic."

Caroline's passion for good clean food is contagious. When she talks about working in her garden with singing birds and the shining sun, you can't help but be inspired to plant one of your own.

Green Sister Gardens

Moose Jaw | greensistergardens.com

Keri Fox at Green Sister Gardens in Moose Jaw.

■ **Keri Fox's chemical-free urban farm** is the only one of its kind in Moose Jaw. She started Green Sister Gardens in 2011 after leaving her career as an electrician. "It was a big transition in my life. I was looking for something that was more sustainable and more in line with my values."

During her search for a new career, a SPIN (Small Plot Intensive) farming workshop got her hooked. She started out with a garden across the street in a neighbour's backyard.

She spread the word about "this crazy idea," explaining that she wanted to have an urban farm and wanted to use peoples' backyards and lawns. Some in her social circle didn't think much of the idea but she persisted.

She now gardens on nine different sites around the city, in total just a third of an acre. She purchased one lot to grow food, built a greenhouse, and converted her basement into an indoor growing space for year-round microgreens.

In order to maximize space, she plants crops she can grow in multiple successions and easily replant, like leafy greens. She collaborates with farmer friends outside the city for root crops and cucumbers.

Green Sister Gardens is at the Moose Jaw Farmers' Market and sells to several Moose Jaw retail locations along with some Regina restaurants.

Treasure Valley Markets

#4 Hwy, Cadillac | 306-785-4602 | treasurevalleymarkets.com

■ **A family holiday in Alberta** inspired Linda Metke to start her own U-pick business, Treasure Valley Markets. Linda had been searching for a career that would take her away from the city and back to the farm her husband Maurice's family started in 1913.

The name comes from a dam built across the nearby valley in the 1930s, that created a large body of water for the farm. Maurice's family survived by running a market garden. "They had an old engine and they'd pump the water via trickle irrigation system from the dam. That's what kept the farm together," says Linda. Today, the fruit orchard spans thirty-three acres. There are several large vegetable gardens and even bountiful rows of watermelons.

Linda sells the produce at the farmers' market in Swift Current and from the farmgate, following in her father-in-law's footsteps. "I like being outside and I like growing things," she says.

The couple also operates an organic grain farm. Though the orchard is not certified organic, they follow organic practices; the strawberry patch's weeds are all hand-picked.

Linda Metke with her goats.

That treasure of a dam still ensures everything stays hydrated and happy. Linda uses an updated version of her father-in-law's trickle irrigation system. She conserves water with trays at the base of the plants that collect condensation in the air.

Treasure Valley is geared toward families. There's a petting zoo, along with paddleboats on the dam. Kids can enjoy their own play area and apple orchard. An ice cream shop sells homemade jams, syrups, and honey from the Treasure Valley bee hives.

Prairie Bee Meadery

23B Main St N, Moose Jaw | 306-692-6323 | prairiebeemeadery.ca

■ **Mead is a relatively new venture** in Saskatchewan. There are just a handful of farms making the fermented honey wine. Prairie Bee Meadery was the province's first and takes pride in handcrafting small batches.

Owner Crystal Milburn says it's important to her to honour her origins. "We've got a real reliance on our bees and our origins in farming and fruit growing." Saskatchewan-grown fruits, like haskaps and sour cherries, are added to the wines before fermentation to create a variety of flavour profiles.

Crystal owns Prairie Bee with her husband Girard and her parents. The honey and much of the fruit comes from the family's vegetable and fruit farm, Grandpa's Garden, west of Moose Jaw. "We really want to keep it local. We want it to be something that's made here—Saskatchewan in a cup," she says, adding they occasionally need to source fruit outside the province.

Crystal's parents began making "really good" mead at home with all the honey from their bees and her mom soon decided opening a cottage winery was the way to go. Crystal, Girard, and their four children moved from Alberta to the farm to run the business. They brought in fruit wine expert Dominic Rivard for advice and launched Prairie Bee Meadery in 2016.

The meadery has a retail outlet in Moose Jaw. The farm is open seasonally for visits. Book on the website, which also lists retail locations.

Due to severe droughts the last several years, Grandpa's Garden is no longer a U-pick operation and is instead growing herbicide- and pesticide-free fruit solely for the meadery.

Crystal Milburn at Prairie Bee Meadery's retail store in Moose Jaw.

Pure T Organics

Pense | 306-757-7012 | farmerstable.localfoodmarketplace.com

■ **When Hazel Tanner** was diagnosed with cancer, she knew it was time to make a drastic change to the way she and her husband David were farming. The couple had been farming grain and pulses conventionally since 1971. In 1998, they sold the sprayer and began the three-year transition process to become certified organic.

"I believe it's the healthy, sustainable way to farm," says Hazel. "Even before cancer, I had been wanting to change. I think women are just more intuitive. They know what it's doing to their kids."

It wasn't an easy process to transition to organic farming. "We made a lot of mistakes to start off with," says David. "Rebuilding your soil back up again is a big learning curve."

David and Hazel Tanner with their antique tractor.

At the time they went organic, it was an industry on the fringe of Saskatchewan agriculture. The Tanners faced opposition but say they're happy with their decision. "You have to go into it with your heart and not just an economic viewpoint because it won't work," adds Hazel. They've learned all kinds of things along the way. "The mustard that looks horrible in a field of lentils will help hold them up, shield them from getting disease, and from the sun," explains Hazel.

The couple sells a range of grains and pulses, complete with recipe cards, at the Regina Farmers' Market and on the Local and Fresh and Farmers' Table websites. One of their most popular products is a splentil mix (a spelt and lentil ground beef substitute).

Ian Crosbie

Saskatchewan Snow Beef | Caronport | 306-631-3466

■ **What do you get when you cross** a Wagyu bull with a Holstein heifer? You get some darn good beef, that's what! Ian Crosbie runs Benbie Holsteins with his dad, Neil, and wanted to expand the operation by finding uses for the dairy farm's replacement heifers.

He's doing that by crossing Wagyu with Holsteins and creating a market for his high-end, ultra-marbled Saskatchewan Snow Beef. "With Holsteins, no one ever talks about how good of beef they actually make. And the Wagyu is on a whole other level."

It's an extensive process to finish the animals properly. After a year and a half living with the regular dairy herd, Ian transitions his calves to a controlled finishing program for three hundred days. He works with a

Ian Crosbie in his dairy barn.

Wagyu nutritionist and imports the cattle's specialized grain ration from Texas. All that specialized care pays off. The snow beef is melt-in-your-mouth tender and full of buttery marbling—people are usually hooked after one bite.

But creating a market for premium beef is easier said than done. And his experience in running the dairy never included marketing. "I'm the one who everyone is trying to sell to, so it was very different. But it's been fun, too."

Ian's go big or go home attitude will help build appetites for his beef. "There's no market cut out for you. The only way to do it is to market yourself."

Saskatchewan Snow Beef is on the menu at the Capitol and Crave Kitchen + Wine Bar in Regina. Give Ian a call for farmgate sales or find it at Regina's Local Market.

Heyer Forest Gardens
Neville | 306-741-0315

■ **It's easy to forget** you're on the plains of southwestern Saskatchewan at Heyer Forest Gardens. Billy Bryan's twenty-five-acre forest looks decidedly out of place in an area where treeless fields stretch for miles. Towering spruce trees line a long driveway that curves up toward the house. The sound reaches you first: warbling, chirping undulations.

Soon, the turkeys emerge, an almost prehistoric vision, their tall, strong bodies covered in

Billy Bryan and his Narragansett turkeys.

white and black feathers, offset against bright red heads. Billy raises Narragansett turkeys, a hardy heritage breed unique to North America.

The term free-range is an apt expression for Billy's poultry—he also raises heritage chickens—and the animals roam the entire property. Since his turkeys spend their days walking and flying, the meat is much leaner than your average domesticated bird. "We want to be known as high-quality food or an alternative to mass [production]. So that's what I'm really shooting for."

Billy moved to Saskatchewan from Vancouver Island fifteen years ago. He says it was love at first sight when he saw Adolph Heyer's forest. Heyer immigrated from Norway in 1905. Shocked by the bald prairie, he began planting trees on his property, eventually amassing the forest that's there now.

Billy shares the Norwegian's thirst for horticulture. He wants to reduce his dependence on annual crops to feed his birds through a silvopasture, which combines trees and perennial forage plants with grazing animals.

Billy sells turkey jerky from the farmgate and welcomes visitors. Purchase his eggs and poultry at Moose Jaw's Wandering Market.

Kerkain Farms

Ranch House Meat Co. | Shaunavon | 306-297-4050

Vince Stevenson works his cattle as much as possible on horseback.

■ **Vince Stevenson** was born and raised on the farm. A cattleman to the bone, he worked in the oil patch for fifteen years, but when he had an opportunity to get back to ranch life, he jumped at the chance.

Stevenson and his family run a thousand head of cattle at Kerkain Farms and own Ranch House Meat Co. (profile on page 279) in Shaunavon.

Along with his main breeds, Shorthorn and Angus, he's been trying Speckle Park. "They're known for their docility and their carcass traits. They win lots of awards for that and that's why I wanted to try them," he explains. Stevenson also acquired a Wagyu bull—Wagyu beef is known for its rich flavour and tenderness thanks to the animals' natural marbling— and has been crossing it with Angus and Speckle Park.

His ranch is in an area with a lot of marginal land where prairie grasses grow best. And cattle have a knack for turning grass into protein. He grazes his cattle as much as possible, even swath grazing (leaving the hay swath in the field instead of making bales) to save costs.

Stevenson wouldn't trade ranching for anything. He does his work by horseback whenever he can. "There's nothing better than early morning; going out on a horse ride and clearing your thoughts."

Kerkain Farms' Speckle Park beef is on the menu at Harvest Eatery in Shaunavon.

Prairie Pearl's Homestead

Admiral | 306-297-6457

■ **The Pearl family's free-range, bio-diverse farm** is a real wonder to visit. Brian and Jen, with help from their three children, raise pigs, poultry, rabbits, and sheep using a permaculture system. "While trying to raise things more naturally, I've noticed a huge difference in flavours and in quality. When I do things the way nature intended, I don't fight nature. I don't need chemicals," says Brian.

Permaculture creates healthy soil and organism diversity. One way Brian does this is by using maggot buckets for his chickens. It may seem weird, but in nature if a chicken dies, the other chickens will eat it. "I'm taking it a step further to not expose them to a rotting carcass, but rather feed them the worms that naturally feed on that carcass."

When a critter dies on the farm, the carcass goes in the pail. Flies lay eggs which fall to the ground through holes in the pail and the chickens eat them. (Brian barbecued a chicken when I visited and it was some of the best meat I've ever tasted.)

The Pearls sell their meat locally and through the Wandering Market in Moose Jaw. "I think local product should stay local," Brian says. "It keeps costs down and it creates jobs for small family operations like mine as opposed to large corporations."

Brian Pearl in his underground, temperature-controlled chicken coop.

Spring Valley Natural Meats

Spring Valley | 306-704-0140 | springvalleynaturalmeats.ca

Ralph and Rhonda Martin at Spring Valley Natural Meats.

■ **Southern Saskatchewan** is full of historic agricultural relics, like the big red barn at Spring Valley Natural Meats. There, Rhonda and Ralph Martin help improve soil conditions with organic and regenerative practices while raising their grass-fed cattle and pigs, chickens and turkeys.

"My tree-hugging, bohemian, hippie side thinks this is the way of feeding people in the future, because commodity farming is getting top heavy and people are starting to notice the chemicals," says Rhonda.

When she bought the farm, the land was extremely overgrazed; fifty acres of grassland didn't feed ten cattle through to August. She's noticed vast improvements since starting rotational grazing. "Now you can rack up a nice pile of wonderful, fluffy organic matter."

They experimented with finishing pigs outdoors but found the feed costs too high. "That's just silly," says Rhonda. "One thing a lot of people don't remember about sustainable farming is it has to be sustainable financially or you won't be doing it for very long."

The Wandering Market in Moose Jaw carries their products or visit the website for online ordering with delivery options.

And what about that big red barn? It was built in 1928 in Spring Valley, then moved to the farm in 1957. It's never been vacant. It was a livery barn at one time, then a home for purebred Hereford cattle, and horses, and now it's part of a farming operation helping to feed Saskatchewan families.

The Wandering Market

461 Athabasca St E, Moose Jaw | 306-648-8067 | thewanderingmarket.com

■ **If urban life** has made you a bit disconnected from agriculture, Nadine Lee has a solution. Nadine has devoted the last decade of her life to making partnerships between urban dwellers and those producing food using holistic practices. In so doing, she's also helping small-scale farmers become economically viable. "Food is a really great way for people to get back their connection that we've really been separated from," she says.

Nadine and her partner Michael Neuman operate the Wandering Market, Moose Jaw's (and likely Saskatchewan's) first local food hub. Farmers and food producers can sell or trade their products to the Wandering Market, which does the marketing work and resells products to the public. "The farms need help," says Nadine. "A long time ago, when people were farming, it would've been whole families. They would've had all those resources of knowledge and equipment."

The grocery store sells seasonal produce, meat, eggs, dairy items, preserves, tea, coffee, noodles, raw honey, grains, and pulses, along with Nadine's kimchi and sauerkraut. She also hosts cooking, canning, and fermenting workshops and organizes family-friendly farm visits. You can even sign up to help butcher chickens.

Nadine was living in Gravelbourg when she began her local food hunt for her family. (She and Michael welcomed their sixth child in 2018.) "I discovered that … there were tons of people growing food and it was so underappreciated."

The market delivers throughout Saskatchewan via online orders.

Nadine Lee and her partner Michael Neuman with their youngest child.

✪ For gluten- and dairy-free baking in Moose Jaw, visit Alternate Root Organics, which is also a health food store.

SOUTHWEST SASKATCHEWAN FARMERS' MARKETS

Check the website for current hours prior to your visit.

Gravelbourg Farmers' Market
Soucy Park on Main Street
Fridays, 2:00 PM–4:00 PM
June to September
facebook.com/gravelbourgmarket
306-648-8067

Maple Creek Farmers' Market
32 Pacific Avenue
Fridays, 8:45 AM–Noon

Moose Jaw Farmers' Market
400 Block Langdon Crescent
Wednesdays, 5:00 PM–8:00 PM
July and August

Saturdays, 8:00 AM–1:00 PM
September and October
facebook.com/mjhomegrown/

Shaunavon Farmers' Market
Grand Coteau Heritage &
Cultural Centre
Saturdays, 10:00 AM–Noon
July to September
306-297-3882

Swift Current Farmers' Market
Corner of Chaplin and Central
Saturdays, 9:30 AM–2:30 PM
June to September
facebook.com/Swift-
Current-District-Farmers-
Market-166677660057789/
sgalvin@shaw.ca

SOUTHWEST SASKATCHEWAN WATERING HOLES

Check the website for current hours prior to your visit.

Black Bridge Brewery
295 Alexander Drive, Swift Current
306-773-4404
blackbridgebrewery.ca

Tours: By request.
Taproom on site.

Smooth 42 Craft Distillery
400 Cathcart St, Brownlee
306-630-7468
smooth42.ca

Tours: By request.
Visit website for retail locations.

FRUIT IN
SASKATCHEWAN

Saskatoon berries taste like my childhood. Memories of picking berries in the hot sun, swatting away the mosquitoes, sweat soaking my hat brim, belt wrapped around my waist, and a plastic ice cream pail dangling are still fresh in my mind some thirty years later.

I can still hear my younger brother's giggles at the jokes we'd tell to pass the time and my mom's humming as we picked and ate. And ate. And ate some more, until our lips were stained purple and there wasn't much to show in our pails by the end of the row.

My mom was always full of bliss when we went berry picking, even when it was stiflingly hot and my brother and I were picking fights instead of berries. It reminded her of her own childhood when she'd pack a lunch and ride off on her horse for hours, picking berries for my grandma who would then turn them into pies, jellies, and jams.

Berry picking is a way of life in Saskatchewan. U-pick orchards are dotted throughout the province and do a brisk business for people seeking that delicious pop of flavour that only a locally grown fruit can provide. People here don't line up in the grocery store to buy California strawberries, but they'll spend hours in the hot summer sun, picking the year's freshest fruit from their local orchardist.

Fruit researchers and developers at the University of Saskatchewan are responsible for new fruit varieties, like Carmine Jewel cherries and haskap berries, bred to thrive in the long, cold prairie

◔ **Sour cherries are grown in many areas of Saskatchewan.**

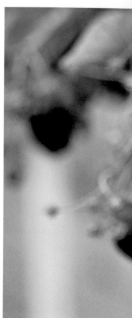

 Saskatoon berries, strawberries, and a huckleberry bush on an urban farm in Regina.

winters and hot, short summers. It's Saskatchewan's climate extremes that produce these robust fruits. And that fruit makes for terrific wine, as the award-winning Living Sky Winery (profile on page 78) has discovered.

Today, you can find plums, sour cherries, haskaps, sea buckthorns, apricots, strawberries, apples, and even grapes in Saskatchewan orchards. But the province is most famous for saskatoons, the name derived from the Cree word misâskwatômina.

People compare saskatoons' taste to blueberries but that comparison doesn't do the deep purple berries justice. The flavour is more complex, with hints of sunshine and good prairie dirt. Once you know the history behind the native plant that provided valuable antioxidants and nutrients to the Plains Indigenous people for thousands

of years, the taste deepens. Eating saskatoon berries is tasting true Saskatchewan terroir.

Our sour cherry industry is booming, too. The province is full of cherry orchards and food producers sell a range of products derived from the tart, juicy fruit.

According to the U of S Fruit Program, Saskatchewan is likely the coldest location in the world where crops like sour cherries are bred.

In 2019, program head Dr. Bob Bors and fellow fruit breeder Rick Sawatzky jointly received the prestigious Stevenson Award for their work developing sour cherries and haskaps. Bob is well-known in Saskatchewan for his efforts marketing these fruits through talks, courses, articles, and leading plot tours. (He's usually got samples for folks to taste wherever he goes, too.) He also co-authored *Growing Fruit in Northern Gardens*, a full-colour handbook aimed at the home gardener.

The fruit program has a collection of about twenty crops, developed over decades of research, and is currently emphasizing breeding haskap, sour cherries, hazelnuts, and apples. They hold an annual plant sale in early June on campus. Proceeds from the sale and royalties from varieties purchased at licenced nurseries go back to the fruit breeding department and an equipment fund that benefits horticulture research at the U of S.

Saskatoon berry shrubs are an economically viable crop for orchardists. In order to thrive, the berries need cold temperatures that stay cold over a number of months. In the summer, the bushes need heat to produce berries. Riverbend Plantation's sasktoons and associated products are well-known in the province. Lee and Grace Whittington and their family grow the berries on an orchard just south of Saskatoon (profile on page 74). Their oldest saskatoons were planted in 1981 and are still going strong. Proper management has maintained a healthy, vigorous orchard that's resistant to pests and disease. The family also runs HomeQuarter Coffeehouse & Bakery where you can enjoy a slice of homemade saskatoon berry pie.

Saskatchewan's fruit industry faces threats from climate change, however. Sue Echlin and Vance Lester own Living Sky Winery near Perdue. They began planting their orchard five years before they opened the winery in 2010. In 2018, winter kill from above zero temperatures in January, combined with below average snowfall the last few years, hurt their orchards. Summer storms are getting more intense, too, and their entire fruit crop was hailed out two years ago.

Like any seasoned farmer will, the couple took the weather setbacks in stride. "Harvest as much as you can, when you can, and then accept that next year you might not have any. Which makes for unfortunate amounts of freezer costs, but you gotta do what you gotta do," Sue says, smiling.

Orchardists in southern Saskatchewan have also struggled through severe drought conditions for the past several years. "I think all of those things will change the terroir," says Sue. "That's going to be an interesting question moving forward: How is fruit going to survive in Saskatchewan?" ■

○ Homemade apple pie, a Saskatchewan favourite, at Yellow
Fender Coffee House and Eatery in Christopher Lake.
○ Following spread: Schimmel's Dutch Bakery in Swift Current.

Acknowledgements

Writing *Flat Out Delicious* was a wild ride. I received assistance and guidance from many during the year it took to produce this book.

When I asked photographer Richard Marjan if he wanted to drive all over the province with me to get the images, he didn't hesitate. He even drove the entire 20,000-plus kilometres so I could rest and plan the next day's farm visits. I could not have done it without you, my friend. Thank you.

My mom, Lori, was my rock throughout the writing process, providing me with notes of encouragement and roast chicken dinners. She was also my secretary, making calls to farmers and coordinating visits. Both my dad, Gordon, and stepdad, Geoff, were always in my corner. Geoff's computer savviness and eye for foundational practices set me up for success and helped with last-minute details. To all of my parents: Your support was everything.

Thank you to my editor at the *StarPhoenix*, Heather Persson. You've always believed in my abilities. Allowing me to write my "Flat Out Food" column for Postmedia Network in Saskatchewan helped spread the word about the artisans featured in this book.

And thank you to all the Saskatchewan media who publicized my story during the research phase. Your support helped connect people with our province's local food system and small-scale agriculture.

Tourism Saskatchewan has been a big supporter of my project since the beginning and made the research travel possible. Thank you.

To the writers and their books in TouchWood's Food Artisans series: I referenced and took inspiration from your books often during my writing process. Thanks to Dan Clapson for his unwavering friendship. It was his recommending me to Taryn Boyd at TouchWood that got this book going. Many, many thanks to the team at TouchWood who made sense of it all and turned out this stunning ode to Saskatchewan. To my dear friend Jackie Clarke: I could not have done this without your love and encouragement.

Thank you to everyone who commented and shared posts and messaged me on social media. Your engagement invigorated me, letting me know there is a demand for and importance in the stories I share.

And, of course, thank you to all the food artisans I met along the way. You have all taught me more than I could have ever anticipated. Your tenacity, drive, determination, and passion got me fired up. Learning from you helped me define my role in Saskatchewan's food future. We can create a better, more connected local food system if we work together. Hearing your stories of joy and hardship made me realize just how important that is—we cannot lose the small-scale family farms. Witnessing my brother Dane's courage in bucking the big ag trend inspired the heck out of me. Farmers like him and the people in this book will save the planet. And consumers have the power to support them.

Cam Fuller, my dear friend and mentor, gave me the title for this book and the accompanying social media project. I'll never forget the look of joy and pride on his face when I first told him I was going to write a book. When I worked with him at the *StarPhoenix*, he helped transform my writing and find my voice as a storyteller. After I left the paper, he remained a source of guidance and positivity as I embarked on a challenging career as a freelancer. He left this life, much too early, in December 2018. I carried his spirit with me during the months of manuscript writing. Thank you for everything, Cam. I will never forget you. ∎

Recommended Resources

BOOKS

Animal, Vegetable, Miracle: A Year of Food Life by Barbara Kingsolver (Harper Collins, 2007; 2017)

Arab Cooking on a Saskatchewan Homestead: Recipes and Recollections by Habeeb Salloum (University of Regina Press, 2005)

Food and the City: Urban Agriculture and the New Food Revolution by Jennifer Cockrall-King (Prometheus Books, 2012)

Growing Fruit in Northern Gardens by Sara Williams and Dr. Bob Bors (Coteau Books, 2017)

Nourishing Traditions: The Cookbook that Challenges Politically Correct Nutrition and Diet Dictocrats by Mary G. Enig and Sally Fallon (NewTrends Publishing, 1999; 2001)

Out of Old Saskatchewan Kitchens by Amy-Jo Ehman (MacIntyre Purcell Publishing, 2018)

Prairie Feast: A Writer's Journey Home for Dinner by Amy-Jo Ehman (Coteau Books, 2010)

Taste: Seasonal Dishes from a Prairie Table by CJ Katz (CPRC Press, 2012)

The New Farm: Our Ten Years on the Front Lines of the Good Food Revolution by Brent Preston (Random House Canada, 2017)

The Soil Will Save Us: How Scientists, Farmers and Foodies are Healing the Soil to Save the Planet by Kristin Ohlson (Rodale, 2014)

MAGAZINES

Flow Magazine is published every two months in Saskatoon and has a great listing of the city's independent restaurants and regular food and drink features.

Merry & Bright and *Sunny & Bright*. These annual magazines are published by Industry West and distributed throughout the province. The magazines tell stories about Saskatchewan artisans, independent business owners, local chefs, food entrepreneurs, and restaurants.

FOOD AND TRAVEL WEBSITES

chep.org—An excellent resource for community gardens, local food boxes, pop-up farmers' markets, and agriculture educational programs in Saskatoon, all run by CHEP Good Food Inc.

farmerstable.localfoodmarketplace.com—The Farmers' Table delivers sustainable, Saskatchewan-grown food to Regina, Saskatoon, and Yorkton/Canora via online ordering.

localandfresh.ca—A farmers' market that comes to your door via online ordering and delivery to Regina and other locations in southern Saskatchewan.

thewanderingmarket.com—Monthly orders with delivery to Moose Jaw, Regina, Saskatoon, and Swift Current are available on this farm-to-folk site.

saskfoodtrucks.ca—The Saskatoon Food Truck Association's website provides a truck tracker and information about their membership.

saskorganics.org—Your connection to organic growers and their events in Saskatchewan.

tourismregina.com—Tourism Regina has comprehensive restaurant listings on their site. Use the #seeyqr tag on social media to find fun food- and drink-related posts.

tourismsaskatchewan.com—Tourism Saskatchewan has listings of food-related events and festivals in the province, along with excellent ideas for places to go and things to do.

tourismsaskatoon.com—Tourism Saskatoon has comprehensive restaurant listings and regularly post food- and drink-related stories on the Saskatooning blog.

twitter.com/yqrfoodtrucks—The YQR Food Trucks account monitors food truck locations in Regina and posts regular updates during the season.

FARMING AND FOOD EDUCATION WEBSITES

aitc.sk.ca—Agriculture in the Classroom Saskatchewan connects kids with agriculture through innovative and experiential programs, while helping encourage the next generations of farmers.

brownsranch.us—Everything you need to know about how Brown's Ranch uses holistic management practices and regenerative agriculture to grow quality food and build healthy soil.

eatnorth.com—This online platform tells a range of stories about the Canadian food scene. Eat North encourages Canadians to look in their backyards for outstanding homegrown ingredients.

ecofarmingdaily.com – A wealth of information from Acres U.S.A. magazine, a world leader in sustainable farming methods.

farmersfootprint.us – The goal? Regenerate five million acres of farmland by 2025. This site and accompanying film will tell you how to support the movement and get involved.

foodwaterwellness.org – This site documents advancing regenerative agriculture practices to support robust ecosystems with healthy soil growing nutrient-dense foods.

fruit.usask.ca – The University of Saskatchewan Fruit Program page is updated frequently with educational articles and news from the department. They post dates for their annual plant sale on their Facebook page.

polyfacefarms.com – The world's most famous farmer is one we can all learn a thing or two from. Joel Salatin advises us to get to know our local farmers, buy their food, and then cook it in our own kitchens.

saskyoungag.ca – The Saskatchewan Young Ag-Entrepreneurs association provides networking, training, and education opportunities to the under-forty generation of farmers and entrepreneurs.

slowfood.com – Since 1989, founder Carlo Petrini has helped create a revolution working to prevent the disappearance of local food cultures and traditions, while counteracting the rise of fast food culture. Conviviums are found throughout the world and the Slow Food Ark of Taste project includes a catalogue of endangered heritage foods.

slowfoodsaskatoon.com – The Saskatoon convivium's website lists their upcoming events and the SK Snail Trail, a map of Saskatchewan producers of good, clean, fair food. The organization has sent several representatives to the Terra Madre conference in Italy.

spinfarming.com – Saskatoon market gardener Wally Satzewich founded SPIN (Small Plot Intensive farming) with Roxanne Christensen. SPIN spearheaded the city's urban farming and community garden movement by making farming accessible to everyone.

westonaprice.org – The Weston A. Price Foundation is the source for accurate information on nutrition and health through nourishing, traditional foods.

zachbushmd.com – Dr. Zach Bush's site is an excellent place to learn about regenerative agriculture, how to improve gut health, and the damaging effects of glyphosate.

Index

Photo credits

First day on the road.

When you spend months on the road with your best friend, hilarity is to be expected. Richard and I developed quite a bond during the road trip gathering information for *Flat Out Delicious,* sharing many a laugh and inappropriate joke. And as you can see, my penchant for outhouses became a bit of a side project.

Thanks to generous funding from Tourism Saskatchewan, we were able to cover a lot of ground. But, as we're both frugal types, we camped for a portion of the trip, which was an adventure in its own rite. We hope you enjoy these road trip outtakes!

The morning after the first night of camping.

Jenn needed a good set of boots for the road trip, which she found at Peavey Mart.

Jenn in Kitako Lake Honey's two-seater outhouse.

Joanna Shepherd and Jenn sharing a laugh at Cobblestone Farm.

Richard posing Bryn Rawlyk at the Night Oven Bakery.

Getting off the beaten path south of La Ronge.

Janeen Covlin shares a moment of stillness with her herd at Cool Springs Ranch.

Best buds for life.

(above) Jenn learning how to forage wild chanterelle mushrooms, thanks to sage advice from the owners of Saskatoon's Hearth restaurant.

(left) Meeting Saskatchewan's small-scale producers, like Joan Merrill, and hearing their stories made the long hours in the car all worth it.

Richard making friends with a baby goat at Red Barn Dairy.

Tom Wilson, an organic gardener and one of Slow Food Saskatoon's founding members, made us a hearty harvest meal using produce from his garden.

Ron Exner started Buns Master Bakery in Moose Jaw. During retirement, he built his pride and joy, the Horse Shoe Saloon, an Old West museum on his farm near Killaly. After a long fight with cancer, he died on February 3, 2019. Happy trails, Ron.

Road tripping is hard work!

Vital bear-sighting strategies, etched into the outhouse wall, at Against the Grain's wild rice camp.

After several long days of editing and writing photo captions, this was the moment after sending off over 200 edited photos to TouchWood Editions.

Jenn Sharp is a writer based in Saskatoon. She was a features writer, columnist, and editor at the Saskatoon *StarPhoenix* for five years. Today, her Flat Out Food column runs in the *StarPhoenix* and the Regina *Leader-Post*. She's a regular contributor to CBC Saskatchewan and Eat North. Her work has appeared in *The Globe and Mail* and numerous other Canadian publications.

A natural entrepreneur and connector, she strives to tell stories that help us determine our place in the world and stories that help people embrace humanity. Jenn loves a good adventure. She's studied in Bangkok, searched for hidden temples in rural Cambodia, canoed the waterways in Honduras's remote La Mosquitia jungle, meditated on the banks of the Ganges, and trained horses in a small village in Spain. While she thrives on discovering new cultures and ways of thinking, exploring the world always brings her renewed passion for how good life is in Saskatchewan.

FIND HER ON SOCIAL MEDIA:

Facebook.com/flatoutfoodsk
Instagram.com/flatoutfoodsk
Twitter.com/JennKSharp

Richard Marjan first picked up a camera when he was ten and has loved everything about taking pictures ever since. After thirty-five years as a photojournalist at the Saskatoon *StarPhoenix*, he's now retired and does occasional freelance photography. He's won several photography awards from the Canadian Press, and his work has appeared in *Canadian Geographic*, *The New York Times*, and *The Globe and Mail*.